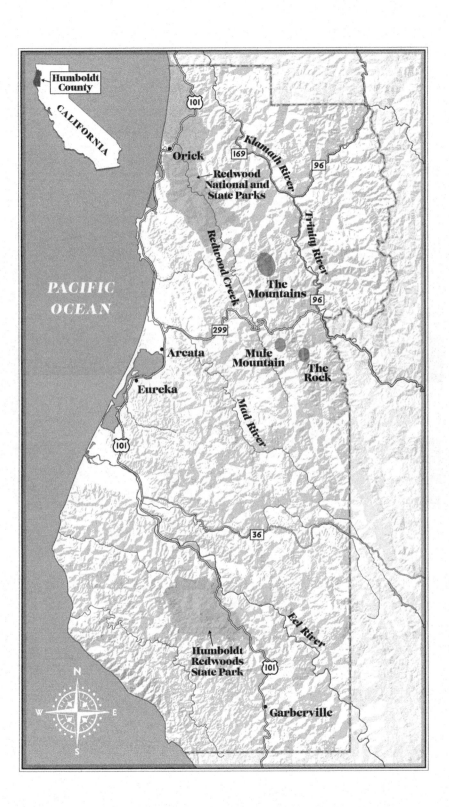

Five Hours North

FIVE HOURS NORTH

A MEMOIR OF OUTLAW FARMING ON CALIFORNIA'S CANNABIS FRONTIER

TY KEARNS

DISRUPTION
BOOKS

New York, NY | Washington, DC

Published by Disruption Books
New York, New York
www.disruptionbooks.com

Distributed by Disruption Books

For information about special discounts for bulk purchases, please contact Disruption Books at info@disruptionbooks.com.

Cover design by David Gee; cover art by MYCALI Designs, Woodland, California; author headshot by Hilary Wolf, Northern California. Interior design and typesetting by Jess LaGreca, Mayfly book design. Writing assistance from Alice Sullivan (alicesullivan.com).

Library of Congress Cataloging-in-Publication Data available.

Printed in the United States of America.

Print ISBN: 978-1-63331-089-6
eBook ISBN: 978-1-63331-090-2

First Edition

IN MEMORY OF UNCLE BOB AND RUE

IN HONOR OF THE INDIGENOUS AMERICAN TRIBES
OF NORTHWESTERN CALIFORNIA

IN GRATITUDE TO THE FARMERS WHO FEED US

Contents

Historical Context of the Emerald Triangle

IF YOU DRIVE FIVE HOURS NORTH on the Pacific Coast Highway from San Francisco, you'll come to the sleepy town of Eureka, California. Set between hills to the east, the Pacific to the west, and Redwood National Park to the north, Eureka has found fortune in each of these dynamic environments.

In the 1850s, the land enclosed by deep-water Humboldt Bay attracted the area's first European settlers during the California gold rush. The estuary allowed the tall nineteenth-century sailing ships a safe place to dock while offloading prospectors and their equipment.

Few of the prospectors who fanned out in the hills came back to town with the sacks full of gold they had hoped to find. The ones who did strike it rich created a community on the bay and christened it for the cry of joy when finding something: *Eureka!* While the town took the name of discovery, the county took the legal name of the bay: Humboldt. Named after a then-famous author and naturalist, Baron Alexander von Humboldt, the 3,600 square miles of Humboldt County was home to residents who turned their attention to nature's bounty to secure their fortunes. Logging giant redwood trees to the north supported Humboldt County for almost a century.

Then, much like the gold rush, the logging industry petered out.

The 1950s were hard on Humboldt County residents. The buzz of sawmills and muted chugs of ship engines grew all but silent. Those with homes on the bay eked out a living from fishing and gathering oysters from the Humboldt Bay estuary. More than half of the oysters farmed in California come from Humboldt County, and that trade kept the seaside residents flush during the lean times. Those who lived in the hills didn't fare as well. The hill people, as they're still known to locals, turned into isolated clans of subsistence farmers and odd job seekers. By the time JFK was elected, those living in the hills were as far away from their president's vision of a utopian "city upon a hill" as it gets.

And then a curious thing happened. The landscape devastated by rampant logging turned Humboldt County around. College graduates at the University of California, Berkeley, who managed to avoid the Vietnam War draft didn't want to put down roots in the communities around San Francisco. The 1960s seekers wanted a more tangible connection to their fellow man and the land than they could find in urban environments. Somehow, the word got out that there was cheap, clear-cut land in Humboldt County, and the hippies started snapping up parcels of land to grow on.

There wasn't a concerted effort or specific movement to relocate and create a utopian society in Humboldt County. The land and its "freedoms" simply called to the 1960s idealists like gold called to prospectors a century before. The hillside forests that were no more started a new chapter as homesteads for hippies who wanted to live off the land. Small farms and food co-ops sprouted up throughout the hills of Humboldt County. The land provided a greater bounty than single families could use, so the new farmers turned their eyes to the cities they had abandoned as a new marketplace. And then, every so often, among the beans and tomatoes, some of the farmers shared another bounty of Humboldt County: *marijuana*.

The pot trade in Humboldt started innocently enough. The Humboldt hippies grew a few plants on their farms for personal use. When the farmers came to town to sell produce, they'd share a little of their weed with friends and good customers. Sharing a lid or two turned into folks asking to buy nickel bags. Through word-of-mouth trade and a little help from groupies of the psychedelic jam band the Grateful Dead, the "buds of Humboldt County" industry was born. The name recognition and capitalist opportunity for the region's new-age crop increased rapidly as the logistics of large-scale trading throughout the United States expanded and flourished.

The cattle ranchers who sold the land to the "back-to-the-land hippies" started noticing the rapid increase in wealth from their buyers' crops. They were envious of their newer equipment, finer homes, better-dressed children, finer amenities, and sun-tanned bodies that came from tropical winter vacations, so they wanted in, as did the struggling mill workers and loggers. Thus, the "rippies," or redneck hippies, were also born.

Vietnam vets found refuge in Humboldt as well, escaping the unwelcome homecoming. They felt betrayed by society and politicians. When they got word of this utopia, they moved up to settle in the new jungle with their Vietnamese wives and fellow soldiers. They began to grow marijuana as well, creating big operations and guarding them with many of the tactics they had learned from the Vietcong—think Steve Earle's song "Copperhead Road."

Today, in the 2020s, growing and selling pot is nothing new. However, in the 1960s, growing in the continental United States was a novel concept. Most of the marijuana in the country was smuggled in from Asia, Mexico, and South America and was old and dried out by the time it hit the US shores. Humboldt County pot was something different. It was fresh, potent, and like nothing that had ever hit the counterculture market.

As it turns out, Humboldt County and the surrounding areas

have the perfect growing conditions for marijuana, much like the Bordeaux region of France does for wine. Moderate temperatures, morning mists, and rich soil come together to form what has become known as the "Emerald Triangle," not to mention the camouflage that comes with tens of thousands of remote acres of dense, lush forests where there is minimal law enforcement and an even smaller budget. Over 3,500 square miles of land are policed by fewer than fifteen deputies. It's the perfect recipe to make this three-county area the largest marijuana-producing region in the United States. Even though the Emerald Triangle comprises Mendocino, Trinity, and Humboldt Counties, Humboldt is the one that became the epicenter of the weed industry.

Though the hippie communities in Humboldt started growing more weed as the 1960s faded into the 1970s, the early pot pioneers could never have foreseen what would happen. Back then, pot fetched around $1,000 per pound, and most of the money flowed back into the Humboldt community. Schools, small businesses, a radio station, and roads were all built using pot money. It probably seemed like the hippies' vision of utopia was just a few years away. But like all dreams, there comes a point when everyone must wake up.

Humboldt County emerged from that dream in the late 1970s and early 1980s. The demand for quality weed was on the rise, and the per-pound price of marijuana shot up to $1,800–$2,400. To put this in perspective, one marijuana plant produces about two pounds of sellable pot. In 1980, the median income in the United States was $21,000. Growing and selling thirty-five pot plants was more than enough to live on back then, and that's what most of the pot growers in Humboldt County did. It was estimated that in the early 1980s, 25 percent of Humboldt County's rural residents were involved in the weed trade. They grew just enough not to be noticed by law enforcement but more than enough to live on and give back to the community.

Unfortunately, the promise of easy money doesn't stay a secret for long. Out-of-towners started coming to cash in on the high pot prices, and these new profiteers weren't the hand-holding and "Kumbaya"-singing types. The Emerald Triangle newcomers were from drug cartels or had connections to East Coast organized crime. The new growers scaled Emerald Triangle pot production to levels the original growers couldn't have imagined. Abandoned logging mills were turned into indoor grow houses. Watersheds that once drained into Humboldt Bay were diverted to large pot farms. Worst of all, they made a concerted effort to muscle out the small-time growers using any method deemed necessary, including those from their criminal underworlds.

The state government could no longer ignore the scope of marijuana farms and the related violence in the early 1980s. As such, California started the Campaign Against Marijuana Planting (CAMP) in 1983 with federal money from the War on Drugs. CAMP was a near military-style operation that used law enforcement, the National Guard, and even active-duty military members to stamp out the Emerald Triangle's weed trade.

At one point, the United States Air Force tasked U-2 spy planes designed to perform high-altitude reconnaissance over the Soviet Union with finding marijuana fields in Humboldt. When a field was found, law enforcement officials came in with helicopters to destroy plants and make arrests (if anyone was around to be arrested). During the harvest time of October 1983, CAMP forces were responsible for destroying one hundred tons of pot, an estimated 5 to 10 percent of the total pot crop in Humboldt County.

From the Humboldt County supervisor to the sheriff, those in power were not always in favor of CAMP's heavy-handed tactics as they applied to local pot growers. Local marijuana farmers from the generational Anglo-Saxon families who had settled those hills were seldom involved in episodes of violence, and they poured money back into Humboldt County businesses. The local political machine was more interested in getting the new, outside growers out of their backyards in the 1980s and early 1990s. In fact, a Humboldt County sheriff's deputy went so far as to say that he steered CAMP activities away from local growers in favor of taking down outside pot growers.

CAMP-style tactics continued throughout the rest of the 1980s and the mid-1990s as the government stepped up the War on Drugs. The enforcement of marijuana farming started to decline in 1996 when the California legislature legalized medical marijuana. Under the California statute, to legally obtain and use marijuana, it had to be prescribed by a doctor and purchased at a state-licensed facility. One would think pot growers in Humboldt County would have welcomed legalization, but it only brought more headaches. Proposition 215 didn't provide a clear set of guidelines; licensing procedures for growing medicinal marijuana were onerous, vague, and still illegal at the federal level, and many local sheriff's offices still shut down medical grows and dispensary outlets. The differential between medical and black-market growers also caused issues for law enforcement. With this half legalization, cops were forced to make judgment calls about how to pursue potential violations of the new California statutes. If cops busted someone who could legally possess and use marijuana, it opened county governments up to costly wrongful arrest lawsuits.

Many factors favored small grow operations as well. Pot plants grow heartier if they are correctly pruned throughout their growth cycle. Dead leaves must be removed from the bottoms of the plants to promote bud growth toward the tops of the plants, and machines cannot effectively trim buds. Also, pot must be harvested at the correct time. Harvest too soon, and you'll have skunk weed. Harvest too late, and the buds lose their narcotic effects. Finally, when pot plants are harvested, the flowering parts (buds) must be separated from the stems, which must be done by a person. Poor trimming can significantly reduce crop yields, and experienced trimmers are highly sought after at harvest.

Speaking of quality trimmers, many are migrant workers who filter into Humboldt County from other agricultural harvest gigs. Marijuana harvest runs from mid-September into early October, a little after traditional farm crop peak harvest times. Because of the influx of trimmers needed to process Emerald Triangle weed, many trimmers erect temporary tent cities on farms and stay throughout the harvest. A migrant workforce naturally brings issues that tend to spill over into the general groovy vibes of Humboldt County life.

Despite the legal risks and logistical headache of growing marijuana, the incentive to farm remained for many locals: jobs, income, a sense of purpose, and the ability to provide. The other longtime industries in the area were quickly going bust, and farming in the rural mountains naturally coincided with many of the labor skill sets of the region's workforce, many of whom had recently lost their jobs. Toward the end of the 1990s and the start of the 2000s, generational mills like Simpson Lumber Company, Flakeboard, the "Pulp Mill," Louisiana-Pacific, Eel River Logging Company, and a score of others around Humboldt Bay began shuttering their operations. The second- and third-growth timber was years, if not decades, from a harvestable value, and the forests of Oregon and British Columbia were catching better returns. Two-by-fours from out-of-town mills were sold to contractors at lumber yards and hardware stores in Eureka, Arcata, and Fortuna, literally within sight of the shadows of the towns' quickly overgrown, graffiti-laden mills.

Over the next fifteen to twenty years, the greed and false dealings of a few on Wall Street would pull the power cords from the massive spinning saw blades at the Pacific Lumber Company, halting the business. In what seemed like an instant, close to 1,200 direct jobs at the mill, plus another eight hundred that were supported by the felling and reshaping of the timbers within Humboldt County's forests, vanished. The paychecks stopped coming. The local community was devastated.

The Pacific Lumber Company went bankrupt in 2007. It seemed like the coffin that had taken almost sixty years to build, shape, sand, and varnish by the wood and workers of the region had been nailed shut, buried beneath a bed of sawdust, smack in the middle of a clear-cut forest surrounded by hundreds of square miles of twenty-year-old second-growth trees.

Amid the immediate aftermath of depression and excessive substance abuse, a new scent took over in the coming decade, a new tree. New jobs and financial opportunities exponentially exploded in the economy. An explosion of greed for a new "money tree" began to write the paychecks—a tree that could be hand-milled, grown and harvested in five months, not sixty years. A tree with a profit margin and sheer financial value that was unlike any other agricultural and most mineral products in the entire country. It was another perfect storm, another resource rush, more environmental destruction for a quick buck.

. . .

As a native of Humboldt County, all of this was "normal" to me. Some might say I was destined to try my hand at the green rush. But I was not raised to grow pot. My parents taught me to study, graduate with a degree, and work a steady career. Their ideal was not for me to enter an illegal industry that most people wanted to stay illegal. Although things look a bit different now with 68 percent of the country behind legalization, that wasn't the case even fifteen years ago.

I was not raised to break the law, especially as a career. I was raised to be a man of honor, respect, and courage. These principles were literally etched into my pocketknife alongside my initials. I was raised to respect education and strive toward college. Outside of work, my goal was to find a wonderful woman to love and create a family with. My future wife and I were to take our nice little children every Sunday to Saint Someone's Catholic Church in the town where we settled down. My childhood was spent in the largest geographical marijuana-producing capital of the world. I had walked to school watching SWAT teams break down garage doors and bust indoor grow houses in my neighborhood. As a child, I was sometimes told that so-and-so's father had to go to jail for a while for "growing something in a bunker behind their house." Huh? I was casually taught and trained not to ask what certain family friends did for a living.

As I entered my teenage years and early twenties, I knew of so many little grows, grow houses, hidden rural diesel grow bunkers, and rural gardens of weed hidden under or in the foliage of trees and bushes. It wasn't that cool to me; it held no novelty or sexiness per se. Maybe it's the feeling that kids of rock stars have toward their parents. Then, after moving out of the area immediately after high school, I realized that people really like this weed stuff. They always asked about the weed of Humboldt, with questions that ranged from simply odd to almost fantastical. "No, it's not quite like that," I would answer.

When someone asked where I was from and I answered Humboldt, they often responded, "Oh, where the . . ."

Before they could finish their sentence, I would answer, "Redwood trees are."

This was the example I was shown on both sides of my family. My parents were incredibly hardworking, they held stable jobs, and they provided my brother and me with a great lower-middle-income childhood. Both sets of my grandparents were married for over sixty years, and both sets had four children. My father met my mother at the start of his last year of college and married her a year and a half later. Everyone in my family worked honest jobs and married fairly young. Many believed strongly in Jesus, and if they weren't so sure about Jesus, they at least believed in working hard.

My example of a working father was as far from a pot grower or self-employed individual as you could get. But I must have subconsciously noticed his willingness to change and the way he took action when he didn't like how something was going.

Regardless of the future that was laid before me, school and academics didn't come easy. My grades were always barely good enough. Through those years, my brain was more interested in building forts, dressing up like Robin Hood, or riding anything with wheels than doing homework. I was interested in constructing things, discussing them, and then analyzing how they could be improved. Teachers came up with unique but truthful ways to describe my struggles in each of their subjects on report cards: *His attention fades away quickly. He doesn't seem to be grasping how to construct a sentence. He can't spell well and has trouble following verbal directions.* I realized I couldn't learn at the same speed as my peers in the first grade when it was deemed a good idea for me to try the first grade a second time.

I was—and still am—a visual learner. I am a person who creates with my hands and uses tools. I wasn't good at creating things from my brain using the structures of grammar, biology, or advanced math. Even when I could focus strongly enough, my brain was more like a brick than a sponge. There were afternoons in class when I could hear topics bouncing off my brick brain, falling atop my desk, and rolling over my notepad onto the dusty old classroom floor, never to be retained. I admired my friends, who seemed to complete their assignments and make good grades with ease. It wasn't that way for me. I was good at construction and had a knack for business, but I wasn't confident in my ability to learn scholastic subjects. I knew how to camp in the woods, how to build things.

I wasn't meant to be a grower. I didn't want to be a grower. I had heard terrible stories of grows gone bad from growers buying soil and building materials at the lumber yard I worked in during my teenage years. I had read the countless articles and press releases in our local paper about who got busted. I witnessed my friends try their hand at growing right out of high school, and most, if not all, failed. I was terrified of creating a scenario where I wouldn't have a choice but to be a grower.

But here I am—a grower all the same.

CHAPTER 1

Five Hours North

FALL 2009

AT LEAST I HAD THE NEIGHBORS for company. A year and a half into the weed business and for the first time in a long time, I was working alone. My girlfriend Rachel had taken off to study abroad in India, leaving me to deal with the farm alone. It was truly all on me. So when I called the neighbors to confirm we were still on for later that night, I was hoping to hear a friendly voice. Instead, I got a double dose of the fear and loneliness that had been dogging me all summer long on that mountain.

"They cut the gates! They cut the gates!"

"What? Who did?" I asked the man on the other end of my call.

"Are you freaking kidding me?" asked my neighbor incredulously. "Are you dumb?"

"What do you mean?" I was confused by his harsh tone.

"Haven't you checked your phone?"

"No, I didn't have any service 'til just now." It was true. I never had service in this location. The few texts that came through were from my side fling.

His voice was staticky from the spotty service, but I made out what sounded like "Bitch worm! You're joking, right?"

"What?" I asked.

"This is not a fire drill. She's as real as herpes," he whisper-yelled into the phone.

"What, what the . . . ?" I asked again.

I was twenty-five and going back to college. It wasn't so bad. I was more focused than when I was younger, and I only had classes from Monday to Thursday. Friday mornings, I got up at 4:00 a.m. and headed up north in my old Ford Ranger I had named Ranger Rick. When I got to the town closest to the farm at about 9:00 a.m., I routinely called my neighbor and fellow farm worker.

That particular morning in 2009, it was abnormally warm for mid-September. I made my normal call at 9:22 a.m., only to be completely confused within seconds.

I didn't understand why my neighbor was acting that way. He was a southerner who had lost his job as a mortgage insurance agent during the 2008 banking crash the summer before. One of his childhood friends had come out west to attend college ten years prior and got into growing pot. After the crash, my neighbor hit him up for a job. The former insurance agent did not have the Mr. Central-Casting-Hill-Growing-Weed-Worker look, but most of us didn't. And while he was also easily the most paranoid worker on the mountain, this level of freakout was new to me.

"They came—all of them with papers! About twenty of them in uniform with two choppers in the sky. They cut the gates and are stuck halfway up." His voice shook like a panicked public speaker.

"They are there?!" I asked, beginning to clue into what was happening.

"The gate held up for well over an hour. The hardened steel lock in the enclosed iron worked. One of the cops said he needed a laser cutter from town to cut through it."

"Oh, good," I managed to squeak out.

Years before, the owners of each parcel on the mountain had hired a welding company to make three sets of custom gates set a half mile apart going up the driveway. Police can usually cut through gates in a few minutes, but it sounded like these custom gates held them off.

"*Not* good, kid!" my neighbor yelled into the phone. "Not good! Clean your truck. Clean your phone, and wear your best gecko face! This is because of you!"

The cell line went dead. I pressed my lips together and exhaled a short breath through my nose. I looked down at my little ring of keys in the cupholder. A dark green key caught my eye.

Sixteen months earlier, an owner of one of the neighboring farms, Jarod, handed me that key and told me, "You only get two keys, one for you and one for your family. Never, ever leave the gate open. Ever. Each key is $120. Four other parcels have keys, and the logging company, Champion International, will get one too. There are 1,920 acres behind the gate. It's a long drive with four gates to go through. That'll give you security and time in case the worst happens. Pot is new-age gold, new-age timber . . . new-age money."

He'd placed the keys in my palm and returned to his massive pickup truck. As he climbed in the cab, he looked back at me and said, "Hey, kid!"

"Yeah?"

"Good luck at this, but don't outsmart your common sense."

Almost a year and a half later, I was looking down at the same key the man in the mammoth pickup truck had given me. That key unlocked the gates to the 5,376 square feet of white industrial greenhouses I had built, which housed hundreds of marijuana plants I had so confidently planted four months earlier.

A redwood-and-hog-wire fence surrounded the perimeter of my greenhouses, and God bless America, we even flew the stars and stripes, though the amenities ended at the American flag. There was no house on the parcel, only one little camping tent hidden in the trees. My mountaintop farm operation didn't stop at my group of greenhouses. I had another thirty-six seed plants at the top of the ridge and 298 more hidden under the surrounding forest's black oak trees.

The owners of one of the other farms had thirteen other greenhouses on two different parcels of land. It was a big operation on the underside of legality. My physician recommendation to grow medical marijuana, commonly called a 215 card, had only been good for twenty-eight days. My request to the doctor to deal with my insomnia with cannabis wasn't received well. You needed this medical card, basically your ID card, to enter a dispensary or grow. And even though the card was supposed to last a full year instead of the twenty-eight days I had been granted, it had expired seven months earlier. I had planted past any reasonable medical amount of need; my garden wasn't fooling anyone.

That technicality was what the cops were trying to take advantage of when Mr. Paranoid picked up my call. He finally had a reason to be apprehensive. I started feeling it too as I thought about Jarod's words: *Don't outsmart your common sense.* Their terrible meaning bounced around my head and sent SOS signals through my body. My right hand shook on the shifter as I drove up the mountain, and my bowels started to cramp. I had been driving for five hours straight, but I couldn't stop now. I had to get to the farm.

Damn. What was I thinking?

I was almost on autopilot as I drove the county road to the farm. Six miles up, where the paved road turned to dirt, I pulled over and ran into the woods. With my Starbucks napkins in hand, I jumped over an old fallen snag, dug at the ground with a stick like a cave person, and let go of my bowels. The napkins were a funny reminder of my double life between the city and the mountain. That took care of the stomach cramps caused by an overdose of nervousness, but I still had a gnawing desperation to get to the farm as soon as humanly possible. I jumped back in Ranger Rick and drove three more miles to the gate I had come to know so well over the previous sixteen months. Large knotty tire marks were everywhere. The gate was wide open, the lock was gone, and the dirt around the gates was damp, I assumed from the laser cutting.

"It's real," I said out loud, standing in front of my worst nightmare.

Just then, my phone vibrated, and a foreign number showed up on the screen. It was my girlfriend calling from India.

"Dammit! She was right," I said to myself. I slammed my fist into the radio on the dash, still mad it hadn't worked the entire five-hour drive. "I went too big."

Flipping the phone open, I declined the call and noticed the two texts from my current fling. I had stopped right before the open gate, as was my habit. The gate had never been open before my arrival.

Over the past eighteen months, I had been pretending I was prospecting in the gold rush era of the 1800s. It kept things exciting and light, and distracted me from the dangerous realities and legal repercussions of this chosen venture.

In my best made-up miner's voice, I urged Rick onward. "Go, Rick! Get your Detroit Steel ass up there, ya mule, ya!"

Ranger Rick didn't move. I punched the radio once more, breaking off the volume knob. My knuckles busted open on impact and began bleeding as Rick finally obeyed. We rolled forward, and five hundred feet later, I passed the first sheriff's truck, windows down. No one seemed to be nearby. The pure exhaustion of my life began to take over my body and mind.

I thought about every pot industry failure I'd ever heard about in Humboldt County. Shootouts, deaths, lockups, houses burning down, and family names in local newspapers. My life flashed before my eyes, ending with less than $4,000 buried in an old Pyrex container, which was all I had to finish the grow year. It was still $3,687 more than I had eighteen months before, but was it worth all of this?

"This never works!" I said aloud to no one. "Why am I still driving to this stupidness?"

I drove fifteen miles an hour, as if that would make my future two miles ahead at the greenhouses go away. Suddenly, two guys on dirt bikes shot out of the trees across the road a hundred feet in front of me and then rocketed out of sight over the ridge to my right. I didn't think they saw me, but I recognized one of them from the operation. They were escaping the scene, and I couldn't blame them—or could I?

"Nah," I said to myself. "Choose to live by the sword, and you choose to die by the sword."

My mother had always said that when I was younger, along with "You take responsibility for your own actions." Consequences were getting closer with every yard I drove. I needed music to take me to my fate. Since Rick's radio was shot, Tool's song "Vicarious" started playing in my head, a song I must have played a thousand times running up and down forgotten roads the summer before. Every bump on the road made my CD player skip, but it only made the song better for me. A few minutes into my mental musical loop, I got to the second gate, which stood as wide open as the first.

"Yes, let's go!" I yelled, pumping myself up to be handcuffed. My crazy gold-prospecting itch was about to be scratched by the reality of getting arrested.

Ranger Rick inched up the ridge toward the greenhouses. I noticed the US Forest Service sign. I'd seen hundreds of the small yellow signs mounted on silver metal posts in my life. This one held a different legal meaning at that moment. *Would the rangers be with them?* I thought. *Is "they" the Humboldt County sheriff? Is "they" the feds? Maybe "they" is the Forest Service rangers?*

Boom! Tool's bass drum thumped along with the guitar riffs in my head as I got closer to the greenhouse. The tunnel of trees overhead disappeared, and the landscape opened. The dirt road inclined and shot straight up the mountain as if into the full sky above. I downshifted as the song launched into the chorus.

Ting Bing Ting Bong!

The song played in perfect time to the metronome of gravel shooting against the wheel wells. A massive rooster tail of dust appeared like Old Faithful in Rick's rearview mirror. I threw up devil fingers out the window as the beat in my head got louder and harder. Everything was becoming clearer. Suddenly, all the sounds changed. The *bong* became a *woop* and the *tang* became a *chup chup chup!* The truck shook violently as I pushed it up the hill. A dust cloud emerged from nothing far behind the thin trail of soil Rick was kicking up. Then I saw it in all its glory: a black helicopter screaming right above the tree line.

"Wow, epic!" I yelled in complete delusive contentment.

Moments later, the bass in my chest and head became real—very real. There were two black 4x4 quads with the word *Sheriff* in yellow block lettering plastered across the grills blocking the roadway.

"They," I said aloud. "Ohhh, '*they.*'"

I let out another long, slow breath and slammed on the brakes. My knee cracked the bottom of the dashboard when my heel kicked into the brake. My forehead kissed my knuckles, clenching to the steering wheel. The tires slid to a halt, and I couldn't look up from the steering wheel. I exited Rick with my tail between my legs, unable to make eye contact with anyone. Walking felt like being on a floating dock. The sound of the helicopter's blades made my stomach curl and my palms sweat. I watched the guys hanging out of the copter and remembered thinking, *That looks like an awesome job,* back when I was a child, before I knew what they were doing. My five-year plan looked like it was going to be planned for me.

I walked up to the clearing. There was truck after truck full of SWAT officers. I heard helicopters even though I was still about a mile from the property. I looked up the road, and a group of officers in full fatigues were gathered around our excavator operator, Tractor Frank, in the middle of the road.

"Hello" was all I could say. My lips quivered.

I recognized a couple of my old baseball teammates among the officers.

"Tyler, good morning!" Tractor Frank said. There was an eight-foot-wide by seven-foot-deep freshly dug ditch across the middle of the dirt road. I could see another one about a hundred feet behind him. The dirt road was impassable for the time being, it seemed.

One of the officers called out my full name.

Oh, I'm done. I'm just done.

"Yes, sir."

"What are you doing?" the officer asked.

"I just drove up from school this morning."

"From school?"

"Well, I live in Sonoma and go to school there."

"Cute hair." One of my old buddies took a jab at my shoulder-length hair with an accompanying nod, making it clear a handshake wasn't happening.

"Oh, this you, huh?" asked Sergeant Dwight Henderson. He pointed at a map that included a couple highlighted property boundaries with names, while fifty cops and two helicopters buzzed around me. I recognized him from the news. "Same name, different first name as the property owner?"

"I'm going to get back to putting in these to-code culverts we talked about, Tyler," Tractor Frank said informatively to us all before I said anything. "Answer their questions only as needed. Come clock in and help me clean this up when you're done. You're already thirty minutes late."

My body felt as if it was in a full spasm.

"Yeah, that's my family name," I said, amazed that the culvert and road construction idea had worked. "This is my aunt's property. She doesn't know what's going on here. She has no idea."

"What's going on out here, Tyler?" The sergeant broke my gaze at the deep pit.

"Putting in culverts and washouts, sir," I said, smiling back, feeling a jolt of confidence.

"Well, those folders contain papers from a judge with passcodes to the parcels past this here temporary roadblock inconvenience. If we see anything in your place, we are taking it and taking the person that's taking the fall."

Oh my gosh, they are going to see it all, take it all, and then take me. How does this work?

"OK . . . do you need to handcuff me or anything?" I asked.

"For digging culverts," Sergeant Henderson said and paused, "or for . . . ?"

"Shit," I said.

"No, no. You are fine until this road is passable again."

"You're a Seawolf?" asked a random deputy as the excavator growled to life.

"What?" I said, unfocused. "I don't know. I can't think correctly right now."

"So, you are not a Seawolf? Well, what's your story?" The deputy pressed me as he pointed at the textbooks on my passenger's seat and the Seawolf decal in the lower corner of Rick's windshield.

"Tyler, just tell them about your school!" yelled Tractor Frank from the controls of the tractor. "Come on, I need your help!"

It finally clicked. *Seawolf! The school mascot.*

I spilled my story of going to college, camping, fishing, and working construction up here on weekends. I talked about spending the night before in the library, how I slept in the back of my truck because I was trying to save enough money to buy next semester's books.

After my long story, the deputy pointed down at my knuckles.

"Anger issues recently, huh?" he asked.

I started to explain, then his radio went off.

"This is Helicopter Two. We have got a flare going up or something over on the south side. We will circle and report back."

"Yes, approval to investigate granted," Sergeant Henderson said.

I looked at Tractor Frank smiling and pointing to a CB radio in the excavator. The two helicopters over us turned and flew off. I glanced down at the dried blood on my knuckles. My hands were shaking violently.

A few hundred pounds of product sat in the warm morning sun a mile up the road in "the largest greenhouse in the north county," and it was a month from harvest. Worse than that, two hundred yards away, across a ravine to the north, were a few hundred more plants. I had let the itch take over. The potential massive fiscal rewards from my new entrepreneurial ventures had cast a blindness over the reality of criminal activities. I thought back again to what Jarod had said: *Don't outsmart your common sense.* Dammit. I had.

The sheriff's radios came to life again, and I heard, "Sergeant, we just found what looks to be over two thousand plants down the ravine on national forest land. Please bring a squad."

Sergeant Henderson looked up from the map he was holding.

"This is the luckiest day of your life," he said.

"Why?" I asked.

He just grunted, locked eyes on me, and shook his head as he circled his finger in the air. All the cops got in their vehicles and left.

What just happened?

As the helicopter followed the dust trail of the two men on dirt bikes leaving the scene, the pilot noticed the riders go right past a major illegal grow on national forest land a few miles away, large enough to be visible from the air. The bikers had unintentionally run a distraction. Our asses were saved.

This time.

CHAPTER 2

No Trespassing and Chemo Pills

SPRING 2008, SEVENTEEN MONTHS EARLIER

"YOU GOING TO HIT THIS?" Bob asked in his tired, cracked voice.

Finally, another voice, I thought. For almost an hour, I had only been listening to my own deep breaths. Each exhale hummed along to the vibrations of the old truck. The tired man with a cracked voice reached across the gear shifter, and his sunburned, freckled hand grasped an old, faded Altoids tin. I lowered my eyes to the tin and was distracted by the aged purple veins protruding across my uncle's knuckles like wet worms in a rainstorm. Bob flipped open the tin with one blackened and cracked thumbnail.

Inside the tin was a nicely rolled joint, healthy in stature. I mentally named the joint Her Majesty for the way it rested against a pack of Zig-Zag Original rolling papers and a couple of small, dry, untrimmed buds. My constant chaotic thoughts of my latest breakup and life losses were registering *what the hell* on the Richter scale. The joint, on the other hand, seemed to be almost relaxing in the tin. I imagined the tin was white sand, the pack of papers was a towel, and the leafy buds were shady palm trees. Tropical life rolled up in plant matter and laid against the towel under the shade of the buds on a warm beach somewhere else—somewhere different— somewhere on the other side of the globe, just like where I had my heart broken and then lost three friends in less than a month.

What am I going to do, dammit? What am I doing? I ranted at myself, still trying to poke my brain into submission.

Bob interrupted my internal dialogue. "I wore gloves when I rolled it and used no saliva to seal her tip."

"Oh yeah?" I replied, lost and gazing ahead.

"You gotta hit it first. I got this hep-C shit, you know? Can't be hitting it after me." Bob trailed off as he looked out the window.

"Nah, it doesn't work for me anymore," I said, gripping the grab handle above the door.

"What? Since when?" Bob smirked.

"Since, well . . . since right now, I guess."

I could feel his eyes look me up and down. He let out a light chuckle.

"Ah, shit. The heartbreak and the hurricane mind got you by your—" He stopped and shook the tin. "After a breakup, life is like a table missing a leg, bud. Hard as hell to balance when that leg is gone, but you're still upright."

I didn't answer.

"Over time, another leg finds her way under ya," he said, chuckling more.

"Right," I said, rolling my eyes. It was all I could muster to appease his attempted wisdom.

"Let's wait to light it up 'til we get wherever we're headed," I said.

"Suit yourself. I can always roll more." He shrugged, ignoring my request.

He dropped the open tin in his lap and began digging aggressively for a lighter in the truck door. He moved aside the remnants of a foil-wrapped breakfast burrito, then handed me a ring of unlabeled keys and a pair of small camouflage binoculars.

His frantic fingers finally found a blue lighter, missing a flame guard and with a rusted top. A few flicks later, weed smoke billowed out the driver's-side window. He seemed to find relief and comfort in the smoke. I was glad he had sparked up Her Majesty. She was better off pressed between his fingers and floating into his lungs than mine. A few years ago, I would have grabbed her myself.

For the last six years, I'd smoked out of a pipe made from an apple almost every workday morning at 5:15 on my way to construction sites. After, the apple was part of my breakfast. I had to do it. Smoking was the only way I could focus enough to run trusses in my DC skater shoes. It was the only way to deal with the grunt labor. Now I was back in my hometown, refusing a hit after seven years of countless joints.

Bob abruptly hit the brakes, flinging us forward. The vehicle snapped back as he downshifted to second gear. He throttled up a sharp turn in the road and snaked up two more. The old Ford Ranger used every bit of its two-wheel drive to push us up the steep, winding road cut almost a century before to harvest the valuable old-growth western red cedars and Douglas firs. It had been built for profits and to promote "horizontal" forestry, not "vertical" forestry—growing weed—and not residences.

Bob sighed. "This mountain has a long history of dark secrets fueled by fear and greed," he said, coughing.

This part of California was full of dark secrets and men who tried to exploit the land. During the early to mid-1800s, a group of Chinese immigrants who were after gold themselves built a small township called China Flat. Gold mining—hydraulic mining in particular—devastated the land, clogging up rivers, eating up timber from the forests, and destroying the natural spawning pools for California's abundant salmon.

There were also the Indian killers—white men formally known as the Settler Protectors who massacred full tribes of Native Americans. The Hupa, Karuk, and Yurok tribes were their targets. These native people hunted in the steep, fertile forested mountains and netted the annual salmon river runs. They danced during the changing seasons in honor of nature's powerful cycles and generosity. They sat around large fires underneath the star-filled sky, sharing the tales of Omah, now known as Bigfoot.

Then there was the logging. The last major logging on this hillside was believed to have happened in the late 1960s, and the first industrial cuts were in the 1920s. Before then, wide-eyed miners whipped their mules along these trails, digging and blasting their greed into the watersheds. They had hard-ons for the gold flakes that paid for their supplies, liquid courage, and debauchery.

Before his last cough subsided, Bob took another deep, slow drag off the joint.

Bigfoot and logging were the farthest things from my mind when I looked across the cab. "It's got to be a seven-hundred-foot steep, guaranteed death down south of the pavement."

"Yep. Just wait. It gets even wilder ahead on your side," said Bob.

Black oaks and madrone trees clung to the rugged earth, reaching for the sun with unmatchable psychedelic bark. Their branches and leaves held in the last drops of the great spring rains. Grasses and the wildflowers at the bases of their stout trunks exploded with vibrant greens and wildflower pastels. As we drove past, a curious doe peeked her head from behind the electrical poles lining the road. My palms began to sweat, and my elbow grew numb from my tight grasp on the handle.

All around us were rugged, dangerous, mountainous prospecting lands—Northern California's Humboldt County, also known as the Emerald Triangle. We were driving up a critical artery of the area's past, a watershed of tough times and a tributary of greedy choices. The turnoff to this artery is where the Oak Creek tributary meets the mighty Trinity River. Every moment the truck climbed, the river basin shrunk in the rearview mirror, a sign we were traveling away from the heartbeat of the township and humanity. We were exiting populous areas and entering a lawless land of lucrative natural beauty. I'd spent many days and nights in the mountains of Humboldt County in my life. Hell, it was my hometown's backyard. However, I had never been on this road or this mountain.

Our silence disappeared as the radio scanned until it landed on some FM radio chatter. A female voice crackled through the speaker and read the daily news over the broken waves of the local public station. "An earthquake has struck in Yunnan Province, China; deaths are over fifty thousand. Microsoft has withdrawn its bid to purchase Yahoo for billions, and in a landmark decision, California's Supreme Court has voted in favor of same-sex marriages. May 2008 saw unemployment increase in the US by 861,000 people this month, bringing the total unemployed to 8.5 million. Filings for foreclosure jumped 48 percent in the states of California, Nevada, and Florida, with another seventy-three thousand families losing their homes this month alone. In other news, the Bush administration has announced that polar bears will be added to the endangered species list."

I reached over and turned the radio off.

"Happy times in the world today," I snarked.

Bob tried his hand at another quote of wisdom. "Hard times never fade. Just got to learn to navigate the river of life better each year."

As he drove and took hits of Her Majesty, he described what he had been trying to do out here the last couple of years, how his plan failed, and why he couldn't try anymore. The day before, I had told him I was willing to go see "the property," as Bob called it, to help him clean up his mess, horticultural artifacts of his unsuccessful and short-lived venture.

Bob tossed the joint to the floorboard and put it out with the heel of his tattered hiking boots. The last bit of smoke crawled up his leg, swirled once, and wisped out the window. I looked at him as he gazed ahead at the dangerous road, red-eyed. I had not spent much time with him over the last five years. His hepatitis C was noticeable now. Not only had the virus eaten away at him, but so had the meds, his constant stress over his eighth-grade daughter, and his excessive consumption of joints. Bob was simultaneously sluggish and anxious, an almost paralyzing combination at times. Bob was no longer the energetic uncle of my childhood. He was lost in drawn-out gazes, awake but slower, quieter, maybe even depressed. He shouldn't have been doing strenuous labor of any kind, let alone on a job site at four thousand feet elevation producing a Schedule I narcotic.

The road widened straight ahead but was cut off by a gate ornamented with signs reading:

PRIVATE.

NO TRESPASSING.

FUCK THE DOG. FEAR THE OWNER.

TRESPASSERS WILL BE SHOT AND SURVIVORS SHOT AGAIN.

WE DON'T CALL 911.

To the right was a sharp, uphill horseshoe turn with a brown marker containing longitude and latitude numbers. This was a US Forest Service road. We took a right. Little did I know as the Ranger's tires spat gravel and struggled to gain traction that I would be making this turn hundreds if not thousands of times over the coming years.

Two miles farther, the road narrowed again, and instant death waited patiently out the passenger's-side window. I winced at the sight of Oak Creek, a small town now some 3,200 feet below. She

was so tiny that she looked make-believe. Her bridges across the
"wild and scenic" Trinity River were thin lines, and the veggie fields
and peach orchards were dots.

"Wow, we climbed fast," I said.

"Lots more earth to cover ahead. Hope the tires hold today,"
Bob said, mostly to himself.

After another mile and two deep washouts that almost snapped
the Ranger's tie-rods in half, another gate appeared ahead. We
rolled to a stop.

"The road that continues to the right leads up to an old Cold
War–era radio relay tower that sits at the actual top of Bear Mountain," Bob said. "It's massive, dark-colored, and overgrown, but it's
still an artifact of this mountain's past. It was used to forward radio
signals, sending information from sonar recordings from the coast
at Requa, a small town on the north bank of the Klamath River,
and to forward sonar signals toward Redding, warning of underwa-
ter Russian intruders. But now she's just covered in spray-painted
hearts, initials, penises, and bullet holes."

"Modern petroglyphs," I replied. According to a local saying that had been passed from generation to generation since the
1850s, there was no law north of the Mad River and no God north of
the Klamath. We were smack between the two. The original settlers
fought among themselves for land, a mirror of the Hatfield-McCoy
feud. Eventually, half moved north and the other half south, settling
in the bay.

"Yeah, lots of history up here," Bob said. "Grab that green key.
It's for this gate."

The brown gate was old and, in true 1970s Forest Service style,
made of solid Pittsburgh steel. It had expanded from the direct
morning sun, so it was almost impossible to open the conventional
way. I squatted with all my weight while pulling the four-inch round
pin out of the tight slot, holding the lock until it finally released.

The skin between my thumb and index finger caught between the sliding metal, breaking my flesh. I flinched and cursed a jumble of words. Too late and still in pain, it dawned on me that I was riding the gate as it swung open. A second later, I was driven into a large Douglas fir, knocking the wind out of me. I fell off and collapsed to the ground.

Bob thought it necessary to heckle me from the truck. "Damn! What an introduction!"

The fir bore a pronounced indent from the many times the gate must have whacked it over the years. Uncle Bob released the parking brake and let the truck roll through the gate down a short way. Still catching my breath, I shut and locked the gate with caution. Surrounded by the light rush of madrone leaves in the wind, the smell of earth, and the sight of spring blossoms, a feeling of calming, instinctual awareness crept into my chest. It was a nice moment to pause after the nonsense my busy brain had been thinking lately.

"Damn gate got me good end of last summer. I had to explain to my doc in town how it happened and disinfect the gate so no one else got this shit I got."

I glanced at the silver water jug in the center console as I finally got the seat belt to latch. *Don't drink from that*, I reminded myself.

The truck bounced and jerked another couple miles through a tunnel of pole-straight black oaks and tanoaks. Every few hundred yards were piles of cut trees stacked and pushed aside by a masticator some years prior. The rear of the truck slid as we slipped through a right turn, followed by an aggressive dip in the road that splashed muddy water onto the hood. Steam rose from the grill.

This poor little beat-up truck, I thought. *This two-wheel drive is going up a road where even four-wheel drivetrains could easily get beat up.*

There were three washout humps spaced out at the perfect distance from one another, like ski moguls. As we climbed to the crest, the sky opened, and the rock patterns and colors changed.

The terrain became more of a gray clay than decomposed mud. The western red cedars, firs, and Jeffrey pines were dwarfed by the unending scenery but stood wise with the experience of seasons past. Vast views expanded west and east as we climbed the spine of the mountain.

We rode in silence. Lost in this new landscape, I found comfort in the journey. We pulled over four times in the next three and a half miles because I needed to stack four-by-six timbers and rocks across the winter washouts for the Ranger to cross. At each stop, I muscled large boulders of Bob's choosing into the truck bed to add the weight we needed. The boulders left fresh dents in the truck, and my gloveless palms left bloody handprints on the tailgate.

"A couple more should do," Bob yelled from the driver's seat. In the side-view mirror, I could see that he was trying to light another joint.

"This shit is ridiculous," I mumbled, returning to the edge of the road for more massive rocks.

The white noise of seasonal snowmelt cascading down the ravine parallel to our path vibrated in my chest. Weed smoke tickled my nostrils once again. I looked at Bob.

Shit. He'll be fine.

Ducking under low branches and sliding down several yards of loose earth, I knelt before the swift churning stream. The feeling of cold water seeped into my torn socks through my cheap, tattered construction boots. I couldn't have cared less. I put my hands in the water until the cuts in my palms were painless. My body warmth and brain fog seemed to leave me, rushing downstream over boulders and across rounded pebbles, slowing in an eddy farther down, swirling in circles with a large maple leaf and two swollen pinecones. *Am I hallucinating from mental exhaustion?* I didn't know and didn't care. I'd had a rough few months—years, really.

When I graduated from high school, I moved away from home

and attended five different junior colleges. My work history was almost as varied. I worked in a video rental store, a lumber yard, and a concrete company before I got into construction. After a few years of never making more than $10.25 an hour on a crew, I took out a loan to build my own home. I sold the house right as the stock market crashed and walked away with $2,350.

Without anywhere else to live, the camper shell of my truck became my new bedroom. I parked my truck at a hotel in Oakland and started a job with a large industrial-scale solar electric contractor. I was young, living in the big city, traveling, and working on huge projects. I became a foreman pretty quickly. After ten months, I saved enough money for a four-month backpacking trip in Costa Rica. The company I worked for encouraged me to go, so I took off to Central America.

Costa Rica, though beautiful, left me feeling empty. My on-and-off relationship of a few years ended in disaster while I was there. And about three months in, I got a call letting me know that my childhood best friend, Joey, had died of a brain aneurysm. My trip was cut short when I flew home to the Bay Area and drove up north for his funeral. On my drive back down to Oakland from the funeral, my brother called and told me another childhood friend had taken his life that evening. I started spiraling. By the end of the next week, another friend who had just returned from Iraq took his own life. Three of my childhood friends were gone in a matter of three weeks.

And now here I was, up north again with Uncle Bob watching my pain, anxiety, and aches go down a creek bed. Despite my exhaustion, I felt good for the first time in a long time—like I belonged. I cupped my hands and splashed the frigid water onto my face, baptizing myself with the snowmelt. I grabbed the largest boulder I could find and returned to the stupid truck.

Growing up, I was taught never to ask how much longer or why we were going when we were on a road trip. "Only ask to pull over if you're going to hurl breakfast all over the back seat or your younger brother," my parents would say. I bet they had never been on a road trip like this. I wondered how many more creek crossings, wash-outs, and downed limbs we would need to move, stack, chainsaw in half, or throw in the bed. How much more debris would I have to move out of the way to avoid flats? How many more gashes would be on my hands by the end of this day?

Uncle Bob had taken me into unfamiliar Humboldt County ter-ritory. I grew up in the Humboldt hills, but these were the Hum-boldt mountains. The difference was striking. The Humboldt hills were my backyard, where we created imaginary fortresses. There were areas for childhood warfare and exploration—BB gun ranges, BMX trails, quad jumps, broken bones, and spin the bottle. There were secret lookouts where we made it to third base with our girl-friends. We sat in the glow of Friday night pallet fires, stolen kegs, and skinny dipping under sunsets that became sunrises on the weekends throughout high school.

The Humboldt mountains, however, demanded a higher level of wilderness education, charged a lot more in tuition, and required keener intuition. The mountain regions were rugged and unforgiv-ing. Bob and I were isolated even by Humboldt County standards, but sometimes isolation has its own opportunities. The Humboldt mountains were a blank canvas for a young prospector.

"See the bent T-post coming out of the washout?" Bob asked.

I saw a tangle of rusted barbed wire wrapped around a rusted post with five rusty NO TRESPASSING signs nailed to a snag just beyond it.

"Yeah, what about it?"

"That's the corner of the property. The property runs northeast of that mangled piece of metal, across this watershed, and up over that mountain. Up that way to the west." He pointed to the left out the window up a fork in the road. "That's the neighbors we bought in with."

Bob flipped open his Altoids tin and started rolling another joint. I stared east at the snowcapped Trinity Alps and then north to the wooded mountains. Fresh knobby tire tracks ran up toward "the neighbors."

"Wait, you own all this land out here?"

Bob didn't reply, so I focused on a culvert in a fork in the road. Beside it were weathered deck boards sporting hundreds of protruding large, rusted nails.

"What's with those? Kind of odd, right?" I asked, pointing.

"Ha! Good eye, dude man. I think they use them for unwanted comers and goers. It's just the neighbors and us. There might not be anyone else around us for maybe ten or fifteen miles in some directions."

Bob sparked his third joint and put the Ranger back in first gear, and we rolled ahead once more. The trees cleared some, and the topography leveled as we drove the saddle to the west side of the mountain. Branches scratched the sides of the truck as the old logging-skid road got tighter and rockier. We turned northeast, and my uncle turned off the engine. We coasted slowly for a quarter mile, finally emerging into a little landing area. Even with the engine off, the truck sounded like a herd of black bears thrashing down the road, banging Detroit Steel against pots, pans, and pebbles.

This is a lot of rugged land.

The truck, dusty and loaded, slowed to a stop. In the silence, we could hear the sound of a spring rushing down the washout some fifty yards ahead. Short manzanita shrubs covered much of the landing, and a couple of firs spiked above, tall, beautiful, and naked. Madrones towered to the sky, their silhouettes in the rising sun's glow. Dew turned to vapor as the shrubs stretched toward the warming sun. The last patches of small spring snowbanks hid beneath the towering fir trees of the northern side of the mountain.

Sitting in the middle of the landing area were two cheap carport frames. Some of the camo-painted framing was bent, and netting hung on cheap pins. Hidden in the madrones fifty feet up the hillside, a shredded camo tarp had been flung atop part of a collapsed canopy over two weathered white plastic chairs covered in pine needles. One chair was missing a leg, and the other was missing half its back and an arm. While I took it all in, Bob took a four-minute piss. He finally walked back to the bed of the truck to grab his tattered leather work gloves, a backpack, and his walking sticks.

"I need to walk up to the water tank and get the hose plugged back in. I'm sure the winter has pulled it loose, and the bears have done their fair share of chewing the line," said Bob.

"Damn," I said, still getting my bearings. Kiddie pools full of soil and moldy stacks of striped branches sat on the ground inside the carport frames. "Why the hell did you spend so much time camouflaging the road here and the structures if you were growing in forty-eight bright blue kiddie pools that could be noticed from the edge of the stratosphere?"

"Dude, it was hell last year. I was all for it, then hid it, then didn't hide it. I'd smoke a doobie and think more about hiding it or not hiding it. It was all screwed. When I went to get the kiddie pools, someone asked me what they were for, and I told 'em I was raising baby ducks for fancy restaurants. Ha!"

I started chuckling but was also sad. The disease had him good those days, physically and mentally. Bob and I got to work, and after over five hours of emptying kiddie pools, my back was on fire, and I smelled like rotten water and fermented soil. I placed the last kiddie pool on top of the stack of the rest in the bed of the truck. We cut all the irrigation into strips and zip-tied them together—dozens of blue, lime-green, red, and white plant tags filled a five-gallon grow pot along with rusted tie wire, a broken utility knife, a cracked turquoise glass pipe, some plant tape, and innumerable pieces of weathered duct tape. The soggy patchwork of a greenhouse cover was stretched out under the trees to be dried and disinfected by the sun.

I sat under a tree, still in amazement that I didn't know this place existed until a couple days ago. As I rested, I listened to the leaves blowing in the wind, the far-off cry of a redtail hawk, and the rushing creek. Clouds passed over, crickets played their instruments, and vultures spiraled in the sky. There was a terminal peace about that place. *My uncle's growing years are done. Maybe his years are done too. This is a heavy time for him and for our family.*

The peace was short-lived as the faint but unmistakable sound of an automatic firearm echoed in the distance. The rapid sound reminded me why warning signs were hung on every post and prominent tree for the last thirteen miles. Bob fired up the Ranger.

"Let's get out of here!" I said as I climbed back in the truck. "I'll come back up with you next week to help get the rest of this crap out of here. This is your property, right?"

Bob didn't answer. A couple miles later, I was closing the aluminum gate, locking it with a piece of tie wire. I put the bullet-riddled private property sign back on a nail. Off in the distance, I heard a couple of men yelling what sounded like directions. It was the first human sound I'd heard other than our own since we hit the gravel road hours prior.

"Damn, sound carries out here. There are some guys up over there." I pointed southwest to the opposite camel hump of the mountain spine and up the dirt road heading in that direction.

"Oh, they're up here today?" he asked, perplexed.

CHAPTER 3

Damned If You Do, Damned If You Don't

SPRING 2008

ON THE WAY OUT, the Ranger handled the road better when Bob used the low gears, plus the trash in the bed of the truck helped ground the truck in the fine gravel as we sped away from Bob's property with the kiddie pools loaded. "Fifty feet from the property's corner," Bob said. Then he looked at me and seemed to consider something. "Hell, might as well."

He took a sharp right up the driveway toward the neighbors' place. He stared ahead, shifting hard from first to second gear. We passed seven newer-looking NO TRESPASSING signs, crossed a spring runoff, and started slamming up the steep road. The two-wheel drive barely held us to the road, and the back tires spewed gravel in every direction.

A single gatepost with a simple KEEP OUT sign nicely mounted in a wood frame came into view as the road ahead disappeared, and for a moment, all we saw was the southern sky. The truck slammed back on the ground as we leveled out, and the dust we kicked up cleared. The sun was blinding as it pierced through the partially cracked windshield. Bob kicked on the emergency brake, turned the truck off, and got out.

The flat emerged as the last of the dust drifted east into the teenage fir trees to our left. To the south, we had vast open views of the radio towers on Mule Mountain. A nice cabin was tucked back inside the hog-wire fence line, both abnormally well-built and con- structed for the elements—luxurious for Humboldt. Four trucks, a quad, and two industrial off-road-ready-looking golf carts were parked in a line to the side of the cabin.

Those are nice new trucks, I thought. *Expensive trucks. No one is buying new construction trucks right now.*

One truck in particular caught my eye—a lifted, massive blue Dodge with mudders, rims, and a bumper set. But what got my at- tention was the camper shell, which was reinforced, windowless, and lockable, surrounded by a built-in contractor's lumber rack.

That's a perfect grower's truck. I think they call 'em . . . um, "grow dozers."

My uncle yelled hello and announced his name, but my eyes and thoughts were so fast and tense that his voice sounded muffled. When I turned toward him, I saw a greenhouse in all her mighty beauty. It was thirty feet wide and seventy feet long with wood- framed end walls, lattice skirting, a white top, and DC fans powered by a small solar array on a single eight-foot post. There was another greenhouse behind it.

"Hey!" a man yelled. "Someone's here! Intruders! Hey!" He jumped off the little deck of the cabin in a full sprint toward us. Two other men came rushing out of the cabin, and a third walked out slowly.

"What are you doing here?" yelled the first man.

"Jarod, it's Bob!" my uncle yelled.

"They're fine!" another man, Jarod, apparently, said as he

entered the half circle of men silhouetted against the midday sun. "They're the neighbors." The man who ran and yelled at us was the tallest. He had shoulder-length reddish hair and wore a cutoff motocross T-shirt, shorts, and worn work boots. I chuckled inside—he reminded me of Bill from *Bill and Ted's Excellent Adventure* crossed with a gold prospector—and then I noticed the sheathed knife under his shirt.

There was also a quiet, good-looking, muscular guy with tattooed arms and what appeared to be Ray-Ban sunglasses and Red Wing boots. He walked over to a black Chevy diesel truck as if he had no urge for introductions. He was packing heat in the back of his jeans.

"Get back to the mini backhoe," Jarod said. "I'll be down there shortly." He stayed with Bob and me.

The three other men headed down the single-track path to the south, disappearing into the sun's rays.

"I'm sorry for your recent losses," Jarod said extra intently, looking into my eyes.

"Thank you. It has been a pretty mournful spring." I was confused about how this man I'd never met knew about my recent life.

"Any good surfing in Costa Rica? How 'bout dancing with those gals?"

"Sorta. I'm not that good at either activity. I was there more for the warm water than the waves. It was my first solo trip out of the country. Cut short, though." My eyes, with a mind of their own, took another quick glance at the greenhouse.

"You grew up here in Humboldt, right?"

"Yeah." I couldn't quite pinpoint this man's accent. It wasn't California.

"Anyone you grew up with know about this property?" he asked, pivoting like a defensive basketball player and looking me directly in the eyes again.

"I just learned about this place five minutes ago as we drove up from the property corner. Nice driveway you got." I spoke with a slight smile and a nervous growl in my throat.

"No!" he fired back. "I mean your property next door—your uncle's."

"Nah, man. I just learned about it a few days ago."

"Haven't told anybody?"

"No. I got a friend staying with me, but I told him I'm cleaning up Bob's vacation cabin. No one knows about this mountain from me. I've told no one, not even my parents, who I guess know about it," I said, coming to some realizations as I answered.

"We bought the whole two logging tracts and all three of these mountains so we can control our neighbors, control ourselves."

"Damn, sounds baller." I was almost laughing.

"Yo, look at me," he said. His voice was deep and solid as he rubbed his hands together. He leaned within inches of my face. "A silent mind will lead to silent lips, which leads to deaf ears, which will lead to us being millionaires. This mountain will give us that if we keep her secret silent. If we protect her and the neighborhood, we will be rewarded."

He was acting like a Native American medicine man in the movies. His words repeated twice over in my head. *Why am I part of the "we"?* My eyes wandered back to the now-open greenhouse doors.

"Do you understand? Never talk about this neighborhood or who you meet or know behind that first gate. Ever. Even if you see them or we see each other in town."

"Get it?" my uncle asked.

"Yeah, I got it, but I'll never be here," I said.

I could tell this operation was different from the Horse Mountain and Southern Humboldt growers I knew in my youth. This was not eight to twelve lights in the garage on the coast; this was the pure agricultural, commercial production of pot, weed, ganja, mota, bud, hippie grass, the devil's lettuce, or whatever you wanted to call marijuana. The going rate for the weed coming out of this area was $3,400 a pound, which was a lot more than the $735 I had to my name that afternoon. It was even more than the incredible wages I made doing industrial solar projects—which I had squandered over the last three and a half months in Costa Rica, moving, and getting back into junior college.

"What do you want to start on?" Jarod asked me.

Although I didn't know how to answer, I could feel the freedom and literally smell the financial reward. If I did this, I would be doing what I loved—being in the woods, building structures, and living how I wanted. My mind was racing, but my eyes were taking in the mountains, a perfect cabin, a level iron gate, the outdoor shower off the side of the quad shed, the Buddha statue sitting content in the veggie garden, and the dirt bike with a cracked helmet hanging from the seat. It was nice to finally see an ideal homestead commercial grow in my homeland, and I was standing in front of the best one I'd ever seen. In fact, I had never seen anything like it at all, not even on the news.

"Let's pick out your ladies then." Jarod smiled and turned toward the greenhouse.

"My ladies?"

"Yeah, your uncle said you wanted to grow some of your own to help pay for college?"

All right then. I didn't think my faint glimmer of the thought of growing weed would actually ever materialize into an opportunity. It had been more of a joke to myself. *Well, I guess I could try growing weed,* I would think, laughing, whenever I considered my next steps.

"Um, yeah . . . yes, I thought about it," I answered rather casually, though I was thinking, *I don't even like smoking weed anymore.* Reality and maybe a glimpse of adulthood grabbed hold of me for a split second—growing wasn't for me, and it wasn't the right time. Ironically the dollars I had to my name had just come from taking apart indoor grow operations for family friends. It was an exorbitant hourly rate for electrical and framing demolition.

In the previous two weeks, 250 federal agents stayed at a local hotel. They'd arranged to block out a huge chunk of rooms a month ahead. Well, the manager got wind of who was staying and got in touch with someone who must have gotten in touch with the local media and gave everyone a few weeks' advance warning of what was coming. "Elbow wireless," two folks talking between two trucks on a dirt road, is what we liked to call our rural game of telephone that could spread partially accurate gossip like wildfire. I had electrical experience and was in the right place at the right time. So I worked twelve-hour days for a couple of weeks, helping some friends take apart their grow houses prior to the federal agents arriving for Operation Southern Sweep in May 2008.

Every failed attempt by my friends to make a quick buck in the weed game had been killed or almost killed. The odds didn't seem in my favor. But I was still walking forward, following my future mentor toward "the ladies" like a blind prodigy who didn't know his destiny.

A circulation pump gargled away in the cattle trough, and the fans hummed in the corners of the corrugated roof as Jarod and my uncle opened the greenhouse doors. They were perfect plants, hundreds of them, all in plastic grow bags. Their little deep green leaves danced in the wind. They looked so innocent. I was stuck at the entrance to the greenhouse, staring and thinking. I knew I could replicate this system. I also knew this system was well-funded. One of Jarod's solar panels cost more than I had to my name. Six months before, I was hanging off buildings in Oakland and installing them.

"It all begins with healthy starts. You must have plants ready to flip by May fourth. They have got to be healthy and stress-free every waking moment and sleeping second." Jarod called me over. "Yo, spaceship cadet! Come here."

I snapped out of my thinking abyss and walked down the center path between squares of what must have been a hundred plants. Some men were crouched, lifting and tipping the plants, pulling them out of their bags, and checking the roots. Sun filtered through the translucent greenhouse top.

Jarod turned to me. "So, you ever tried to grow any weed before?"

"*Try* is the key word."

I had peddled little amounts of weed to friends, roommates, and coworkers for years. I had also attempted to grow a handful of plants, which were eaten by the local deer. My most valiant attempt, I told him, was along a creek bed in the rice fields of the central valley. A coworker had given me some seed starts.

"Well, how'd it go?" he asked.

"I hid my truck a quarter mile away and packed the plants a few hundred yards down the creek bed. Let the groundwater grow them. Actually did all right, but I didn't know about sexing the plants, so they seeded a week before harvest. The farmer found them and shredded them."

"Well, that happens more often than not when you trespass grow," Jarod said.

"It was a lot of stupid risks, and the only reward was a few hundred mosquito bites and a couple of photos," I said, embarrassed.

"That's ballsy, kid. Those farmers really don't like our kind."

"My attempt was only to help decrease the cost of my smoking habit. Wasn't trying to grow them to profit like this."

"No profits here, just some product for donations from the patients," Jarod said. He seemed almost sincere.

I didn't know much about the intricacy of the laws, but I knew bullshit when I heard it. I was standing on a profit-making mountaintop.

"Kneel down, touch them softly, get to know them," Jarod said, his tone a contrast to the way he acted outside the greenhouse. Inside, he was nurturing and soft.

"How old are they?" I asked.

"About seven weeks. Ready for their final transplants this week."
He began to vaguely explain the law and process of their operations,
and added, "We grow for patients."

"Patience, like people waiting around and being calm?" I asked
with an amused smile.

"What the heck are you talking about? No, kid, like patients in
the hospital."

At that time, the sale and growth of medical marijuana was legal
in California. To purchase it, you needed a prescription from a medical doctor and a card that allowed you into dispensaries. I didn't
know much about the growing end of the business, but I was sure
there were permits and state inspections required. This operation
was a little far off the path for a state inspector to visit. But as ad-
amant as Jarod was about getting the product to patients, I wasn't
going to push the issue.

"Listen, Jarod. I appreciate meeting you, man. I appreciate getting to see this setup and property. It's legit. Well, legit-ish, I think.
This place and you guys will never be mentioned from my mouth. I
promise you that on my Catholic faith. The truth is, I would love to
take these plants. But man, I'm not taking these plants anywhere.
I don't have a solid greenhouse. Shoot, man, I drive a 1994 Lumina
with no stereo, on loan from my little brother. That thing won't
make it out of town on a warm day, and it would take an act of the
automobile gods to get it to that first gate."

Looking at the beautiful plants, I knew it would be a sad existence for them if I took them away from their beautiful nursery and
caretakers.

"You can borrow my truck when you need to," Uncle Bob suggested. Yet another risk. He was wishy-washy with his decisions.

Moments later, forty little gallon bags with a lady planted in
each were loaded onto the green nursery cart. Thirty-six of the

little yellow plant stakes read *Mr. Nice,* and four read *Blue Dream.* We looked like people picking out the year's bell pepper and heirloom tomato starters at the local nursery—innocence in the sun.

"I'm still not sure what I'm going to do with these or where the hell I'm going to put them."

"You're going to grow them," Jarod said. "You're going to grow them really well. You got enough soil next door in those piles, I'm sure. I can see that you came to your senses and ditched the stupid swimming pool idea." He pointed to the back of the Ranger with blue half-circle kiddie pools acting as rear bumpers.

"I cleaned those up today," I said. "As of thirty minutes ago, I had no idea there were plants I was supposed to grow, and I'm not even sure what this is. Am I growing them for myself or for you or for Bob? All I know is, shit needs to be hashed out at the beginning in this industry. I've witnessed too many friendships and families get destroyed over this little money leaf. I need to know what the deal is now. I'm confused. What's even happening right now? I ain't never seen that many plants. I know how much those trucks and tractors cost. I even know roughly what that cabin and solar array cost." I was almost yelling. I knew I was being cornered into the offer and didn't want to get caught up in a distraction that would take my attention away from school. No one said a word as I continued. "You all are big-timers. Nothing here is hiding that." I ranted like a basketball coach yelling at a referee.

How did my uncle even meet this guy?

We finally made it over to the Ranger in the shade. I pulled the green nursery cart behind me. I was a twenty-five-year-old looking like a kid with a Radio Flyer wagon waiting for an answer from his father. *Can I play more with the weed plants?*

Steller's jay birds landed on the closest fence post and heckled me with their obnoxious laughter. Not one of us spoke. The hum of the fans played the scene's white noise. My breath was slow and deep, the way I had been trained to breathe in tense times as a child.

"What nutrients am I going to use?" I asked.

"Go get a pen and paper out of the truck, write down what I'm about to tell you, and consider it tuition-free education," Jarod said. He walked off to the quad shed.

I walked back with a ripped-off piece of a local brown grocery bag. The cart of plants sat in the shade of the solar panels.

"And what is your wife going to say about this?" I asked Bob.

"We aren't going to tell your aunt," said Bob. "There's no need."

"What? How are we going to keep this from her? If this goes wrong, I'm going to be the one that will take the fall." I hadn't even agreed to this yet, and I was already lying to someone I loved. Well, maybe not lying, but definitely keeping something from her. Throughout my childhood my aunt was the only extended family member I grew up around. She was my godmother, and she had been present at all major events. This "not telling her" plan was the wrong approach but the right thing to do. So started my time in the weird double life that farming weed in Humboldt often created for many families and now, apparently, mine.

"You're never going to get a better way in than this. Look at those plants. These are really healthy plants," Bob said. "Wish I had had starts like this last year or the year before."

"They seem healthy, but how am I going to be able to take care of them? I leave and move to Sonoma County in late August. I want to, but . . ." I protested.

"Listen, you can borrow the Ranger to come up here once a week to check on them."

"Yeah? And what do you want in return? What's your cut if I do this?"

"Maybe 30 or 40 percent," Bob said.

"Don't give me that wishy-washy shit. Which is it going to be?" I huffed.

"Then it's 40 percent."

It felt like extortion, a setup from my uncle for growing in his soil and using his truck a few times. *Here is your future. Take it or leave it.* But it was a start.

"Just be prepared for 40 percent of nothing," I said. "This never works out. Just look at your last year's harvest." The tall guy with shoulder-length hair yelled up the hill at Jarod, who was still rummaging around in the shed. "All right, if I do this, 40 percent is OK, but I need that truck available when I need it. In the fall, you need to check on these. I'm going to be in college a five-hour-straight drive from where we are standing right now."

Just saying it all out loud—getting involved with Jarod, hiding things from my aunt, giving Bob such a huge cut—made it seem like a stupid plan. But it was a plan that didn't start for three and a half months. The unknowns of the future and the knowns of the moment were comforting. The plants sure did look pretty with their leaves waving hello. They looked like they were almost asking me to give them a chance.

The quad reversed out of the shed and burned out toward us. The beast was loaded with white bags of what looked like soil. Jarod drove with one hand on the handlebars and the other reaching back over the load sitting on the back rack, keeping them from tipping over backward. The quad stopped eighteen inches from my shins.

"What kind of soil is that?"

"It's not soil! It's amendments," Jarod yelled as he got down off the quad. "The ratios are on the bags. You can figure it out, college kid. You need these for that soil you got over there that's two shitty years old."

I noticed one of the price tags on one of the bags that read *worm castings. Huh? Aren't castings poop?* Right next to it, the price tag read *Mad River Gardens, $89.*

"Damn! Eighty-nine dollars for that bag? There are three of those. And what is this? Bat guano for fifty-eight bucks?"

"Yeah. This is the shit."

"Yeah. Quite literally exotic, expensive shit, apparently from the Southern Hemisphere. Here in this white bag on a quad, limited time only for eighty-nine dollars!" The guys chuckled for the first time since we had arrived.

"Dude, you need this stuff," Jarod said.

"Yeah, but I can't afford it. I'm sorry. I can't afford four hundred dollars' worth of exotic cave shit. That's more than half of my savings."

Jarod peered into my eyes with an awkward laser focus for a few deep seconds, then motioned me to follow him back to the door of the largest greenhouse. We stood there looking in. I could hear Bob talking with the other guys over by the trucks. The jays quieted down, but they were sitting on the fence right above the cart of plants.

"You got goals, man?" Jarod asked. It was the calmest he had been since our introduction.

"Yeah. I want to get through school. I start this fall at Sonoma State."

"Has that always been your goal?"

"Well, no," I said honestly.

"What was your last goal before this school goal?"

"I always wanted to have my own home on the river and not have any debt."

"You got debt now?"

"No. No credit card, no car loan—just a debit card with a couple hundred bucks on it and a little over five hundred in cash from working last week. I was actually taking down an operation before the feds got there. I will get more next week—maybe seven, eight hundred. But nothing is on the horizon after that."

"I didn't have all this when I started, and I will have more than this when I'm finished," Jarod said. It almost seemed like he was talking to himself. "As I see it, college isn't going to get you any of those goals completed fast, and we are in the worst recession in over eighty years. Those plants over there are not in a recession. Look at them shining." He whispered, "They're in veg."

"What?" I naturally whispered back.

He snapped back to his naturally aggressive personality. "Veg!"

"What? What is veg?"

"They're growing there, not decreasing like homes and Wall Street," he said, reminding me of the news on the radio that morning. "Look, kid. You clearly can work hard. Your uncle told me you built houses with convicts and journeymen in hundred-degree weather for the last five years. You know these hills. You understand keeping your mouth shut. You got no debt, and you can borrow a truck to get your butt out here."

That was true. I worked with construction crews for years, where I was the youngest by over twelve years. That was tough, and I grew up fast. It honed my work ethic and my focus on being on time, waking up crazy early every day, and showing up, no matter how late I was up the night before. And I knew how to build.

"I know him. He won't let me borrow that truck very often."

"Then walk up from the gate. Man up, kid, you're about to complete your second astrological age." Jarod kicked dirt in my direction. I chose not to ask what the hell he was talking about or its relevance.

"Fact: You guys are going to get busted," I spat back. "What are you doing? I don't even want to be here anymore."

"What do you mean? Everybody just got busted. Over the last three weeks, there was the biggest bust ever in Humboldt County history. You even helped clean it up. We weren't part of it, and we're right out front. Why is that?" For thirty seconds, my eyes blurred, and I could only hear the sound of dry air passing through my nostrils as I processed his questions and the surrounding scene. I exhaled. My eyes came back into focus.

I looked at the plants again, over at the greenhouse, and down again at my bloody, dirty, stinky clothes. I wiggled my toes in my soggy socks. The hours of sweating started to chill me as the sun lowered on the horizon. This was a different approach to this industry—incredibly different from anything I had ever seen or heard of growing up. Jarod was running a focused, clean, industrial farm. It almost didn't matter what was inside the greenhouses. If they were growing lettuce or raising chickens, the level of professionalism would be the same. There could have easily been $10 million worth of weed growing on 1,920 acres, but no one knew this farm existed. These guys knew the laws, and they had the money for attorneys.

I guess if you're going to do wrong, there is a right way to do it, I thought as I soaked in the operation. *This is wild. Not quite OK but an opportunity maybe.*

"Go to school in the fall and do well," he said. "But with this opportunity, you got me on one side of you and those plants on the other side of you. You're damned if you take 'em and grow 'em, sure. But after next week, it sounds like you're damned if you don't."

I looked at my cheap digital watch, trying to buy some time. It was 5:43 p.m., Tuesday, May 20, 2008. "What the hell," I said. My shoulders fell, relaxed, and I caved. "I'll give it a shot."

CHAPTER 4

A Recipe

SPRING 2008

I BOUGHT FORTY GROW BAGS at $3.39 apiece from the same nursery where I'd purchased almost every birthday and Mother's Day gift for my mother for a decade. They knew these bags weren't for her, nor were the six bags of chicken shit, two hundred feet of black irrigation line, fifty plant labels, forty pieces of bamboo, hose stakes, two bags of hose clamps, end caps, splitters, valves, tie wire, granular mycorrhizae (which was supposed to help the roots or something), perlite, or pack of peanut M&Ms.

The lady at the counter asked about my mother.

"Ah, yeah, she's good. Living in Los Angeles. My father works down there now too."

"Did her blueberry bushes produce this year?"

My mother had purchased some blueberry bushes from the nursery a couple years back, and my father had built her the Taj Mahal of redwood blueberry cages to keep out birds.

"Yes, she got some off the bushes this year. Enjoyed them during one of her long weekends up here recently. She's kind of like the people who want to raise chickens for eggs, but after all the costs and time, each egg costs fifteen dollars. I always thought it was kinda funny, but it makes her happy, knowing she's got those blueberries for her breakfast."

That reminded me that I needed to keep track of all my expenses, just like any business, including travel costs. *Got to keep gas receipts*, I thought, distracting myself from the longest, most awkward checkout line ever. I'd tried to avoid any other locals by arriving the moment the garden supply store opened on a Tuesday. I didn't need any Humboldt gossip about me clearly buying weed-farming supplies. I could have gone to one of the grow stores, but then I truly would have been tagged a grower, and I didn't want to be seen as one. I hadn't really grown anything yet anyway. This thought made me feel a bit more comfortable with the slow checkout process and chitchat.

"Two hundred sixty-eight dollars and fifty-four cents. Cash?" she asked, cementing to me that she knew what I was up to.

"Yes."

I pulled out my wallet. The bills were in perfect order. I had heard so many complaints in my life about "growers and their wads of cash." The stereotype was that growers never seemed to care how much money they had and would just throw it around indiscriminately. At a restaurant, they'd lay down a mess of cash without even asking the server to bring a ticket. I didn't want to be like that. Plus, I wasn't a grower.

"Trey will help you out and load up the chicken poop and perlite," she said.

She closed the cash register and handed me the smallest little receipt with *River Gardens* printed across the top. I noticed that each item I purchased was listed as *Garden Goods* with a multiplier of how many of each I had purchased, the price, and a total at the bottom.

Well, my first receipt for the Receipts envelope. I spent over 60 percent of my funds that day.

"Pull your Ranger around back, and I'll load you up by the soil shed, OK?" Trey said.

Trey was good people. An older brother to one of my closest and oldest friends, he also may or may not have grown the best weed ever in his closet. Everyone knew it was the cleanest, strongest, most beautiful organic small-batch bud you could find in the Humboldt shire, and he didn't even grow it to sell. Trey grew for the art and appreciation of it. He grew for himself and those around him. I trusted his skill, friendship, and discretion.

The wipers cleared the morning mist on my windshield as I drove around the store where they warehoused large, expensive garden statues. Past the garish lawn cupids, lion heads, fountains, Buddhas, and St. Francis statues was a secluded soil shed. It brought back memories of smoking bowls in the "insulation shed" at the lumber yard while on the clock with customers.

The soil shed had a similar vibe. It was a sanctuary for discreet conversations, a place amid Humboldt County's persistent coastal rainy fog where you could take a few minutes under the metal roof with like-minded individuals. This was my first trip to the soil shed. Little did I know I would be going to that shed thirty times a year in the future.

"I haven't seen you in a few years," Trey said. "Last I heard, my brother said you were living in the Bay Area somewhere doing solar and then went down to Costa Rica. Heard you were down there when Joey got sick too."

"Yeah, I was working down there for a year or so, living in Berkeley. Then decided I wanted to travel on my own. Then spent all my money and then came up here to stay for the summer. I'm going back to school this fall."

"Joey's illness and death was shocking and so sad."

"Yep, still processing it all."

"The Fredrick and Terry losses were really sad too," he mused.

"The mind is more dangerous than that enemy over in the sandbox, it seems. They got back, and the enemy of the conscience joined forces with the devil and won with self-inflicted friendly fire."

"Yeah. Heard on the news our soldiers are killing themselves faster than the enemy. This war doesn't have an end, it seems."

"Yeah, it has been a tough spring and start to summer for sure. But let's talk about something better, huh? Like the economy!"

We both laughed.

"Like chicken poop," I replied, laughing harder.

"So, where are you growing?"

"Honestly, in the middle of the middle of nowhere. Toward Oak Creek. I'd tell you more, but that's all I can say."

"Out there, huh?"

We traipsed back and forth from the shed to the tailgate with the supplies. The wet concrete floor was half-covered with soil and manure from bags punctured by the forks of an old forklift. The smell of shit and the seashore filled the air as a few curious dairy cows in the pasture next door wandered over to the fence line to watch us. After we secured the tarp, a quiet hung in the moment. I gazed west through dwarfed spruces and pasture toward the coast. The morning fog was still dense, and the hum of the morning commuter traffic on Highway 101 moaned in the distance.

"You good?" Trey's voice interrupted my space-cadet moment.

"Ah, man, you know, to be honest, I don't know what I'm doing," I said.

"Yeah?"

"I mean, I've kinda grown a few veggies. That might not even be true. Now I'm setting out to grow forty pounds of weed. I have only seen a few pounds at a time once or twice in my life. I got nothing to base what I'm about to do on. I got to grow some frickin' good weed to make this damned mountain rodeo worth it. I know I need water, sun, and some soil to make it grow, but I don't even know how much of those or what else. I got eighty-dollar bags of Peruvian bat guano. I don't even know how much to put in or not to put in or when to put it in. Damn, I sound like I'm about to lose my virginity talking to an older experienced friend," I rambled.

The confidence I had in my purchases twenty minutes prior was gone.

"Well, that's all a bit extreme," he said.

"I'm nervous, man."

"You didn't buy any soil today. Got some at your spot?"

"Yeah, actually, it's the only thing I got a lot of. I think I got enough of it. I need your help with this—not growing it but here at the nursery. Picking the right stuff, how much nutrient to use, and all the other shit about how to grow. And I need to grow on an almost zero-funds budget too."

"I can help. You're a customer, for Christ's sake."

"Dude, you grew the best Salmon Creek big bud this county has ever seen."

"OK, OK, easy. Tell you what, you've got to get those plants in this week. It's getting late. Go up and plant the plants."

"Plants planted in the ground. Boom, baby! Yeah, yeah, let's go!"

In those years, I was hyperactive. My intense ADHD and natural energy were running the show as Trey looked on, clearly amused.

I explained the products Jarod had given me. Trey walked over to the shed, found an old cardboard box, ripped off a piece, and grabbed a dusty Sharpie. He was like a chef putting together his recipe with the spices I had in my kitchen. No fluff, just the recipe and cooking instructions. On one side of the oil-stained cardboard, he wrote how to mix the soil, how to transplant the plants, and what to give them in the first two weeks. On the other side, he listed what nutrients to give them.

After Trey gave me a few other pointers, he said, "At the beginning of August, you'll stop everything written on this cardboard."

"OK, and?"

"Then come back, and I will line you up with what you will need for the flower stage."

"The flower stage, huh?"

"When they start to bud, it's called flowering. You're going to need to save up five to seven hundred dollars in the next couple of months to pay for those nutrients. It's super important. That's where the difference in your quality will be the difference in your wallet. Roger that?"

"Hell yeah, roger that, roger this Holy Grail of a piece of dirty cardboard."

"Be patient and calm with the plants. They will appreciate you for it. They're your livelihood now."

"Thanks, Trey. Appreciate this. And please keep it quiet."

"I know, dude. Of course. It's my business to keep my friends and customers' choice of plants quiet as they grow their business."

"Speaking of business, can I ask you something else?"

"Maybe. What's up?"

"I know the grow shops are in the business of selling the dream and everything one needs to 'live the dream.' But do you know anyone who actually lived the dream, retired from growing weed, and won the dream? I mean, really. Were any able to change their lives, buy a nice house or investment properties, retire, or be, as they say, a baller, set for life?"

At that point, I didn't know anyone who had won the weed game. While I had no judgments about anyone I knew who tried their luck at the green-to-gold reward, everyone I knew who tried had failed. They either got busted or spent everything they made in the first three months.

"A baller, huh?" He laughed and reached for his coffee mug. "I thought you were just trying to grow a small garden for one summer—nowhere near an enterprise."

"I am just growing a small plot of forty plants. But I saw something last week that looked like someone could maybe make this whole thing a lucrative career."

"It's a hustle, sure. But a secure career—no way. Not in the sense of what we grew up thinking of as a career. It's still farming, and in most seasons, fields across this nation are full of farmers crying no matter what was grown in their fields. Farming is a bitch, and gardening is a joy. Your size is a garden."

I was shocked.

"There's not *anyone* you can think of?" I asked again as the feeling of being a destined failure settled in my gut.

"I know two individuals it worked out for, and they are both set for life. Both now live out of the area," he said.

My curiosity was piqued. "Really?"

"The majority of the men and women who come here, well, we take their money, and they fill their trucks with all these products. They head up into the hills all around us with those small little plants. And every fall, not all but most come out of those woods more broke than when they went in. They're less sober, with longer, untamed hair, and way more detached from a structured life. Then they try again the following season and fall deeper into the spiral. They're like gamblers trying to win back their losses before the sun rises, the lights go up, and the cocktails are cut off," he concluded with conviction.

"Is that why you don't try?" I asked. "I mean, you have all the resources, knowledge, access to successful people who own land, and the examples of those who are waiting for the sun to come up."

"No, that's not why. I don't try because I understand the odds and the long list of risks. The farming odds and risks are way worse than the legal odds. Safety in numbers has a good chance of beating the legal odds, but farming is another story. It's going to be a long season of farming. You against the rugged natural world. It's a war against the elements, and I just don't want to suit up for such a fight when I know too much about the most common outcome. The sudden storms, deer that eat up your plants, wood rats that dig in your roots, bears that tear apart your water and nutrient lines, little microscopic pests that devour your plants in a matter of hours, the agitated rattlesnakes of the summer and the mighty molds of the early fall. All the while camping with the bare minimum surrounded by *actual* bears as you dig at the earth and brace yourself against a tree to shit every day. It's a fool's errand to roll those dice. I'm not willing to roll."

Trey took a swig of his coffee and continued. "It's so much more than just planting, hiding, harvesting, processing, and God forbid, selling. It's . . ."

He paused and turned away. The mist had become droplets of rain streaking down our backs. My hands were soaked. I stuck them in the front pocket of my hoodie, trying to restart my circulation.

"Here's the deal. I will tell you, but don't let it kill your naive mind. With a budget like this, your mind, willpower, and quiet demeanor will be the deciding factors this year. Here, give me that back." Trey snatched the soggy cardboard recipe from my hand. He wrote a list of about thirty things to watch out for, from deer and mold to disgruntled girlfriends and predators, both animal and business.

"It's better to know it and grow it than grow it and blow it," he said to me, smiling with pride. I felt blessed to take such a valuable piece of soggy cardboard from his hand. It was my first guide to the game board of weed season.

"Thanks, man. It's good to see you. Your help really means a lot too." I shook his hand, started Rick, and turned the defroster on full. I gently placed the cardboard on the dash to dry.

"Hey!" Trey yelled, motioning for me to roll down the window. "Don't buy anything from the grow stores if you don't have to. This here is a way safer and quieter option. You are family here. You're gossip there."

CHAPTER 5

The Sound of Captured Water

2008

FIFTY-THREE MILES AWAY from the garden center and 4,200 feet higher in elevation, it was planting time on the mountain. I had already been up a few times and built the greenhouse structures. Patched a lot of the water line. Cleaned the area. Carried the pickle barrel up to the spring and built my little camp and tent in the woods.

The morning was already hot—mountain hot. There was no wind or clouds—just heat. When you're four thousand feet closer to the sun, you feel it.

I wanted to arrive at 7:30 a.m. and start by 8:00 a.m., but I had to stop in the small rural neighborhood of Horse to grab Noah and then visit the hardware store in Oak Creek for a couple of last-minute things.

Noah had been a transient presence. I met him five years before in the Humboldt hills the night the neighbors gave me the tools to shoot him when he'd been scouting at their property. That early encounter years before had been a disaster. My friends and I found Noah and his party of drifters on the neighbors' property in the middle of the night after we had already chased them off once. Everyone was drunk, high, or some combination of the two, and it only didn't turn violent because they agreed to leave the property that night. The next morning, I found Noah on the side of the road, separated from his companions and trying to hitchhike to the nearest town. In daylight hours and relatively sober, he turned out to be a good man. We exchanged apologies, I gave him some food, and he had since become a sort of property caretaker for those same neighbors and a trusted friend to me. I always thought he looked like Adonis from Greek mythology but with white-guy dreads. A former youth pastor who struggled with alcoholism, he still loved God with all his soul and found comfort in the mountain.

We made it to the flat at 10:48 a.m., already behind. With the late start, it was clear we wouldn't complete our planned duties for the day. The goal was to mix the soil, add the dry amendments, fill the thirty-five-gallon bags with it, then plant and water. Two hours in, our plan seemed more of a joke than a goal. I noted for future runs that everything needed to be ready to go the night before. As we prepped to plant the ladies, dry manure and dust rose into the air after each shovel scoop. We had wet T-shirts tied around our heads as respirators. The only worse planting condition I could imagine would be a thunderstorm.

It was imperative that this little garden be self-reliant. In the fall, I'd be in class five hours away from the plants. There would be times I would not come to the garden for two or three weeks. The timers and plumbing had to be a solid enough operation that also allowed me to eat two meals a day and have gas money. Most importantly, I didn't want to be up on the property during the week-days so that I could avoid any run-ins with CAMP or the Six Rivers National Forest rangers, either of which would spell the end of our operation before it began.

Still, I tried to prepare for any encounters with law enforcement. I developed a plausible cover story for why I was at the ass end of nowhere. My summertime story on the weekends was to claim I was in the area for recreation. During the week, I would say I worked down at the lumber yard. By the fall, I would need to create an alibi that wasn't hunting; I didn't have tags, and I didn't want to have a gun. I also knew that I was unlikely to be able to borrow a truck after planting, so it would be a grueling three-mile hike up each time.

Noah interrupted my contemplation of future alibis.

"That's twenty-four blessed little homes for the wonderful plants to live, brother," Noah said, tying back his dreadlocks with a copper wire.

We had just finished building a ten-by-forty-foot greenhouse with Bob's bent, rusted metal carports as the frame, wooden closet dowels as the rafters, and clear painter's plastic as the walls. The two carports connected longways, stitched together by rebar and runners. "Rickety" would have been a compliment. We knew the structure needed bracing to hold up against the mountain elements, so we used scrap wood we found in the free box at the lumber yard and pallets from the feed store. When we were done, we arranged the grow bags in four rows, ten plants long.

"There, under those saplings, is the tarp hiding a couple of chairs," I said. It was time for lunch. "Use a stick to flick that tarp. Heard a rattler up on this flat yesterday during my exploring."

"Looks prime for them here," Noah replied. "Was going to ask about the wildlife earlier. Saw a healthy bear yesterday, had a rear end like a Volkswagen bug. That sucker got my heart pounding."

Noah and I called it a day after we planted twenty-four of the forty ladies and filled and prepped the rest of the bags. Our backs were bright red, our fingernails black, our necks and forearms black with dirt and manure. Stiff from ten hours of hard labor, we retreated to the campsite I'd set up after my trip to the garden center.

"Are you going to be able to finish this up on your own?" Noah asked.

I had agreed to pay him for the day's work and add a twelve-pack of Coors. As of right then, my labor budget had been spent.

"I will make do," I said. "Thank you. Your help and company was needed. Let's get on out of here. I'll finish up tomorrow morning. Rain is forecasted for tomorrow evening. Want to get plastic over the top of the ladies in the morning."

"You're not going to have any of those beers?" he asked. "They're calling out our names like a siren song."

"Nah, I don't drink much these days."

"This was one hell of a day, though, kid. Sure you going to stay out here alone?"

"Yep, staying here for a few nights has broken me in. It was comforting just being with myself and this mountain."

"I'm an isolationist, man," Noah said. "I ain't about no Babylonian life if you didn't know." He always referred to towns, people who worked jobs, and a long list of civilization's trappings as "Babylonian," and he found a way to bring it up at least once a day. "But this out here, this is like, like Alaskan bush life or modern gold prospecting. But alone, alone, alone, like an old pack mule miner without even the mule to chat it up with."

"Those small weed plants are my livelihood now, my non-Babylonian responsibility, my flock or biblical herd even," I said, trying to connect to Noah's devoted relationship with Jesus and the Bible. I'm going to treat it as close to a job as I can, and I only have the truck for two more days."

"If you look past our pieced-together shack of a greenhouse, they do look happy. Their leaves are already praying to the sun, praising the light of the Almighty. Amen, a faithful flock you have."

"Ha, it kinda does look like it."

"Not kinda, my brother," said Noah reverently.

I gave him a sandwich, a jug of water, and ten dollars when I dropped him off.

. . .

On Saturday morning, I loaded up the Ranger at 5:00 a.m., drove out of Arcata, and made it to the grow site by 6:32 a.m. I spent the next two hours fixing all the bear holes in the water line and making my way up the mountain to the spring that fed it. Even though the spring was just over six hundred feet above the flat, over 1,600 feet of line was needed to deliver the fresh mountain water to a huge 1,200-gallon water tank, which was the water's last stop before irrigating the plants. I cut branches, moved logs, and used tie wires to secure the waterline from tree to tree.

Getting to the spring was a workout. As I came over the little landing through the low brush, I could hear the pounding water pouring into the thirty-five-gallon drum that served to build pressure for the flow. I wore work boots, camo shorts, and a long-sleeve green shirt because I wanted to blend in with the surroundings, although I doubted anyone was anywhere nearby. It gave me a sense of comfort and power to have the correct jersey for the arena.

The earth was soggy, and the rocks around the drum were slippery. As I approached, the earth gave, and I tumbled into the brush, scraping my calves and shins, which were already covered in scabs. *Shorts are not an option in the future, even on hot days,* I noted as I regained my footing and sat my heavy backpack on an old stump. I unstrapped the piece of green metal roofing from my pack and set it to the side, happy it didn't catch on the branches or tear at my shirt on the way up. I unbuckled the top straps on the old pack and laid out my tools and parts on a large fir stump like it was a surgical tray. I was preparing to do surgery on this spring so it would move the water where and how I wanted.

Working in the spring was tight. Branches arched over it, and jagged moss-covered boulders buffered a crack the size of a soda can where the water entered our world. During that time of year, the spring gushed more than sixty gallons a minute. To direct the water, I needed to dig a spillway lined with old metal roofing. The metal would keep the water as silt-free as possible so my water lines wouldn't clog with soil. It might have been 2008, but I was operating like a mid-1800s gold miner breaking ground on his claim.

It didn't take long before my knees were raw from the friction of kneeling on damp rocks. I used the claws of the hammer to dig, and frigid water kept splashing against my hands. Every couple of minutes, I set my hammer down and put my hands under my armpits to keep from getting frostbite. That solution didn't help for long. My hands were fully frozen; I could barely feel the handle of the hammer.

I'd dug out and lined about half the spillway when I noticed that the metal wasn't lining up with the spring. I didn't realize how much water was soaking into the ground until I moved the roofing material just a few inches over to catch the spring's outflow. Water rushed down the metal sheet and hit my chest with such force that it knocked me to the side. Unable to get traction on the slippery rocks, I fell over the barrel to my right, and my hip landed on the barrel's spigot. Soaked and aching, I grabbed the hammer out of the mud at my feet and smashed it the last three inches under the mouth of the spring. I turned with just enough time to dodge the brunt of the gushing stream of frigid water on its new diverted path.

"Piece of shit!" I yelled to the mountains.

I flung the hammer into the dirt embankment below the spring. Grabbing my pack, I walked south, leaving the vibrant brush of the spring for the sun. The sound of gurgling water was faint. I kicked some sticks aside and raked a small space with the last of the energy left in my frozen feet. My hands were barely able to untie my bootlaces. Bruises and lesions bloomed on my knuckles. I cut my white undershirt off my body with my small Leatherman blade, channeling my testosterone and forgetting the throbbing pain in my wrist and hip for a moment.

After I removed the rest of my clothes, I took a black sweat-shirt from the pack and laid it out like a beach towel. I rested with my white ass and bare feet on the backpack and my torso and head on the sweatshirt. The beating sun caused my damp hands and drenched hair to steam with evaporation. My icy chest rose and fell as my lungs slowly caught back up to a normal stride. I draped my arm over my forehead to block the bright rays from my eyes. I was alone, naked, and defeated with only half of my task completed. There was no one to call for help. My cell phone was down in the tent, a fact that didn't matter anyway because the nearest cell service was fifteen miles away and the nearest person was five to ten miles away, depending on the day.

Cold and exhaustion overcame me. I drifted into sleep and dreamed that the mountain was speaking to me. I was fully submitting to its will as its servant. The mountain required my silence, and I had to accept that. If I served it with respect, caution, protection, and care, the mountain would fulfill my goals.

I woke to crashing branches and falling rocks somewhere up the hill above the spring. By the time I got to my feet, still naked, the crashing had moved toward me and eventually manifested in the form of a brown bear twenty feet from me, in a full run down the hillside. My heart pounded in abject terror. I had fallen asleep naked on the side of a mountain. Despite, or because of, the horror of potentially becoming a bear snack, I laughed aloud at the absurdity of the moment. A bear, out for an afternoon jog, whizzing by a naked, sleeping, defenseless human. Thank God the bear had no interest in me.

Counting my lucky stars, I knew it was time to get moving. I needed to get the water system running right before the next day. Noah and I had used the last of what was in the tank to plant, and the ladies needed watering. After another thirty minutes of work, I started my walk down the line. On the way down, I connected each section of my makeshift spillway back together, getting drenched at each connection. I liked the pure and rewarding sound of the gushing water. It was the sound of an accomplished goal and future security.

The last connection to the water tank was at the base of a massive madrone tree that shaded me from the peeping eyes of helicopters. It was almost as if the madrone was holding the tank like a baby against the mountain. Once I made the last connection, I placed my mouth at the tank's spigot. Beautiful, clear mountain water gushed into my mouth. With a few adjustments, the whole system was watering my plants. The bear, the bruises on my hip and shoulders, my cut hand, and the dangerous two-hour drive home were all worth it.

I had grown accustomed to using hard physical work to block my mind from anger, jealousy, loneliness, and the feeling of failure. I began applying the same strategy on the mountain. I hid from life's issues by throwing myself into growing pot. The trick was to work harder and more efficiently than my emotions and thoughts. Somehow the mountain gave me a special strength to accomplish this no matter how afraid I was. And after the dream, I knew at least now I wasn't alone. I was with the mountain and hoped it would continue being with me.

CHAPTER 6

Spicy Chicken Sandwich

SUMMER 2008

BACK DOWN THE MOUNTAIN after my irrigation success, I snuck Ranger Rick into the back-alley parking area near my uncle's house. My little cousin was nosy, and I didn't want her to have a clue I was borrowing the truck. I wasn't interested in my aunt seeing anything either. As my aunt put it years later, she would never lie in a court of law. I found it honorable. If she honestly knew nothing, having nothing to say would be honest. She was a hard worker, a good, conscientious Catholic woman.

After locking the Ranger and leaving the keys in a hidey-hole behind their house, I leaned down, kissed the hood, and said, "Thank you," like a cowboy does to his horse. "I'll see you toward the end of September, God willing and the creek don't rise—or I guess in this case don't dry up among a million other things."

I walked down the alley to get my brother's '94 Lumina and drove five miles south to Arcata. I was beat and dirty, and I had the stink of a working man. The upside was that over the last few weeks, I was feeling ripped and muscular for the first time in a while. Most of the day, I had worked without a shirt on. I had put on some sunscreen later in the day, but it was too late. I was as red as a lobster.

As I merged onto the 101 South, my tummy growled. I hadn't eaten much that day and wanted a meal I didn't have to cook. I decided, between my fatigue and unsure feelings about my mountain venture, that I needed to take myself on a date. I drove to a café in downtown Arcata to grab a sandwich. I'd maxed out my debit card at the hardware store the day before, so I hoped the cash in my pocket and change rattling around in the console would be enough for dinner. Little did I know that the café and sandwich would be a turning point for my whole life.

I pulled into town and found a flat place to park. I didn't trust the Lumina's parking brake, so I turned the tires hard against the curb before I got out. It was the first time I had been to downtown Arcata in some weeks. The small coastal town, my hometown, was also the location of Humboldt State University, home of the Lumberjacks. The semester had ended a few weeks before. The students had clearly done their annual summer exodus of the little town. The streets were mostly bare, and only a few locals roamed around.

Walking down the quaint street that led to the town plaza, I passed the old head shop with its bumper stickers hinting at the county's connections to the weed trade. It had been there my whole life. As much as the landscape of Humboldt had changed, that little corner head shop represented the good old days of Humboldt County. The back corner of the store was a twenty-one-and-older section full of pipes, bongs, and rolling papers. I stood in the doorway for a few minutes, getting whiffs of frankincense-and-myrrh incense sticks burning on the counter above the display of classic weed magazines. It looked different to me now that I was growing.

In the past, I came when I needed a new little tin for my stash, a pack of coconut-flavored rolling papers, or maybe even a sticker for my laptop. What better way to show my rebellious side while studying in the library than a pot leaf sticker? But at that moment, I saw my new self within this plant's cultural, financial, judicial, criminal, historical, and nonsensical context, which was stuck to various apparel and other counterculture knickknacks.

I'm in the weed industry now. What the hell? I realized then that, actually, all the money I had made in the last month had come, indirectly, from the pot industry. Even if I wasn't a grower yet, I had made my living working for the people who had made their living off of weed sales. A lot of us in Humboldt were paid in green rush greenbacks. In my case, the money came from taking down operations, but it was still weed money. And now I was going in another direction and would hopefully turn a much bigger profit.

I left the store behind and entered a mostly empty café. The only other customers were two older women drinking wine and sharing a basket of cheesy garlic fries. I walked to the counter and read the chalkboard menu to confirm the price I had in my head for the sandwich. *Perfect. I have enough.*

"I'll be right there," a young lady said as she banged through the swinging doors with a five-gallon bucket of ice. Gorgeous and petite but strong, she walked to the back of the soda machine behind the front counter, set the bucket of ice down, lifted the ice chest door, and poured the ice in. Then she stepped behind the register, looked up, and caught me staring. She smiled and looked down. I was done. My heart fluttered for the first time in years. *This woman might change my current one-night-stands-only status.*

"What would you like?" she asked. Her long wavy blonde hair was up in a ponytail and fell straight down her back. She wore a cute cream-colored tank top with little blue anchors stamped all over it. Her fingernails were painted light blue with a pair of white stripes on each index nail. This alone showed she hadn't been in town long. There weren't many, if any, nail places up there.

"I'll have the spicy chicken club sandwich with no sprouts and a cup for some water, please."

"No fries?"

"No, thanks."

"Do you like fries?" she asked again.

"Yeah, I like fries, but . . ." I said, not wanting to let on that fries were outside my budget.

"We have some extra, and it has been kinda slow the last hour. I'll throw them on your plate if that's OK."

"OK."

"You are crazy burned," she said, looking me up and down as I reached out to give her the cash. She took it, rang up the order, and handed me my change. I placed a few bucks in the "Feeling Tipsy" jar. It was a very valuable tip, the last few paper dollars I had as my hand fidgeted the remaining coins around in my pocket.

"What have you been doing," she pressed, "and where have you been doing it? It hasn't been that hot here for a burn like that."

"I was helping a family friend at his vacation property near Oak Creek. Getting it cleaned and ready for the summer. I started enjoying the sun a little too much without sunscreen—first real sun rays of the year." It wasn't perfectly true, but it was accurate enough.

"Well, you wear lobster well," she said.

We both laughed.

"I'm Ty. I grew up here and just moved back a few weeks ago for the summer. I know you're not from here because I would have noticed you and never forgotten. Where you from?"

She chuckled. "I'm Rachel. I'm from over the hill, a small town called Bakersfield, but have been moving around for the last few years. I'm very new in town myself. Been here a week. It's nice to meet you."

"You too, Rachel," I said.

She reappeared five minutes later with my steaming sandwich

and fries. The smell reminded me how hungry I was. I hoped my stomach wouldn't audibly growl. I got up to grab the plate from the counter, half caught a glimpse of her eyes, and smiled. It was the closest we had gotten in the nine minutes we'd known one another.

"Thank you."

"You're welcome," Rachel quickly replied with a smile, and I could sense she knew I wanted another conversation. Sparks had well and truly flown.

I walked back to my table and ate my well-deserved dinner. It was now only her and me in the restaurant. She turned up the music slightly and went about her duties as I managed to eat half my meal. She grabbed a spray bottle and a white washrag to clean the tables even though most of them seemed clean already. Getting up, I walked to the table she was leaning over.

"Miss Rachel," I said.

"Yeah, do you need a box?" Rachel asked.

"Yes, but I want to let you know I'm having a little cookout this Saturday with my roommate and some friends. I want to give you my number, and you're more than welcome to bring some friends, roommates, what have you. I would like to see you again and talk some more."

The truth was, there was no cookout. But if she accepted, I'd throw one together and make it an event.

"You didn't ask if I have a boyfriend," Rachel said.

My heart skipped. Rachel was right. I hadn't asked that most crucial of questions. She brushed past me toward the cash register.

"Hold on a minute. Let me grab you a box and a pen to write with." She looked back and smiled. She handed me a box for my sandwich, a piece of paper, and a pen. I wrote *Lobster Ty* and my number with a drawing of a redwood tree and a lobster raising its claws to the sun.

CHAPTER 7

A Farming Revolution on Independence Day

SUMMER 2008

THE NIGHT AFTER the fateful chicken sandwich, Rachel called and invited me to a local AAA baseball game with her and her friends. Since I passed the group date test, we spent every day together. We were in the blind bliss of summer love overnight.

A few weeks later, on Independence Day, I woke up extra early after calling it an early night; Rachel and I had plans for fireworks and a barbecue. It was going to be a long day for me. I had been working odd jobs and making the drive up to check on the plants every four days. Since I was always home by the early evening and didn't disappear on Sundays when Rachel was off, she hadn't noticed anything unusual about my schedule. I hadn't told Rachel what I was doing yet and didn't plan on it, but she had different ideas about me working on a holiday. When I told her the night before that I needed to get up early and check on some things before the evening's festivities, she balked.

"I'll be back in town by 10:30 in the morning," I told her.

"On the Fourth of July?" Rachel asked.

I shrugged my shoulders, nodded, and left for the night.

60

Fourth of July morning was a hot one on the mountain. I had stashed my old bike in the trees the last time I drove Ranger Rick up a few days before. To avoid the day's heat, I made it to the gate by 6:10 a.m. When the washout road got steep, I pushed the bike up the next couple of miles because I always enjoyed the ride back down to where the car was parked. Surprisingly, hiking up with the bike didn't take much longer than driving from that point.

Once I arrived, I started the day with a good morning to my thirty-eight little plants. I'd given two of them to an old family friend as a gesture of goodwill. The man had cancer and wanted to grow them on his deck. Jarod had given me the plants, so it only made sense to pass a couple along.

After our greetings, I kissed the hose nozzle with a "thank you," unzipped my tattered backpack, and pulled out a brand-new folded American flag. I walked over to the edge of the clearing and hung Old Glory on a post in the corner. The morning air immediately caught her and had her rippling in the wind.

"Ha, would you look at that," I said and saluted, alone in the middle of nowhere on the Fourth of July in my weed garden.

I turned and looked back at the small plants dancing in the wind. All the conventional farms I knew had flags flying. Why not me, a child of September 11 and the Great Recession? Why not my garden?

"Plants," I whispered. "They're just sweet little plants that have become so valuable because they were made so illegal."

These plants were grown by all the fathers of our country. They grew hemp, the same species as marijuana but without the psychoactive properties. They used hemp stalks to make the paper for the constitutional guidelines of our nation. These same plants were smoked by law enforcement after raids on barrels of booze during Prohibition. Now law enforcement enjoyed beers after raiding pot farms.

"You're your own little revolution out here, and I'm honored to serve as your general," I crooned, remembering that it had long been rumored that George Washington and Thomas Jefferson smoked hemp and possibly marijuana.

A great wave of patriotism in my new profession washed over me. While part of the wave was due to the holiday and the allure of living a rebellious lifestyle, I had a gut feeling that it wouldn't be a rebellious lifestyle for long. California was leading the way in the medical marijuana industry. I knew these little revolutionary warrior plants would be fully legal in my lifetime.

"I might be completely crazy for hanging you up here," I said, patting the new flag post. "Nuts, really." In truth, though, crazy seemed to be the uniting thread of our mountain community. *You've got to stop talking to everything in this garden*, I thought.

I spent the rest of the early hours that morning maintaining my little patch of freedom. Once I was done with my chores, I went back down the mountain to meet Rachel. We had planned to go to a party that evening, but Rachel wanted to talk first.

"Listen, I know you are growing weed out there," she started. "Nobody drives all the way from Arcata to the middle of nowhere on the Fourth of July to check on something. Just don't lie to me, and take me out there. I want to see it."

"Do you like hiking?" I asked without confirming or denying what I was doing.

"Yes."

That night, we went to the cookout, and I debated with myself about whether to let Rachel, my summer fling, in on the secret. *I'm not going to do this forever. I'm not going to live in Humboldt County forever. Why not?*

The next day, we drove up to the mountain. Rachel didn't ask anything about my business all the way up. I hid the Lumina in the trees. That way, we had transport off the mountain if the cops came, and the car wouldn't draw any undue attention.

We hiked the three and a half miles up the mountain, and when she saw the operation, she smiled. As I began my water checks, she walked up the hillside, found a large stump, sat cross-legged with her back straight and her eyes closed, and slipped into a quiet moment of meditation while I tended to the plants. The stillness and beauty of the mountain setting made it a perfect spot for a little reflection. Maybe it was just that, or maybe she was trying to process what she saw unfold in front of her after the hike. I wasn't sure but couldn't blame her either way.

Thirty minutes later, as I was finishing up my duties with the plants, she walked down from the stump.

"I'm a little surprised at all of this, but this place, it's so peaceful. The plants are stunning," she said. I thought she was offering her support, but we were still just feeling it out, testing each other out. I was just glad she hadn't turned around and run for the hills. "Tell me more."

I had to give her full disclosure about the risks.

"There is no pay all summer and no guarantee there ever will be. If we're lucky, we'll get some free weed to share with people come Christmas plus a lot of exercise and a story."

None of this seemed to bother Rachel. I showed her around the now fully functional grow operation. All the plants had the proper emitters. There was an old utility sink I had gotten at the recycling center. I connected the sink to a plastic folding table and added a new leg. My nutrient-mixing station was situated at the base of a fir tree in the shade and out of view. It was my mountain office.

I had two large gray totes of supplies as well. I'd put a broken cinder block on top of each tote to keep squirrels and other curious creatures from getting into its contents. I called one of the containers the "night tote"; the other was the "work tote."

The night tote was just as it sounded. It housed all the possible things one would need to get through five days on the mountain, from a first aid kit and socks to food, water, and solar charging technology. I figured if I ever saw that CAMP was landing or the sheriff was coming up the hill, I would have to ditch the grow and hide out while they cut it down. I hid the night tote under a camouflage tarp tucked under a giant root ball of a fallen tree.

The work tote was less focused on mountain survival and more focused on the day-to-day operations. It was basically an extensive toolbox, with saws, levels, tape, nails, and even a couple gallons of gasoline. I also had an extra gray fifty-foot hose with a shower nozzle that I borrowed long-term from the local thrift shop. I sank a post next to the table and bought a hose hanger for a dollar at the recycling center.

It was all very mix-and-match. For instance, I used a spaghetti serving spoon from the thrift store to help mix the nutrients, and I scored some pieces of metal out of the free bin at the recycling center to make irrigation stakes. It was tedious, repurposing the pieces of metal, but I only needed to make sixty of them. That saved me about eighteen dollars, and since I didn't have anything to invest in an operation in the first place, every penny counted.

Mismatched or not, I kept it all very clean and organized. I took pride in putting everything away properly and raking my little area at the base of the fir tree. I brushed off the table and packed out any trash. I figured if someone, namely the police, came to this little place, they might just think of it as a quaint little garden. The joy I felt when arriving at my office, spotless and waiting for me, was like the joy of returning from a vacation to find you had vacuumed and put new sheets on the bed right before leaving.

After I showed Rachel the full operation, she still wanted to help. From that moment, we spent almost no time apart, and we grew into more than a summer fling. Our relationship grew on that rural mountain with nothing to distract us from each other or ourselves. We began hiking up twice a week, even staying overnight one or two nights a week. Not because we necessarily had to but because we were beginning to really enjoy the solitude and natural surroundings more than the town. We had no money to afford town life, and mountain life was pretty darn close to free. And wasn't freedom the reason I was doing all of this?

CHAPTER 8

Five Hours South

FALL 2008

FOR THE FIRST THREE WEEKS or so after I went back to college, I lived out of the little '94 Lumina at the Kampgrounds of America (KOA) close to the campus. I set up a small tent next to the car, which was slightly more comfortable than sleeping in the back seat. Since I had been sleeping in a tent on the mountain, it didn't bother me. Also, this wasn't the first time I'd had alternative living conditions. When I worked in construction, I had lived in a campground sometimes. And when I was working in Berkeley, I lived in the back of my locked-up camper. Really, I was back to my old ways while I saved up for a deposit to possibly rent a place.

This time around, I did have the advantage of access to school facilities. I used the school's athletic locker rooms to shower and shave. The building had a brand-new workout facility and a pool, which was a bonus. Even with those amenities, living in a tent and trying to study wears a man thin. After the first month, I found a place.

During the semester, I drove up to the grow site every other week; I didn't have the money to spend on gas to get up north any more often than that. So we'd pray that the garden was fine during the weeks I couldn't drive north. My income dwindled fast, and there were periods when I didn't see Rachel or the plants for three weeks due to scheduling issues. I hoped the timer system we had put in place to open and close the irrigation system's valves worked well enough.

I was always anxious about leaving the garden unattended. I imagined dozens of catastrophes—from the cops cutting it down to a bear trampling the plants; something bad felt right around the corner. On my drives up, I trained my mind to "accept the business as a mandala." A mandala is intricate sand art used for meditation, and once the mandala is finished, the creator sweeps all the sand away. The lesson is that nothing lasts forever. I saw the garden as my mandala. I created the garden, and like that art, the plants could be destroyed, taken, or dead. I had to accept every outcome, whether success, failure, or something in between.

"It will be what it will be," I often said on the five-hour drive.

My only companions during those drives were music and public news from the solar radio I propped up on the dashboard. The car radio had been stolen. Signals came and went with the sun and shade during the drive. Fiddling with a tuning knob was often fruitless, so silence became my preferred soundtrack.

During one of my visits to the garden toward the end of that September, I brought Noah along with me. Since he had helped me plant at the start of my first season and had grown a few plants for some years, he wanted to see how it was coming along. Three more weekends and the plants would be ready to pick. I was glad to have a friend tag along for the day.

"I forgot how far out this place is, brother," Noah said. "Wow."

"Almost to the first gate. Another fifteen minutes after that 'til we hit God's country," I said, stealing his lingo.

Noah spoke philosophically as he placed his hands together in prayer. "God doesn't have a country or believe in borders, brother. He doesn't discriminate like those Babylonian places you are living in down there in Babylon City." He stuck his prayer hands out the window toward the east mountains.

"Who's that?" Noah asked as we approached the first gate. A clean, well-kept '90-something blue Chevy pickup with a small flat-bed trailer was parked outside.

"Uh, I don't know."

By then, I knew all the vehicles up there by heart from all my hiking, biking, and hiding in the brush as trucks passed on the road. Despite our odd feeling, we continued through the gates and forged ahead to the garden. When we got there, Noah's reaction was immediate.

"These are massive, my brother. I have never seen anything like them!" He held his muscular forearms next to the different bud kolas on each plant to compare, and all the plants outmuscled him.

"Knocked it out of the park so far, I think," I said. I didn't have much to compare them to but was happy with his strong reaction.

"You could harvest them today, and they would be bigger than mine or any I've ever seen."

"Thanks for the compliment—God's work," I said, poking fun at him.

Noah looked up to the sky. "Righteousness."

Right then, a human-made noise caught our ears, a faint but distinct sound of squeaking breaks and the muffled backfire of an engine turning off. We froze and shot glances at each other.

"What was that?" I mouthed.

I tiptoed in flip-flops over the irrigation lines, though it wasn't stealthy as my sandals hit my heels with a *fwap* at each step.

"Sounded like an engine turning off, up the driveway at the lookout," I whispered, pointing in the direction trucks normally drove up. We had parked a quarter mile away near my tent and walked, as I had for months.

I told Noah to stay put, but I knew he wouldn't. I began walking up the drive. About two hundred yards up, the road cleared, and I saw a forest-green four-wheeler with a custom hunting rack on the back and a gun rack on the front. Resting on the rack was a hunting rifle with a scope. *Damn*, I thought. My heart began thumping hard. I was in flip-flops and had nothing more than my hands for weapons.

I saw the back of a man in camo looking out over the point beyond the four-wheeler with binoculars. There was no way to spot or hit a deer from there. The landscape was too steep, and it wouldn't be possible to retrieve a deer carcass even if he did shoot one. I looked back at the four-wheeler and noticed the bill of his orange hat under his game bag. I almost coughed out loud when I saw the handles of large pruning shears slightly protruding from his game bag. *A ripper. Holy shit. I knew it.*

As a person who crafted alibis daily, I could spot another false persona and intent. The ripper was prepared to cut, carry, and hide plants in that game bag. However, he still had a gun. I had a flashback to a construction site on the south side of Oroville, California, where I had worked years before. A teenager, high on meth and mad at the world, pointed a gun at me. I had gotten out of that, and I'd get out of this. *At least this ripper isn't holding his gun yet*, I thought. It was time to act.

"Hey, you're on private property," I yelled. "No hunting here." The ripper's body jerked. "I got two guys right up on that hillside behind me with scopes on both of us, but sights are only on you. You're on private property."

"I . . . I . . . I thought this was Eel River. Loggin' land," the ripper said uneasily.

I was in the mode of a small alpha dog. The type of dog the larger, more fierce dogs cower before because *that tiny dog is pure crazy.*

"Hasn't been for years. Now you are over three miles behind three locked gates and at least forty NO TRESPASSING signs."

"I, uh, saw a deer."

"We see them every day. You know better. We all saw your damn blue truck this morning, and our trail cams caught your quad on that trailer at dawn," I lied.

"I . . . I . . ." he stuttered.

He was in shock. He glanced at my damn flip-flops, board shorts, and hoodie.

"Get out of here now!" I raised my right arm high. "If I raise my left arm, they are free to fire."

He stood still and looked at me for about ten seconds. He took measured steps to his quad and started it. His hand was less than six inches from his rifle. He took one more glance at me and then at his rifle. Then he made a slow U-turn with his knee on the seat and left. As the quad's engine faded, Noah walked up.

"That was an insane thing to say, brother," he said.

"Yeah, I thought I was going to throw up when he reached his four-wheeler."

I looked down at my dusty feet and overgrown toenails. *Always have on running shoes,* I heard Trey from the garden store say in my head.

"Those plants are going to be just fine until harvest, brother. That was a sign and test from the Almighty."

"As long as the next test involves some rain. Enough of the Universe and Almighty for today," I replied, remembering the spring had stopped producing enough water for gravity to move water into our tank. We were almost out.

"OK, one more because it might make you smile."

"Hit me with it. Let's get out of here."

As we started walking down the path to the garden, Noah said, "God loves you. God loves me. Man made the brew, but God made the weed."

I laughed. "Well, then, why do you love drinking the sauce so much?"

"'Cause of the devil," replied Noah without hesitation.

"Ah, well, let's get back to watering the *devil's lettuce*, shall we?" I patted his back.

. . .

A week later, in early October of 2008, it was one week to harvest, and I had a dreadful thought. I worried that the battery-operated timers Rachel and I had set up were still opening and closing the irrigation system's valves on their programmed schedule, but no water was flowing through the system. The tank was empty, and more than likely, I had dry, dead plants. I couldn't handle the thought of it. So I left midweek after class and drove up. After switching out the old sedan for Bob's little truck, I arrived at Rachel's house around 3:00 a.m.

Rachel and I took the camper shell off Ranger Rick and placed a fifty-gallon drum in the bed. To camouflage the barrel, we cut a circular hole in the bottom of a kitchen range box and put the box over the barrel. It looked like we had just gotten a new range—instant alibi. The box hid enough of the barrel that no one would notice at a glance. We'd filled the barrel with about forty gallons of tap water in town and capped it. The plan was to make two full trips that day with water, one and a half hours each way. If my fears were correct, the plants were desperate for water, and trucking it in was the only solution.

Rachel drove most of the way that morning to give me a break.

"Your anxiety needs to cool off before we see the ladies," she said. She wasn't wrong, and I tried to relax.

After an hour and a half of slow driving, we turned up the mountain road.

"These clouds look like it's going to rain," Rachel said.

"Weather report shows first torrential thunderstorms of the fall. The irony."

As Ranger Rick made it to the garden, the first drops of rain began splashing against the dusty truck.

"Hurry," Rachel said. "Get out. I got an idea." She ran off toward the camo tarp, covering our nutrients and twenty-gallon black plastic mixing totes. "Come on!" she yelled as I laced up my boots. She made it to the little greenhouse before me with two totes and a rechargeable drill. "Grab a couple of the two-by-fours from the scrap pile!"

I unscrewed the bottom board that held the plastic tops to the greenhouse. Then with a mallet, I hammered the two-by-fours into the ground as best I could. Finally, I screwed the other end to the running board that held the plastic. We created two chutes of plastic the length of the greenhouse that sloped down to a tote at each end.

"It's a rain catchment," Rachel yelled out as the sky opened up in a torrential downpour. We crawled into the packed little greenhouse, trying to stay a little dry, and listened to the beautiful sound of rain pounding on the plastic above. The smell of mountain rain on dry dust and fall leaves mixed with the ripe buds was intoxicating and all the motivation we needed to finish our work.

"Wonderful thinking," I said with pure respect.

As the rain slacked up, we both got five-gallon buckets out of Rick's bed and started the process of watering. We scooped water from our catchment chutes and gave each of the thirty-eight plants a drink. Once the plants were watered, we took the barrel out of the truck and hid it under the trees. From there, we each carried two mostly full five-gallon buckets up the trail some fifty yards to our 1,200-gallon water tank. I climbed on top of the tank, and Rachel handed me the buckets, one at a time, so I could dump them in.

Our clothes were drenched, our hands pruned up, and our wet hair stuck to our faces. In the cold October storm, our lips chattered, and hypothermia was always a concern. Over the next twenty-four hours, we used the bucket method to store and protect about eighty gallons of the chute catchment water, which was enough to finish the season. It was comical that we were collecting water in the middle of a deluge, but we had to—it would take a few days of solid rain and feet of snowmelt for the spring to start charging again. Our little ladies didn't have that kind of time.

We were swollen and exhausted by the end of it all. In the only standing space of the greenhouse, there was a solitary dry side where we attempted to dry off and change our clothes. We ducked into the tent for the next four hours until nightfall, reading and rolling around. Then we camped the night and prepped for next week's harvest.

I added an item to the list Trey had written down for me on that piece of cardboard back in May: *You can never have enough water reserved.*

CHAPTER 9

First Harvest

FALL 2008

IT WAS GETTING DARK in the driveway of my house. Ranger Rick was backed up to the open garage door. The neighbor's master bedroom light was still on. Rachel unwound the last of the straps. In silence, we nodded and lifted the sea kayak on top of the Ranger. It sat perfectly on the lumber rack mounted to the camper shell.

"Hooked on my side," she whispered.

I proceeded to ratchet the kayak down snugly. Rachel took a box fan off Rick's tailgate and walked it over to the edge of the garage to blow air out.

"Ha. The garage smells so bad," she said. "Like spray paint. You have to open the back window."

"It's almost dried back there," I said.

The day before, I'd spray-painted the inside of the camper shell windows with semi-gloss, pure black spray paint. The windows looked like a limo tint, but you couldn't see inside even with a flashlight—a trick I tried to keep secret for years. In silence, we lifted two fifty-five-gallon drums into the truck's bed and quietly rolled them against the cab. Then we placed eight plastic totes into the bed.

She handed me an old thick burlap painter's blanket and a tin gas can full of unleaded. "Do you have the sheers, change of clothes, gloves, duct tape, rainboots, and plastic suits?"

"Yes, yes, and yes. I put them all in the last tote," I confirmed.

"Ty, put a note on this dash to remind you to fill up in Oak Creek in the morning. Don't forget your debit card. They might not be open yet for cash. I'll be waiting at Mule Mountain with a surprise for you." She whispered her directions while blowing in my ear.

"Sounds great," I replied.

I scribbled a reminder on the yellow pad, released the parking brake, and let the truck roll quietly for twenty feet out of the garage. It was completely dark. Rachel followed the truck. She had placed a tackle box in the cab, a life jacket on the passenger-side floor, and a lanyard attached to an expired fishing license around the stick shift. I tossed my waders over the passenger-side seat.

"Check the lights," I said.

Rachel confirmed that Rick's lights were working and that my tags were up to date. Ranger Rick was spotless and ready for his early morning mountain-to-mountain smuggling adventure. We looked at the truck in silence, feeling the intensity of what was about to happen. Our months of effort all came down to a drive from one mountain to another.

"It's worth it," I whispered.

"The Universe has our back," she replied.

The next day was going to be a big one, and we went inside to sleep. As I lay in bed, I visualized success like a sports star getting ready for the big game. *Visualize, execute, and complete the job*, I thought. It became my routine and mantra in all dealings. I knew I would make it. I had to. I knew a young skinny college kid like me wouldn't fare well in jail. I would probably be kicked out of school, have a felony on my record, and get my uncle's little old truck, Ranger Rick, confiscated.

Every law enforcement agency within three hundred miles of Humboldt County was well aware that it was harvest season. Everyone from CAMP to the California Highway Patrol (CHP) was patrolling diligently and fishing for busts. Any one of the thousand petty reasons to pull someone over was more than enough: a broken taillight, an expired license plate, the exhaust smoking too much. All they needed was a whiff of weed as probable cause to search a vehicle or call out the drug dogs. Then it was game over. Jail time. Liberty, property, and life lost.

I personally didn't have much to lose except my freedom. I had no car registered under my name. I didn't own a house or expensive toys. But I would lose time, and that was my most treasured asset. The reality was that I had been doing all of this to *have* something to lose someday: a paid-off education, a home, and a positive bank account. I wanted to travel again and better understand cultures around the globe. I had a girlfriend to spoil. I wanted to take her out to restaurants with views and romantic lighting. Eventually, my thoughts became dreams. Sleep finally came.

The alarm sounded the next morning. I wolfed down some breakfast. While draining a glass of orange juice, I wrote a quick love letter and kissed Rachel goodbye. Before grabbing my lunch pail, I splashed ice-cold water on my face and walked out of the house shy of 4:00 a.m. The dark and predawn mist made the roads difficult to navigate, but I made it to Oak Creek to fuel up at 5:18 a.m. I was thankful that the gas station was a ghost town. No early bird cops were ducking in for a cup of coffee.

I made my way up the mountain as I had countless times over the past few months. Even with the ripper incident, every time I went to the garden, I felt less and less like I was being watched. I knew the garden or one of the gates was where I would be most likely to get jacked, but today was the first time I was carrying anything worth jacking.

I got to the garden at 5:37 a.m., almost on time. Timing was going to be everything that day. I had exactly one hour and forty-three minutes to be back down to Oak Creek and heading to my destination. The first CHP usually made it to the area between 7:30 and 7:45 a.m. on weekends. I had been trying to get a sense of their routine all summer. They were consistent enough that I knew I had to make it past their normal speed traps and turn off the main road before they set up.

The vulnerability of being so remote at such an hour doing something illegal with something so valuable was almost overwhelming. My upper body shook and spasmed with pure nervousness. I pulled it together enough to light two kerosene lanterns so I could pull out all the Rubbermaid totes and the two large barrels and placed their lids far enough away not to have bud resin fall onto the outside edges. Then I suited up—surgical scrubs, a plastic rain suit, old boots, and two layers of latex gloves. I carefully duct-taped my latex gloves to my sleeves and boots to my pant legs. Finally, I pulled the rain suit's hood over my trucker cap. The intense level of protection was meant to keep the buds' resin, which was impossible to remove without a mixture of mechanic's soap and rubbing alcohol, from coming in contact with my skin.

I glanced at the little digital thermometer hanging in the center of the greenhouse. It read Oct 17, 2008, 5:46 a.m., 42 degrees Fahrenheit, and 76 percent humidity. The ladies looked so beautiful and clean under the glow of the lanterns. I pulled the folding table out from under the tree as a workstation to buck (or de-stem and de-bud) the plants down into twelve-to-eighteen-inch sticks I stacked like firewood in the barrels and totes. I had grown accustomed to working in silence in the middle of nowhere. But in the dark at dawn with only my hatchet nearby, every waking animal's chirp, pat, and scuffle played a beat in my stomach.

"Just start, dammit," I told myself to break my three-minute stare at my crop.

I could hear Rachel's voice from the previous night, saying, "Remember to say 'thank you' for what they are doing for us and 'I love you' to each one before you cut her down." She always told every plant she loved her and appreciated what she was doing for us. Rachel brought an attitude of deep gratitude, and for a while now she had thanked every plant for her contribution. Rachel told me she often channeled the positive vibe that these plants would bring to people. She wanted to acknowledge the plants in a positive way. In a real way, these little ladies were sacrificing their lives in the harvest. This wasn't apple picking. To harvest weed, you have to chop off the plant's head. The least we could do was express thanks.

The snip and crack of the first stalk hit my ears. Then the weight of the first plant was tight in my grip. I tossed it in the outside tarp. I cut down twelve before I started bucking the plants so they would be broken down into smaller pieces. I thought that if I couldn't get them all today, it would be OK. What wouldn't be OK was if I missed my timing.

I could fit eight plants, broken down into branches, into each barrel. I wrote this ratio down in my work tote notebook. At the halfway point of the second barrel, I knew I would only be able to take about twenty-four plants with me that morning, but I had already cut down twenty-six. I hung the remaining two plants high in an old snag where they would be able to capture the afternoon wind but be shaded from direct sunlight. Then I changed into my fishing attire.

It was 6:26 a.m. when I duct-taped the last of the totes. I took a deep breath and sat in the fir duff at the front of the truck. If I was to spend most of this day in custody, I didn't want to be hungry or tired. I drank my first cup of coffee of the day and had a snack with trees turning colors under the changing dawn sky as a backdrop.

"Ah, shit, let's do this," I said aloud.

I grabbed the can of gas from the truck as something jumped on the hillside forty yards away. It spooked me, but I was past the point of caring. I believed the mountain had my back. The mountain wasn't going to let a bear or cougar jump me at that point. I returned to filling a sprayer with gas and then lightly hosed down the barrels and totes. When that was done, I grabbed the painter's blanket and flung it over everything. The blanket, tailgate, and passenger's-side door got a light misting of gas for good measure. As dangerous as it sounds, gas is the best way to cover up the pungent smell of freshly cut pot.

I fired up Ranger Rick and drove to the gate as slowly and quietly as possible. When I was almost to the gate, I knew I'd made a miscalculation. I felt queasy, and my stomach began to churn. When I started out, I thought I could make it, but I was wrong. I couldn't clench my ass muscles any tighter, and I couldn't hold it any longer. I shut the truck off and ran behind the nearest tree. Anxiety, a nasty breakfast, and coffee were a ripe combination for not number one or number two but number three. To add insult to injury, I had no toilet paper. Saved by Starbucks napkins once again.

All that mess sucked up any margin of error on timing. I made it down the mountain to the intersection where I'd hoped to be by 7:10 a.m. at 7:23 a.m. instead. I had time for a quick pullover to tighten a loose kayak strap, and I was off again. *Tick, tick, tick,* the invisible clock ran in my head. I tried not to look at a real clock because if I did, I'd be tempted to speed. *Where is the ranch road? Tick, tick, tick, Ranger Rick. Are you going to make it?* I got to the road with five minutes to spare.

"Boom!" I yelled.

I got to the cabin gate. It was closed. Rachel must not have made it yet, and all the better. I smelled horrible and needed a minute to appreciate my first win and clean up before her arrival. As I opened

Rick's camper shell, the fumes struck me. The mix of scents was so strong that I coughed, gagged, and almost vomited. I wanted to get the branches out of their containers as fast as possible, but it was no use. The truck needed to air out for at least an hour. The sun hadn't made it over the hill; it was still in the low forties. I made a fire in the cabin and started to lay the plastic down along the floor of the big southwest-facing room.

My aunt, Bob's wife, would have killed me if she saw the remodeling job I was about to do on her quaint getaway home. I started heating three gallons of water on the stovetop. I grabbed the clean kiddie pool from an outside shed and laid it on a tarp in front of the wood stove. After grabbing a towel and bar of old soap from the dresser, I sat in the recliner, waiting for my shower to be ready. Standing in a kiddie pool and using a ladle to pour lukewarm water over yourself is usually OK-ish at best. That morning's shower was a blissful baptism.

Once I finished bathing, I stepped onto the tarp, finished drying off, and burst into laughter.

"Hey, Ty, what were you laughing about?" Rachel asked.

"Sweet pea! You made it. I didn't hear you pull up."

"I parked at the gate and walked up," she said as she stepped into the cabin carrying a large backpack and two bags full of groceries. She was dressed in her signature mountain style for those days, one part all-American cowgirl, another part bohemian princess, and that didn't bother me at all. "Glad you made it here," she said with a nervous laugh.

It was the only location I knew that would work in October. The cabin was remote, and no one had gone there for a few years. The neighbors would never have thought we were there. My uncle and aunt were a couple of the few non-growers on the hill, so no one would suspect product to be there.

Rachel and I suited up like I had in the garden. We hung plastic sheets all over the cabin. It looked like a cheap version of a slaughterhouse by the time we were finally ready to start hanging the buds. The whole room was one big plastic bag. Our goal was to dry the plants over the next week. We didn't have an industrial dehumidifier, so we worked with what we had. We placed an old fan by the stove to circulate warm, dry air around the plants. Then we constructed a large free-standing trellis-web of wires inside the drying room and hung the plants up.

We stayed for a couple of days to make sure everything was going well and left everything else up to Mother Nature. I returned to class the following Monday and went through the motions, business as usual. Rachel and I returned to the cabin that Friday.

When I opened the door to the cabin, very warm air gushed out. It was like we had opened a natural oven door. Over the week, the moisture had been completely sucked out of our marijuana branches hanging on the wire lines. Crispy would have been a generous term—not what we wanted. Shocked and bummed, I called an old friend whose father was a large-scale grower and had immigrated to the area from Asia.

An hour later, my friend's father got back to me and quizzed me about the plants and their condition. After sharing my assessment, he suggested boiling pots of water in the cabin to humidify the buds and get the plants to an 8–10 percent moisture content. I had no clue what that meant, but he walked me through an expedient way to tell when the plants were ready. I thanked him. Moments later, my friend called back and said one more thing.

"Yo, bro. Don't get sucked into those hills and that industry. It ain't worth it."

After his warning, he hung up the phone without a goodbye.

CHAPTER 10

Open for Business

WINTER 2009

AFTER PAINSTAKINGLY BRINGING our product back from the desert, we trimmed our thirty-eight plants and packaged our crop. Since it was the first season and we'd had no idea if we would even get to the point of sales, we didn't have too many connections to sell our product. However, we made up rules. We decided that part of keeping ourselves safe in this venture would be following all of them. At this stage of the process, we really had no idea what we were doing. But we knew how to research, take notes, and learn. So we Googled as many news articles, press releases, and court cases as we could. How did people get caught? What were they doing? What weren't they doing? The wheres, the hows, the whys. Then we made a list of what we thought might keep us secure. Well, secure-*ish*.

1. Never communicate on the phone.
2. Never meet up at hotels.
3. Meet early in the morning; preferably be done by 7:15 a.m.
4. Don't make it complicated.
5. Never use more than one middle person.
6. Always have a full tank of gas, a jumpstarter, and an alibi.

7. If you have any lights out on your vehicle, it's a no-go—every time.

8. Make the connections cut open the bags and reseal them themselves.

9. Don't ask or be told where it's going.

10. No need for real names.

11. There are no second chances. There is someone else who will buy it tomorrow.

12. Never do anything where you live.

13. There's never a need to tell your girlfriend, close friends, family, or anyone who the connections are.

14. No drinking during deals.

15. Never keep the product and the money in the same place.

16. No guns; legal penalties are too great.

17. Stash the "donations" away deep in the truck as you leave the deal.

18. Never go home first in case anyone is following you.

19. Don't talk about money; don't look like you're doing good or spending money you shouldn't have.

We figured that if we might be dealing with people on the underside of the law, we were better safe than sorry. The law was written so that you couldn't sell weed, so *most* people spoke about getting rid of the product by saying they were receiving donations in exchange for the weed.

Our first official "donations" were from other college kids in Rachel's classes.

"Oh yeah, I take stuff down every time I go back to visit my family," one kid said. "Can I buy some?"

I thought a little bit, but I couldn't see any harm coming from it. "Sure, yeah."

"I'll take like twelve thousand dollars' worth," he said.

He gave us the equivalent of three thousand dollars a pound, $275 more than I had made building and selling a house over a ten-month period. *Holy shit. This is wild.*

We rode that twelve-thousand-dollar-high for a week. It was kind of nice. We made some money. I was able to pay for my next semester of college. Unfortunately, we still had a bunch of product. I didn't know who to sell it to, and I didn't want to talk to anybody about having it. With that approach, sales weren't going to happen, but I had no idea what I was doing, and school was my top priority. I didn't want to push too hard and end up making a mistake or working with the wrong type of people, so I stayed patient.

After two months with no sales, I received my first karmic business lesson. The family friend I paid forward with my thirty-ninth and fortieth plants at the beginning of the season called me out of the blue.

"I heard you got some extra weed," he said.

Other than giving him the plants through my uncle, I hadn't talked to him in over a decade.

"Well, I've got a little bit if you want to come get a joint or something," I said.

"No," he came back, "I hear you need some help."

"Yeah, maybe," I said. "But what are you talking about?"

"Let me come grab it from you. I'll call you."

"Sure, OK. You can keep 30 percent of what you get for it."

"No, I'm not going to keep 30 percent. I'll put a few points on each."

"OK," I agreed blindly. I had no clue what he meant by "points." He could have been referring to basketball or the number of antlers on a deer for all I knew. I found out later a point meant a hundred dollars.

He picked up the weed, and more than three weeks passed. I didn't care. I figured the pounds were gone and I would just carry on with my life. These things never worked out. Then I got a text while I was in class one day: *Call me. Come up this weekend.* I called him an hour later, and we arranged to meet.

Rachel and I met him in the back parking lot of a local brewery that weekend, where he handed us a big paper bag.

"Congratulations on your first real lunch," he said.

"Huh?"

We didn't get it. He pointed at the brown lunch bag I was holding.

"Wait to eat it until you're in a safe place so you won't spill it," he said. "Kid, that was some of the best stuff I've seen all season. What strain was that?"

"Strain?" I asked. "What's that mean?"

"Really?" He cocked his head and looked at us. "You really are a couple greenhorns."

When we finally got to a safe place, we opened the bag. It was more than our parents had ever made in a year—combined. After we counted it, we looked at each other in disbelief; "Whoa, now what?"

We did what we always did, research and learn. What would Warren Buffett do? What mistakes did professional athletes make? Lottery winners? How does one financially plan a large sum of money? We walked into a bookstore and bought a couple of money management books.

A few days after our biggest sale, it was precisely twenty-eight minutes before Kmart closed. We knew exactly what we needed, but as we walked in, we were both happy and kind of concerned. Neither of us had ever had that much money before, let alone kept all of it in a brown bag. After walking the aisles and not finding what we needed, we stopped an employee.

"Do you have money boxes and envelopes?"

She looked at us oddly and pointed us in the right direction. We realized we had just told her we probably had a lot of cash we needed to hide. We'd already failed.

"It has to be fire safe if it's gonna be in the attic," Rachel said as we made our way to the correct aisle.

"Yeah, you're right, but the safe is eighty-nine dollars," I hedged.

"But we're going to put a six-figure sum in there!" she said.

"Yeah, it's crazy. Well, only about 60 percent of that is ours. But still!"

For the first three years, Uncle Bob was guaranteed 40 percent of our profits for the use of his property and truck. We were still making bank.

We picked out a $280 safe and grabbed a few envelopes, Sharpies, and rubber bands. We checked out with a few minutes to spare and walked out to the parking lot, getting wet from the rain. The parking lot was mostly empty and gave us an eerie feeling. *Is anyone watching us?* I thought for a second. Of course, they were not, but we had so much cash back at Rachel's rental house that it felt like someone was bound to know.

"Are we going to leave the cash in the attic?" Rachel asked as we drove along the dark roads back to the house.

"For now, I think so. Then maybe take it out on the hill and bury it? I don't know," I rambled.

We got back to the house a little after midnight, made ourselves a couple of drinks, and got to work. Rachel laid out sixteen envelopes, and I set up the cash box. I put all the cash box's packaging in a trash bag to throw in a random dumpster the next day. I didn't want anyone to see it in our trash. Then we laid out all the money on the floor; it was mostly twenties.

It was a Scrooge McDuck moment. Less than a year before, neither of us had more than $450 to our names. But that night, we had literal piles of cash. They represented power, opportunity, and security. Months of rent and groceries were paid for up front. We'd worked hard, but in some ways, it was still unbelievable.

The dynamic between Rachel and I was changing slightly. We looked at each other not necessarily as a couple but as two survivors. Each of us wanted to make it out of our twenties without crushing debt. We wanted to skip that part and launch straight into our dreams. Amid the Great Recession, chasing dreams was a luxury, and the piles of cash were the only opportunity we had to get to that point.

"What should the first envelope say?" she asked. "School for you and another one for my school. Then two for rent, one for clones and plants next year, one for gas, one for food next summer," Rachel said succinctly.

"How much should we keep for the project next summer?" I asked.

"Thirty-two thousand, maybe? What are the costs? Let's write those down on paper."

"How much should be spent in Hawaii? Twenty-eight hundred for the whole trip. Plus, I spent seventeen hundred to pay off the truck."

The budget meeting went on until all the envelopes were filled and marked with their purpose. We hid the cash box in the attic underneath insulation and other boxes of old family records and pictures in a location we agreed only the two of us would know. If one of us needed to open it for any reason, we would let the other know. The last thing we needed was distrust between us.

As I rearranged the boxes of papers and pictures, I realized there were a ton of other boxes in the attic. It was perfect. All the boxes were decoys and helped hide the cash. *The hunters will always come looking for the ducks. It's our job to make sure they never find the prize mallard.* Everything we did had to have a cover story. Anything Rachel and I did had to look legit and shield our operation. Now that we were selling, we didn't only have to worry about the cops.

We had to worry about getting our stash jacked from just about any dishonest person.

Afterward, we took a little bit and went to visit my brother in Hawaii. He was living on the Big Island on a large cattle ranch out there. That was winter break for my first year back at school. It was as frugal a vacation as possible. One pound paid for our whole trip.

. . .

Just one season in, the people next door taught me to do wrong right. If you are going to do it, do it the best you can. We studied agriculture. We harvested our product, cleaned it, trimmed it, and then sold it for good donations—hell, great donations! And now that we had the funds, we accepted that this was what we would do to make it through our college educations.

I called Jarod, whom I had only spoken to once or twice since he gave me my forty ladies.

"Hey, where do you get those greenhouses? I want to do this."

"What do you mean?" he asked.

"I'm going to do exactly what you guys are doing, but even bigger."

"Well, you're away at college. How are you going to do this—just you and Miss Button Nose?" he pressed.

"We'll figure it out. We always do."

"You were pretty small potatoes this year at best, kid. Now you're standing here setting out to become the next French fry kingpin. Careful." Jarod had the same intensity he had on our first day of introductions.

"Yes, sir," I replied, still oblivious.

We were open for business.

CHAPTER 11

Gothic Gables

LATE WINTER 2009

"WITH SHIPPING, that will be $4,650."

In the courtyard below, students were walking out of the lunch hall, gossiping, sipping coffee, and power-lifting their textbooks. I should have been studying, not ordering new greenhouses for my illegal business. I took an environmental law class that semester and learned that California's medical marijuana laws were more of a sword than a shield. I wasn't licensed as an authorized grower, and the penalty for illegal grows was stiffer under the narrowly defined legalization laws.

I put that out of my head for the moment to enjoy the order I had just placed. I felt like I was getting a dream toy or even a new home—no more janky carports with plastic sheeting and old splinter-ridden wooden slats. The operation was about to receive its matriarchal chapel of worship and sanctuary of fiscal gardening. And it was time for more space—we had grown from forty plants to six hundred.

As with everything in our venture, there were rules, and there was a cover-up. Rachel was still living at her rented house, but we had started our first nursery in a secret grow room in the garage of my parents' house while my parents were away. Since I was far away at school, Rachel was at the house more than I was and helped with the upkeep, mowing the lawn, checking the mail, and, of course, caring for our crop to make sure the plants were big enough to go up the mountain in May. When she mowed the lawn or got the mail, she left the garage door open so the neighbors could peek inside as they drove or walked by and see the most normal garage ever. We didn't want anyone to have any reason to snoop around or call the cops or the codes department.

However, one afternoon while we were transplanting our little clones in the garage, a couple of police officers stopped by to do a wellness check. I'm not sure if someone called something in or if they were fishing for information, but they walked up the driveway and stopped with just ten feet of pavement and the garage door between them and hundreds of plants. Channeling the same confidence from when I talked to the ripper a few months earlier, I walked up to them, my soil-stained hand outstretched. Rachel and I introduced ourselves to the officers and spoke to them as if everything was above board. I'd even pulled a lawn mower out of the garage to make a little more space to work. I pointed to it and said, "Just waiting a little longer for the morning dew to dry before we handle the chores."

"Do your parents still live here?" one of them asked.

"Yes," I said, "but they are staying in the southern part of the state. Here is my ID, too, if you need it. You'll be seeing her around too." I gestured to Rachel. "She'll be swinging by weekly to pick up the newspapers and mow."

Our alibi beyond reasonable suspicion, the cops left. It was still a close call. Even with all our efforts to hide our activities, someone was going to notice something.

I thought about how fortunate I was that my parents lived fourteen hours away in Long Beach. I didn't have to hide any of my comings and goings from their house while I fed them suitable fiction in case something slipped. I also made a deal with them to put the utilities in my name and pay the property tax and insurance as my way of paying rent for the house. I didn't want them to notice how much more water and electricity we were using for the secret grow room we'd constructed.

In January, we had built a false wall, making the back six feet of the garage its own entity. On the garage side of the wall, we hung shelving, rakes, shovels, and bike helmets to make it look normal. We hid the door with a bookshelf on wheels, which were hidden by trim boards, so it looked solid, but it made the six-by-fourteen-foot room easily accessible. On the other side of the door, the secret room contained a small workbench, a utility sink, and fully lit shelving lined with trays full of our second-season starter crop in four-inch plastic grow containers.

My parents also didn't know about the impending delivery that would surely draw some eyes to their property. As far as they knew, Rachel and I were growing a few plants to make some money for school, and I was doing electrician jobs for Humboldt growers on some weekends. The best lies have a tinge of truth to them.

The day the big greenhouse was delivered, I skipped class, and it still didn't go as smoothly as I'd have liked. Building delivery in a semi-truck was not something you saw every day in the suburbs. The driver and I unloaded the pipes—which were so heavy that I had to drag them across the driveway and left huge dents and scratches in old 1970s concrete—one by one. About halfway through, I dropped one of the pipes. The *bang* and *clang* rang out in the quiet neighborhood air of the early Thursday midmorning.

"Dammit, that was loud," I said to the driver.

"Yep, boom, right? They're heavier than you think. Dat's why I'm serving you one at a time." He laughed.

"Roger that. I got to pace this, man."

The process continued, and the same loud symphony played

with every piece we pulled from the trailer. Discretion, which I always preferred, was impossible. The best I could do was cover the
pieces with a couple of tarps, which probably wouldn't keep questions at bay. Just as I pulled the last corner of the massive blue tarp
over the pile of galvanized metal, my parents' neighbor peeked over
the fence.

"Man, that was a lot of commotion unloading that pile of something you got there," he said in his quiet but stern voice.

Startled, I looked up to see him smiling at the long tarp pile
sitting next to the shared fence line. It was like a scene out of the
sitcom *Home Improvement*, when Wilson would pop his head over
the fence to talk to Tim. I chuckled, though he was no Wilson. He
was a pilot and member of the California Department of Forestry
and Fire Protection (CAL FIRE). He had grown up locally, in the
heart of growing country, but was never part of the hills industry.
He did, however, know the impact the industry had on the land and
Humboldt County's residents. I chattered nervously, updating him
on school, my ventures for the coming summer, and where it was to
go down. I never saw him as a threat. He'd been a great neighbor to
my parents, and I didn't want to lie to him.

"Well," he said, "I've seen many little ones, but that's a big building for sure. You're going to have one nice little spaceship sitting on
top of that mountain."

"Ha, yeah, I hope. Right here, right now, it's just a whole bunch
of metal sitting in my parents' yard. I have to find a way to get to the
top of a mountain in the middle of nowhere."

"Yeah, it's going to take a bigger truck than that little Ranger,"
he said. "Either that or it'll take ten trips."

We talked about the little medical operations he had seen in
northern Humboldt over the last fall and summer. It sounded like
he had only seen a couple of rural parcels with buildings the size
of mine.

"I'll try to call you later in the summer when we're doing fly-overs. Maybe you can show me where exactly 'your ranch' and this new 'hay barn' will be located," he said with a laugh.

We said our goodbyes and retreated to our separate sides of the fence. I stacked patio chairs and lumber by the corner of the tarp closest to the street. If someone walked up, it would look like a construction project waiting to happen—my alibi.

The greenhouse was sort of an alibi in and of itself. It would shield our plants from severe weather and create a visual barrier for air and satellite surveillance. It also offered legal protection in the form of curtilage laws, which make homes and buildings on property exempt from police searches unless a judge issues a warrant. It was not a magical barrier, but it was something.

CHAPTER 12

Tractor Frank and a Flat

SPRING 2009

DURING A FREEZING, torrential rainstorm the prior November, while cleaning up the evidence of the summer's success, I marked with pink logger's tape the corners where the future "flat" that I hoped to have someday would be. A flat was the Emerald Triangle term for the foundation, field, or clearing where you built a greenhouse. Alternatively, if you didn't have a greenhouse, a flat was where you planted your crop. The term originated in the logging industry, and like most of the remnants of logging in Humboldt, we used whatever we could. I hadn't even sold any of that first year's crop, but I had faith, a plan, and some crazy-brained foreknowledge that I would need those marked corners.

I called Tractor Frank and asked him to help with the flat.

Tractor Frank had earned the title because he operated heavy equipment like bulldozers and single-arm bucket tractors. Tractor Frank was another straight-out-of-central-casting character in our mountain community. He was skinny as a plant stake but as strong as an ox. We never saw Tractor Frank without grease under his fingernails, a camo hat, and a pack of Marlboros in his front shirt pocket.

All that gear came with a smile on his face and a positive attitude in his soul. Tractor Frank was an amazing, caring, and honest man. Jarod used him as an excavator operator, and we followed in kind.

Over the years, Tractor Frank would become one of my favorite people to run into on the road or to catch up with over burritos down at the Mexican restaurant. He didn't drink, and his wisdom on those hills ran deep. Tractor Frank's respect for others was solid, and his friendship meant more than he knew.

The plan was for Tractor Frank to use an old bulldozer owned by the boys next door to doze a flat spot where my two shit attempts at greenhouses were built the summer before. I wanted them gone and a proper flat installed. Rachel and I wanted to make sure Tractor Frank didn't cut any new roads while he was excavating. We only wanted the old logging area cleared for the greenhouses plus five feet to the tree line on the short sides, ten feet on one long end, and thirty feet on the other. This was where my preemptive logger tape came in.

To make sure he did this, I drove all the way up there one November night to mark our corners and pathways with reflective tape. I slept in the bed of the truck, did my homework by candle and headlamp, and drove all the way back to school the next morning—ten hours of driving for thirty minutes of work.

After hearing the basics of my plan, Tractor Frank agreed to the gig in the early spring.

"There's still a couple of snow drifts down there, but we'll get down in there and get'r done come Wednesday of next week," he said over the poor signal of the cell phones.

"Thank you so much, sir. I'd be lost and up Shit's Creek without you."

"Well, maybe not, but you sure would be spending a good few weeks hand-tilling yourself a flat space to raise the greenhouse on," Tractor Frank replied in his rusty smoker's voice.

"Don't knock over any trees, and please bury all the brush."

"Will do, and after a couple of strong rains at the end of this month, the place will look older, and the tracks from the dozer will be flattened out," he said.

"Sweet! That will be dope."

"Whatever that means nowadays. We'll get'r done. Over and out!"

Our plan was one step closer to coming together. I knew construction. I knew land prep for a build. The sight of the flat earth excited me and saddened me at the same time. Clearing that old logging flat bare again meant something different. I was starting to blend my past knowledge, skills, and work discipline with a new venture. Excitement and entrepreneurial conquest brewed inside me.

CHAPTER 13

Shifting Focus

SPRING 2009

MY BIKE HAD GOTTEN A FLAT TIRE the night before, so I had had to walk the mile and a half to school that morning, which was actually a blessing. The walk gave me the time I needed to focus. I was weary from all the trips up north the previous fall and wanted a college experience. The problem was that the college experience as an on-the-side pot farmer isn't quite the same as it is for folks pledging fraternities or sororities.

My program was on the small side, with around fifty students. We took many of the same classes for two years straight. We got to know each other. But there was always a weird feeling spinning inside of me. My double life and double thought processes had started to weigh on my social life at school. I made friends but never went out of my way to keep them. I always had to keep the conversation in my control, even though my mind was racing about the plants, plans, or Rachel. I could never give too much information. I dodged questions about why I was always visiting her or how I had managed not to work or take many loans out for school.

Adding to the social pressure was the question everyone asked everyone: "What comes next?" I lived in two different situations, but the writing was on the wall. At the end of the school year, I would have to pick which path would win. Would I walk off the graduation stage with my cap and gown to design a future of renewable energy projects? Or would I walk back into the woods and become an organized, rational, opportunistic outlaw with a college degree?

At that point, I couldn't tell. Even when I was focused on energy calculations of some huge natural gas power plant, my mind drifted back to the problems that needed to be solved on the mountain. In those days, the problem was who I was and how I could build a gigantic greenhouse. It would take more than Rachel and me, but I didn't want anyone to know where the hell the grow site was. What was I going to do—blindfold anyone who helped me? I laughed at the thought. Would I be able to find capable people who weren't convicts or locals? All I needed was a few guys with some building experience who were lackadaisical enough not to care about what the hell we were building.

The greenhouse may have been a heavy pile of galvanized metal sitting in the front yard, but it was a structure of longevity. The greenhouse was not a single summer's use like our plywood and plastic the year before. Sure, it had made us enough to get through the school year and go to Hawaii. And yes, if we did exactly the same thing this year that we did last year, we would have more than enough money to make it to graduation with little or no debt. But that wasn't good enough for me.

"How big is enough?" Rachel asked me one day.

"Big enough?" I asked. "People pay money for it and then consume it. Then when they are out of it, they *buy more*. As long as customers are purchasing and we are running out before the next batch, I don't know."

"That greenhouse sitting in the yard will be the deciding factor of this little venture we did last year," she said. "If that is built and a crop is planted, this will go from hobby to business."

I had it figured out. "The short-term plan is to make some money, get through school, and have some fun. The long-term goal is to graduate and get jobs in our fields. We'll slowly put the cash in the bank over a few years, pay the taxes on it, and have enough for a down payment for a home."

"You're crazy," she said.

"And we will live happily ever after, crazy in love."

"We're going to have to live up there."

"In the woods, on the dirt, shower in the creek with the animals," I sang back.

"Seriously, though, we will!" Rachel snapped. "It's too many plants and too far to drive every day. Have you thought that through on your long drives?"

Moments like these reminded me of the delicate balance our relationship required as both business and romantic partners. It was also moments like this that reminded me that I had not kept up my end of the deal on the latter. The double life had started to wear us thin, and I leaned into it. When classmates came onto me, I couldn't really resist. Would she even know? But such was our closeness that she knew almost immediately. Drama, tears, and a series of blow-up fights ensued. I knew Rachel hadn't forgotten, of course, considering she'd made me change my phone number and checked my messages often once she found out I'd been unfaithful. But a year ago, it had all been so temporary. So light. So free. Now resentment had crept in, and it began to be the third wheel in our relationship.

I hadn't expected to fall so hard or so fast for Rachel. Neither of us had experienced that kind of attraction or love before. Once I moved down to Sonoma, my subconscious was bent on sabotage, and soon I was thinking there was no way this could work with the distance.

When the gal I cheated on Rachel with came on to me very strongly, I wasn't yet mature enough to stop it or to ignore the attention.

So now, it was heavier. We had baggage.

Either way, I think we both knew the mountain operation would become the beacon that pulled me from the path of my higher education and conventional career goals. Because of the lull in the job market, a corporate gig didn't seem attainable. People weren't hiring. But in this case, the grass was literally greener, although illegal, on the other side. *We are damned if we do and damned if we don't, right?* I would think.

CHAPTER 14

More Hands

SPRING 2009

"HE LEADS THE BUILDING and construction class," Laura said. "He works hard and efficiently. He goes to Alaska to fish every summer and makes enough money to help get by."

Laura was Rachel's best friend. She had started dating Jesse five or six months before winter break, and their relationship lasted through the spring semester. Laura hoped it would last the rest of their lives.

"Do you think he can be quiet about it all?" I asked.

"Yes, I can barely get him to talk to me about how his classes are. Getting a feeling out of him is like getting a cork out of a bottle of wine using your bare hands," Laura replied.

I laughed at the response. It reminded me of all the times Rachel wanted to know how something made me feel or how my actions had gotten us where we were. She wanted to know how to read my feelings deep down to make soul-directed life decisions. The damn fact was, I was a twenty-five-year-old boy with a secret, operating on natural octane and industrial drive. Sitting and divulging my deepest thoughts and feelings was not on my priority list. If the topic of conversation wasn't paying for the rent or my next meal, it was out of the question.

I listened to Laura's fairy-tale thoughts because the man she was dreaming about would be our best bet to help build our green-house. I agreed to meet her boyfriend. He was exactly as advertised.

Jesse spoke loudly and walked up as I was viciously chewing the last of a seeded bagel slathered with an obnoxious amount of cream cheese, smoked salmon, and mustard sauce. "What happening, brudda? Good to see you!"

"You too, man," I said. I spoke from the corner of my mouth while reaching for a napkin.

It was a chilly late-April morning, and I was the only patron at the local bagel café willing to brave the cold metal chairs and outside air. I wanted to have a private chat with Jesse in a public place. I couldn't be too careful. If Jesse meshed with the idea I had in my head, it would turn into a preconstruction job meeting. I already had a feeling I would be OK with him working on the project. After all, we had no other viable human options. However, severity and secrecy needed to be sworn upon in a blood oath over some bagels and coffee first.

The door of the café swung open again, and Jesse appeared with his own version of a bagel fortress of toppings and garnish. Jesse was twenty-two and about six feet tall with a strong, athletic build. He had a dark complexion and an unkempt appearance most gals considered attractive. Rounding out his rugged image was the fact that he was a fisherman in Alaska over the summers.

"Got to love living in a cold coastal town every morning, huh?" he said. He pulled out the metal chair with an awful screeching sound and sat down with purpose.

"I had forgotten how cold and uninviting this weather is in the mornings," I said.

"Sun sallies every day, bro, but not here," he said, looking so far up in the sky that he almost tipped over his chair.

I found out that "sun sallies" was short for "sun salutations." Jesse, I would find out, spoke in a shorthand mixture of Cali surfer dude, bro, hillbilly, and abbreviated lawyer.

We shared small talk about school and our relationships. I told him Rachel had decided to do a year abroad in India and would be leaving at the end of the summer, which I would deal with as it came. We were in love but ill-equipped to talk about the implications of a year apart.

More and more customers were making their way to grab fresh bagels, so I had to cut to the chase.

"So Rachel and Laura gave you the CliffsNotes about the subject of our little early weekend breakfast meeting here?" I asked, leaning in and talking low.

"I got the gist. When do you want to start?"

I liked his confident way of telling me he was in for it before I had formally asked or even offered.

"May twentieth. That's the Tuesday after school gets out."

"OK, I can work every day for you 'til the twelfth of June. Then I have to start my migration to Alaska. I start tying nets up there on the eighteenth."

I explained where it was, where we would be staying, and that I needed to find another helper.

"I don't have anyone or want any of my friends or people from campus helping us," he said. He was in the same boat as me with this, even without plants present on the property during the build. He was cautious but willing, able but not naive, and ultimately hungry—he knew how to work and make money.

"I'll find another outsider to be our third," I confirmed.

We walked in separate directions down the street, disappearing into the fog, one of us with a new employee and the other with a new job. All I had to do was find one more person. The neighbors had started referring to us as "the kids next door," meaning we were just college students trying to grow. They were nonchalant about us and didn't think we would become so massive so quickly—or at all for that matter. I wanted it to stay that way, and I knew I had to be particular. We didn't want to upset them by bringing randoms up to work or to learn about the neighborhood.

One of the other rules I'd made for myself through the first season was to *never collaborate with the neighbors*. We would have each other's backs on the mountains, but our business ties had to be completely separate. It wasn't an ongoing "can I borrow a cup of sugar" kind of situation, and I didn't want it to be. That's how things got messy.

Thankfully, I already had a vague idea of who our third would be.

I'd met Daniel a month before while Noah and I were trying to fix the wood and PVC greenhouse where our starts were growing, which had been crushed by the snow. That afternoon, I heard hammering off in the distance, down by one of the neighbors' homes, an unexpected sound. The pieces of land were so big that you could go months without seeing your next-door neighbor.

"What's all the racket, man?" I asked, scratching Noah's red ridgeback mutt behind the ears.

"There's a couple guys building an addition to the house down there—a single room off the upstairs. There's the sound of banging nails and whines of saws all day, man."

"You think any of those guys might be looking for more work in the next month? I need another hand to help 'up top' putting the building together. They seem capable."

"Both are capable," he said. "But one of them isn't your guy." He wrapped a thick rubber band around his dreads. "The other might be interested; he's part native—Sioux tribe from Wyoming. I do think he's an after-hours drunk."

I didn't love the "after-hours drunk" part of the resume, but my choices were growing slimmer by the day.

"Come by at five. They stop a little before then. He heads down the hill shortly after," Noah continued.

"I'll be over."

"Don't be late. Daniel starts to get saucy soon after the six o'clock hour," he said.

"Noted." I was concerned but a little desperate.

When I came back down that evening, Daniel and I had our introductions. He was a veteran, a young guy who had done two tours in a war zone overseas, and before his third deployment, he chose not to show up. He started walking the western slope, then the western states, then the West Coast, peddling his carpentry and hard work ethic to fund his incredible daily volume of needed liquor intake.

He and the neighbor he was working for, a Vietnam veteran, had similar stories and traumas. They solidified their bond over their mutual ability to consume unfathomable amounts of cheap vodka in a single evening. "Vodka is my favorite medicine for this disease of alcoholism I have," the neighbor once told me.

I explained very little, telling him there would be more construction labor for him after the addition, should he want it. He'd get paid a good hourly rate for a couple weeks of work. He agreed.

I had found our third hand.

CHAPTER 15

The Itch

SPRING 2009

"DUDE," JESSE SAID, "everyone has their O-face on and is pointing at us. You have the hazards on, right?"

"Oh yeah, flashing like Rudolph the red-nosed Rick," I said. Ranger Rick rolled toward the old Simpson Mill. Ten years before, the mill had employed hundreds. Now it looked like it was running on a shoestring staff at best. We passed the old logging scales and a small one-room shack where the CHP officers congregated. The light was glowing inside the shack, but we could see that it was vacant on that stormy day. We supposed the weather had already caused so much carnage that the officers had to take a day off from the cat-and-mouse game they usually played on the winding mountain highway, just waiting for a reason to hit the jackpot by pulling over people hauling something illegal—people like us.

"I don't plan on going over forty-five," I said, "maybe thirty-five in the turns. This here weight, the barn we got on this carriage, man—it might tip us clear on over the road and down into that river below." I laughed.

"You're a crazy cowboy, know that?" Jesse said. He turned the radio off.

"Yeehaw, in the name of the hippie grass, partner," I said nervously, trying to keep the humor alive. Humor didn't make the drive safer, but it did take our minds off what we faced.

"Not any faster, bro!" Jesse snapped. "Also, you are never allowed to make knots or tie anything down again when I am around." He eyed the clamps and bolts holding the greenhouse frames to the lumber rack.

"Roger, captain. Don't fret. This Ranger's engine is stronger than I thought."

"I'm not worried about the engine. I'm worried about the metal in the sky above our heads and the tie job."

"It'll buff, brah," I said. I tried to be reassuring, but he was anxious; he only replied with a disapproving grunt.

The situation was dangerous—stupid and dangerous. We were in the middle of a lightning storm, transporting our building to a place where I was going to grow something illegal. It was not an ideal situation by any means, but I wasn't about to turn around.

"Forward, forward, ya mule, ya!" Jesse shouted.

Looking back, I wonder if God or some greater power might have been helping us a little extra the day we drove that Gothic-gabled metal greenhouse frame up to the top of the mountain. The day we should have just spent thirty-five dollars to rent a flattop trailer, the day we should have waited for better weather, the day we tried to make a mark in history like Benjamin Franklin with his kite and key. Like with Franklin, the rains were torrential, and lightning riddled the sky. Unlike Franklin, we were sober from substances but not from the miner's itch.

I guess there was a God that day, but there was also the itch.

The miner's itch was as old as time. It was the feeling a man got when setting out to find buried treasure. It was the compulsion men had in the 1840s to find gold in the hills of California. It was what drove the Wall Street folks who plundered cash by selling off parts of a company or a mortgage. It was the feeling of crazy confidence, focus, and drive to succeed and conquer whatever lucrative opportunity had presented itself. Ah, the itch. The itch made a man pillage the beautiful resources of Mother Nature. The itch pushed minds away from common sense and toward too-good-to-be-true wealth and reward.

Since the day the greenhouse was delivered, the itch had taken hold of me. If my brand of the itch were coffee, it would be a highly caffeinated dark roast. The itch shackled all my common sense and propelled me to a new level—octane itch. This new octane itch had me dead set on getting the greenhouse built in the next two weeks before Jesse had to head north for his own itch—catching salmon in a net and money in his pocket.

The only option was to get this greenhouse to the top of that mountain on that day, grow weed all summer, and make a ton of money. There hadn't been an itch the year before; it had been more of a curiosity. The curiosity had proved successful enough to keep ourselves fed, but the octane itch was for profit, success, investment, growth, and reward. The plan was Business 101, but I was too focused on this exciting new itch to notice that I wasn't acting like a businessman.

I pushed Rick through the rain and treacherous mountain roads. From time to time, cars lined up behind us as we rode down the hill in second gear, but no one seemed mad. Perhaps the sheer amazement of what we were trying to accomplish kept the other drivers at bay until we gave them ample room to pass safely. At the base of Benjamin Mountain Road, we pulled over to let the engine rest and to check our MacGyvered system. The rigging was impressively solid, and we'd made it that far. The next seven miles were on pavement, but the six miles after that would be on dirt with streams running down the middle.

Jesse and I knew we might have to untie the framing and stack it along the dirt road before driving up the big hill—the triple step up, as we called it. It was a steep section with three large rolling washouts cut into the incline. It was a gnarly part of the drive, and I wasn't sure if Rick could make it up the triple step up with the extra weight of the framing.

Jesse inspected our cargo. "She's tight."

"Just how I like her," I said.

"I'm worried about the climb at the triples," he said.

"I am too. If it's got water rushing down, we won't do it with the load in the truck. It dries fast, though."

"Good. I wonder how Daniel's doing up there?"

We both slid back into the truck. Ranger Rick roared to life. We simultaneously tapped the dash and gave thanks to all six of his cylinders. It had been exactly one year to the day since I had been the passenger in the same truck as my uncle drove up this mountain, her secrets unknown to me. Now I was building my own secrets atop her.

"Let's do it with our seat belts off," Jesse said. "If the truck loses traction, we'll just have to set the emergency brake and bail out." We looked at the terrifying climb ahead.

Judging by the lack of top water on the road, the rain must have stopped over an hour before. Each mountaintop was still in the grasp of a dark cloud, though, occasionally flashing with bursts of lightning in all directions. The clouds approaching fast from the west were full of thick droplets ready to fall fast and hard. We sat for a moment weighing the odds of us making it up to the flat before the rain hit.

"Ready?" I asked just loud enough for Jesse to hear.

"Yeah."

"You can get out and walk it if you'd like," I said in one last attempt to free Jesse's mind from the grip of the miner's itch.

"Made it this far," he said. "Go!" His head was level, his eyes fixed on the top of the triples.

I released the clutch, and we rolled forward. Seconds later, I engaged second gear. The truck tilted back with the slope.

"Go, baby, go," I whispered over and over again, using the force of the small downhill of the first washout to propel us up the next rise. I knew Ranger Rick had it.

"If we make it to the next washout . . ." Jesse's voice trailed off.

"Yes, hell yes!" I yelled as the hood of the truck tipped forward into the second of the three washouts.

The engine growled a bit deeper, but the wheels kept traction, and we continued upward. Rick's hood finally leveled after what felt like hours, but only forty seconds had passed. We pressed forward, and at that moment, I knew we would build this structure in time. I knew we would have her planted by the fifteenth of June. I also knew the itch was part of me forever. My hobby had officially walked across the stage with a cap and gown, graduating into something bigger and more meaningful.

I saw Jesse's clenched fist hovering over the stick shift. I released my white knuckles from the adhesive grip atop the shifting knob and gave him a solid fist bump in admiration for our success and our survival.

"Let's get to business, brah!" he shouted.

Over the remainder of the bumpy and slow five-minute drive to the flat, my thoughts returned to our third compadre, Daniel, and his dog, June. We had left him that morning to make our trip to the coast and back. His job was to pour concrete and install fence posts.

"I wonder how he weathered the storm," Jesse said.

"Yeah, the poor guy—should have let him bring his warming juice with him today," I said, referring to his love for whiskey.

"No. He's not allowed to be that person up here on the job," Jesse replied with conviction.

As we reached the level section of the road, there was evidence beyond a reasonable doubt of how vicious the storm had been.

What had been puddles when we left that morning were now long sections of water-filled ruts. Approaching the flat, we noticed Daniel had set another dozen fence posts since we left. I had expected him to finish, but the storm must have stopped his progress. As we parked, we scanned the flat for any signs of Daniel. We heard barking and saw brush moving by the water tank.

"Yes, yes, yes, hallelujah!" Daniel yelled from the wooded hillside. His words were punctuated with June's barks. "The rain was so hard, the lightning splintered everywhere, and that thunder vibrated my bones. Oh heavens, I'm happy to see you guys!"

I smiled. "How you doin'?"

"Well, I'm officially a mountain man now," Daniel said.

"Yeah, well, first let's see if you can grow more of a beard than you have on your cheeks and that predator goatee-'stache thing," Jesse grumbled.

Jesse didn't have much fondness for Daniel, nor did Rachel, who felt he could snap at any point. I thought the same, but I knew where the nearest rifle was most of the time. Every night since our work started, Daniel drank himself stupid, yelled into the sky, then vomited outside his tent before passing out, unshowered. Though I tried to keep my cool because of his issues as a veteran of the conflict in Afghanistan, over the last few days, I had lost my respect for him too. However, he worked a lot better than he made friends, and we needed him, so we kept him on for the full two weeks. Then the plan was that he would head out, distracting himself by walking off his PTSD down hundreds of more miles of dotted yellow lines.

"Boys, it was nuts up here," Daniel said. "It must have rained an inch in thirty minutes. I think a couple of the trees up at the top of this mountain got hit with lightning. Loudest thunder I ever heard in my life."

"We were worried about you," I said.

"Shucks, fellas. I thought you were going to leave me on my own up here."

"We don't leave men behind," Jesse said.

"Doesn't look like you left her behind either," Daniel said, pointing to the metal poles weighing down Rick.

"Well, we're here, and so is that heavy piece of metal," Jesse said rather matter-of-factly. "We've got material for hours of work now."

"You young men be batshit crazy," Daniel said.

"Let's unload this and get out of here," I said. "This mountain is acting rude today."

. . .

When we returned the next day, it was no easy task to raise the metal framing of the greenhouse. Two men positioned themselves at the ends of a rafter, with the third man on the inside with our giant Y-fork made of two-by-fours. The man with the fork created enough push to get the metal arch to rise. It was the opposite of a game of tug-of-war. It was a game of "push against me harder, dammit." It took a full day to raise all the rafter arches and tighten their double bolts. By the end of that day, we could see what was taking shape, and it was glorious.

The itch kept crawling up my timeline, and I wanted everything done faster. I wanted the plants in the ground one week before the summer solstice, and that meant everything else had to be done well before then.

The following day, four of us plus June were crammed in the small truck on the way to work. We needed Rachel's help driving the truck to construct the mobile scaffolding that connected the purlins and the center beam. We arrived at the flat by 8:00 a.m., excited and ready even amid the tight, long, and stinky drive.

We rolled up to the job site. "Look at him," Jesse said. "Our green claim is taking shape."

"It's a *her*," Rachel said with confidence.

"OK, finish your latte, fancy pants," Daniel chimed in.

"Fuck you!" Rachel snapped. "This is my building." I appreciated her sense of ownership.

We spent the day standing on top of a plywood deck we had hand-built into the top rails of the lumber rack in Rick's bed. Rachel drove four feet forward on our signal. At each stop, we leaned the ladder against the rafter. Then two of us slid a purlin through the hanging brackets into the female purlin end a couple of rafters behind us. The plywood deck bowed every moment the three of us men stood on it. We were an OSHA poster titled "What Not to Do," but it didn't matter. Even if we had been doing things to code, we were still building a greenhouse to house a God-created plant and man-labeled Schedule I narcotic.

The workday ended with the entire metal portion of the structure done. We had sunk the main framing posts on the end walls some days before. It was maybe thirty minutes from sunset.

"That's it, the last screw for now!" Jesse yelled.

He had attached the fourth and final end wall post to the arch with some metal plumbing tape and a couple of two-inch wood screws with flat washers. I jumped down from the plywood deck and landed on the ground beneath our new structure.

"Hey, Ty," Rachel whispered over Rick's engine and the static of the job site radio, "I don't want Daniel coming up here anymore. He weirds me out."

Rachel had learned Daniel always had a supply of pills from his VA doctors. On top of all his obvious problems, we never trusted people with pills. None of us were angels, but using harder drugs was a bridge neither Rachel nor I had crossed.

"I need him to help put the poly film top on in the morning."

"Let's do it now and get it over with." She pulled out a bottle of whiskey and a liter of soda. "Share this with them, and I will drive home."

I was exhausted, but she was right. Within ten minutes, the three of us men were watching the sunset on June 4, 2009. Ten minutes later, the entire bottle of whiskey had also faded away.

We walked back down to the flat and laid the cover out perpendicular to the framing of the greenhouse so we could roll it out parallel to the farm. Once all the rocks and possible puncture menaces were gone, we began to unroll the large roof of the structure.

Rachel tried to correct us in our tipsy stupidity. "Your dusty footsteps are going to be all over the ceiling now!" she yelled.

We dusted off the plastic as best we could and strung it half-lit. The sun had crept below the western ridge by the time we pulled and pushed the roof over the greenhouse. We had no clue about how to get this accomplished, but somewhere in the whiskey haze, we engineered a way. The roof was finally on.

"It freaking worked!" I shouted with glee.

The only light left on the horizon was an orange glow. Smiles covered our tired faces. We had been working for a solid fourteen hours, but the top was on, and the day was over.

A couple of days later, I picked up Daniel and June and gave them a ride down to the highway intersection. We said our goodbyes and parted ways. He turned and started walking down the highway, shouldering a big backpack. As a car passed, Daniel's right hand gripped tight on June's leash, and his left hand went up with his thumb turned skyward. That was the last I ever saw or heard of him. Jesse worked with us for another four days building the end walls and large doors of the greenhouse. The rain had stopped, and the ground was drying fast. Our goal of being fully planted by mid-June was nearly achieved.

CHAPTER 16

Anne

SPRING 2009

BETWEEN THE GREENHOUSE, the plot under the oaks, and our plants at the top of the mountain, our garden had increased in size almost eight times compared to our first season, which meant the workload had increased eight times as well. We had finished filling half of the bags inside our greenhouse, a total of 168 plants. We had another thirty plants in the trees nearby, eighty-four plants at a different location, twenty-four seed plants at the top of the mountain's eastern slope, and 280 plants under the oaks.

I quickly found out that my itch was stronger than my back. Before putting our plants in their summer homes, one of our tasks was to mix a soil bag for each plant. These bags, about sixty pounds each, contained a precise, thoroughly mixed recipe of a few different types of soil and fertilizers.

Though they reeked of shit and decaying earth, there was an underlying beauty to filling bags. Once a few bags were mixed, Rachel and I loaded up the cart we'd named Massy, our "little metal ass," like a donkey. We rolled a fully loaded Massy down to the greenhouse and started unloading the bags. With both hands, each of us grabbed on to the edge of the bag and rolled the plastic in over the soil for a better grip. After the count of "one, two, three," we heaved the bag up off the cart, down onto the ground, and into its resting place in the row of all its sister bags.

After the five bags were heaved, it felt like we had done weight training at a local gym. To rest some, we took turns taking Massy back up to the soil piles. Then we started filling and mixing bags again—just the two of us repeatedly for days and days.

Rachel was keeping count of our progress, and after one of the trips, she yelled, "Eighty-four, Ty! Yes, we made it to the halfway point."

"Lunch!" I yelled out into the mountain air like a foreman on a construction site. My coworker was much prettier than the salty ex-cons, chimney smokers, oil riggers, and vets I used to work with back in my framing days. How funny was it that after working with a crew of rough and tough men, my girlfriend and I were doing something way more rough and tough?

Rachel and I stood with our hearts pumping, dust hanging in the still, hot air around us, and the shadows of vultures racing across the greenhouse roof. We didn't conceptualize it this way then, but looking back, we were everything to that business: employees, board-confirmed CEOs, accountants, gullible investors, and on top of that—outlaws. Lunch that day for the CEOs was a couple of PB&J sandwiches, apple slices, carrots, and chocolate chip cookies. We sat in our executive dining room—the shade of a big fir tree.

"I have the name for our greenhouse," Rachel said.

"Yeah, what is it?" I said back, signaling with my wrist that I was ready for another carrot.

"Anne of Green Gables," she said matter-of-factly.

"What?" I said and chuckled.

"Yeah, Anne for short."

"What is Anne of Green Gables?" I asked.

"It's a character from a book. You never heard of it?"

"No," I said with my mouth half-full of a crunched baby carrot.

"It's a classic. It's a book that was written after the turn of the last century by a woman author about a young orphan girl named Anne. The girl is sent to another family, and it's about her life at school and in the town and her family."

"OK, perfect, Anne of Green Gables it is." I wondered how this had any plausible connection to our greenhouse or goal of making it through school by growing weed.

"Like I said, we can call her Anne for short. Our greenhouse is the orphan. She's the only thing out here on the property, and she will know how to take care of all the little orphan girls we're putting inside. It's perfect. Do you like it?"

"I love it," I said. From that moment on, the greenhouse was forever called Anne of Green Gables—Anne for short.

For those short days, we lived an almost magical life. It felt and looked like a scene from the garden in Genesis. We were Adam and Eve, working and living in the woods. We had no tangible consumer luxuries but rarely spent seconds without smiles or lust. We often went a week at a time without talking to any other humans. We didn't have cell service for about fifteen miles, so there were no calls to make or receive. Our only contact with the outside world was an AM/FM radio.

After the workday was over, we tried to make the best use of our time by expanding on the hard-knocks education we'd received the previous year. We bought some literature to perfect our skills and to care better for our ladies. We sat bare bottom on the chairs in the greenhouse and read books on botany, growing weed, hydrology, agriculture climate, and farming vegetables. We read aloud to each other and discussed actions for the plants and system with our newly gained knowledge.

Neither of us was really a hippie; she had been recently employed on military bases and was very well put together. I was somewhat of a country-bro type who cared about how I dressed and looked. Besides, we weren't firmly any one thing or another. Such is the beauty of your twenties. Humboldt County, the mountain, and our Anne had quickly shaped us, and we let it all bend us toward a more natural way of life. I grew to prefer working naked or in boxer briefs with my Red Wing boots. She preferred cowgirl boots, cut-off jean shorts, and a bikini top at most. We'd never known this rare level of freedom where our hearts, souls, and egos were free from outside worries.

We finished planting everything ten days before our goal of having it done by the summer solstice. Large patches of snow still sat at the bases of the mossy northern sides of the large fir trees. The native dogwoods, western azaleas, Sulphur buckwheats, phlox, Indian paintbrush, and mountain death bush were all in full bloom. Monarch butterflies and bees flew from flower to flower, pollinating the surrounding mountain scene. The backbreaking days of building Anne and filling bags swiftly faded into the past. Ten days after the last plant for the season was planted, the solstice arrived, and we decided it was time for some improvements.

"I'm tired of sleeping on that old used air mattress in the cabin loft when we stay there," Rachel said one night. It had been given an overdose of rubber patches over the years, and we still woke each morning pressed against each other in a V against the wood floor.

While we stayed in tents up at the grow site some nights, we mostly lived about forty minutes west in my Uncle Bob's cabin on forty acres at the top of Mule Mountain. My uncle allowed us to stay and live there as long as we were working on it (and we kept our other dealings firmly away from anything my aunt might see, hear, touch, or *smell!*). This was a perfect opportunity to make improvements.

To start, we got a broken wooden futon frame at a thrift store in town after asking one of the employees if they had any full-size wooden bed frames.

"No," he said, "but I have a broken one out by the donation drop-off area. If you screw a few pieces of wood to it and secure the corners, it could work."

After some scary moments on the ladder pushing each broken portion of the frame up into the loft, twenty minutes, and a broken Sawzall blade, the bed had new slats from a pallet we got from a feed store. Rachel was outside smacking the old futon mattress with a closet rod, trying to get the last decade's worth of dust from its innards.

"It's sturdy and ready," I yelled from the loft.

The loft was vaulted, about five feet at its peak, where the ladder and thirty-inch-wide landing were. Then it slanted downward the length of the bed. It had a two-by-three-foot window, and the knotty pine ceiling was six inches above our feet at the end of the bed. You could lie in bed and look out for miles in the distance over the valley and see all the way to the whitecaps of the Pacific Ocean.

Next to our new bed, an old wooden peach box served as our nightstand and housed a tall candle in an old brass holder, a couple of golf-ball-sized quartz rocks, a roll of toilet paper, a small alarm clock, and two headlamps. On the inside of the stand, there was a deck of playing cards, a gallon of water, and three books. One book for each of us, and the other we would read out loud to each other.

Under the bed was a large cooking pot for Rachel to squat over and pee in at night no more than eight inches from my forehead. It wasn't pleasant, but it was safer than her braving the dark climb down the ladder and squatting outside in the pitch black. Each morning, I safely carried the fluid down the ladder, hoping not to slip and start my day with a golden shower.

Next to the piss pot was a hatchet with a chipped and rusted head and a Rambo knife with sticky duct tape around the handle. At the foot of the bed, tucked under the mattress and against the pallet slats, was a loaded twelve-gauge shotgun with the safety on. The thought of it was enough to keep our feet warm at night. We always locked the doors.

Rachel made a home of the big room where the massive windows reached from the floor to the vaulted pine ceiling—the same room where we had accidentally overdried and cooked our previous year's crop. We made a seating area with a couple of old Swedish chairs I bought at a thrift store, an oak coffee table, and a torn recliner covered with a small blanket that hid most of its wounds. We planted succulents, aloe, and indoor shade plants in ceramic pots and placed them in one corner of the living room area. In the other corner, we hung a hammock chair. We found old but trendy Navajo rugs in the other loft that had been bought decades before. We had decorative pillows from foreign lands on the chairs, framed French art on the walls, and tall grasses and sticks with moss in rare vases atop tables with tablecloths.

The windows were covered with functional but inoperative 1970s bamboo blinds. Each morning, we lifted them to keep the cabin cool, and each evening we took them down to have the spectacular sunset rays fill our little off-grid home, which brought just enough warmth to the space before darkness fell.

Our kitchen was more basic than one in an old RV. There was a large, unreasonably heavy cabinet Uncle Bob had taken from an elementary school during a remodel—also from the 1970s. The oven didn't work, but its three propane burners were our culinary lifelines. The counter space was made of two thirty-inch sections of countertop on either side of the old aluminum RV stove.

We found a three-drawer cabinet on Craigslist and filled it with secondhand utensils, bread knives, ladles, measuring cups, and, of course, a can opener. We had all the basics except for running water. We washed dishes outside against the south side of the cabin at the washing station we had fashioned from two gray sawhorses, an old piece of plywood, a sink from a thrift store, and a short garden hose. It was janky but functional, fun, and alluring for the animals. Each night, we were sure our neighborhood mountain lion, the mama brown bear, the fox family, and the dogs all walked by our system, took a sniff, and checked to see if anything was left out. We always brought all the dishes in at night.

We kept the rest of the entry room open because we needed a place to bathe. We purchased a blue plastic kiddie pool with Disney's *Little Mermaid* characters all over it at the Kmart on the coast. Each evening, we brought it inside and placed it on the wood floor a few feet in front of the woodstove, which had a three-gallon stew pot on top, heating to a boil. Another plastic five-gallon bucket full of cool hose water stood inside the pool. Next to the bucket of hose water was a plastic kitchen jug. Next to the kiddie pool was a watering can that had been in the free box at the reuse center.

During those late spring and early summer weeks, we "showered" every night, not wanting to be dirty in the cabin or before bed because washing laundry, pillowcases, and sheets by hand was crazy daunting. The person receiving the shower stripped nude. A bar of soap sat waiting in the middle of the tub. The showeree sat inside the *Little Mermaid* pool, and the showerer dipped the juice jug into the boiling water and poured the contents into the watering can.

"Are you ready?" the showerer asked.

"Yes, let it go," the showeree said.

Lifting the water jug up and over the other person's naked body, the showerer slowly turned on the shower head. In speedy fashion, the showeree soaped themselves.

As the showerer filled another jug, the showeree lathered themselves, paying special attention to their underarms, booty funk, private parts, and the dirt and grime on their calves and ankles.

"Ready?" the showerer asked again.

"Rinse me."

Each shower took four mixes in total. The first gave fluid to the soap, mixes two and three were for rinsing, and the fourth mix was delivered the slowest and the hottest. We liked to call it the luxury pour. Once the showeree was dried and robed, the other knelt in the cool water of the shower to receive their washing.

Even though trying to keep ourselves clean at the end of our dirty days was taxing, it was an exchange of love—tribal love. It was like an ancient display of royal nurturing for one another. Bathing your partner each night is not something that happens in most relationships; when it does, it is usually romantic foreplay. For us, though, it was, first and foremost, a labor of trust, caring, and, of course, love.

The little cabin may have just been two open rooms, 624 square feet, and two small sleeping lofts, but it was our home.

CHAPTER 17

7,728 Miles

SUMMER 2009

DESPITE OUR MAGICAL Adam and Eve summer, I was already becoming annoyed by what was to come: long and lonely commutes to long and quiet weekends on the mountain alone. Rachel, on the other hand, would be experiencing an exciting far-off land and culture in India—not alone. She would have friends. She would have adventures. I would live in a tent deep in the woods five hours north with a single headlamp, the creek for a shower, and a hole for a toilet. I would be harvesting our massive crop—alone.

I would drive out on Thursday nights and be back at school Monday morning and in class by 10:00 a.m. I would be alone, deep in the woods of Humboldt County, to tend the garden and go to school.

I could feel the shift in my gut as the school year approached. Each morning, I started the day flying a white flag, hoping it would keep us from getting into an argument. The looming separation had us both on edge. We didn't talk about it. We didn't want to. Maybe we should have, but it wouldn't have changed anything. I wanted her to experience India, but we had to leave each other. We had to say goodbye to each other and to our ladies.

I felt the double life of growing and being a student intensify. The energy it took to keep up was stealing a part of my soul and love for my school life. I could already hear how conversations would go for me.

"How was your weekend? Do anything cool?" my classmates would ask.

"It was chill. I did a lot of studying and cooking," I would say, even though I was thinking, *God, if you only knew.*

Rachel's departure had taken a major portion of the joy out of the venture. With her gone, I was confronted with the fact that the task was too large and too far in the middle of nowhere for a single person to handle both mentally and physically. I was alone. Then a few weeks after she left, I faced down Sergeant Dwight Henderson, saved only by the quick thinking of Tractor Frank. After that near-miss encounter, my thoughts dwelled on a day months earlier, when the two of us were curious as to what exactly we could see from the air over the mountain grow site. We chose to investigate ourselves and chartered a flight. Our pilot was a Vietnam vet who flew commercial after he left the military. Then he only did small-scale gigs. We booked the flight as a joyride with the bonus alibi that Rachel was an environmental science major doing a project. It provided an excuse to request a specific flight path without drawing too much attention to why we wanted to fly over a certain patch of land.

Our flight was glamorous but unnerving. Glamorous for the pure rush of being able to charter a plane and fly over the gorgeous countryside of the Emerald Triangle. Unnerving because we were afraid we'd see greenhouses and grow operations stick out of the landscape like sore thumbs.

The flight path first took us over the ocean and down the coast. The sights were blissful, and our pilot pointed out seals on rocks and the faint shadows of a pod of whales. For a moment, Rachel and I forgot our mission. We took selfies with disposable cameras. Our pilot let us take the controls. It really was a joyride.

"Starting our track overland east," the pilot said. He banked the plane left to go inland.

We didn't think we'd be able to pick out pot plants from the air going 150 miles per hour, but we could. As soon as we were back over the Emerald Triangle proper, we saw scads of little gardens of what looked like thirty to forty plants. The pilot even identified some of the grow spots.

"Shoot," he said, "there are five, ten, twenty, thirty, or close to even eighty thousand plants down at some of those. Packed with illegals trafficked up from Mexico working 'em."

"There seem to be lots of them," Rachel said.

"Oh yeah, been lots of them for decades. It's the sheer size of them that's changed."

"Really?" I asked over our headsets.

We still hadn't seen anything like ours or our neighbor Jarod's greenhouses. We decided it was time to get a closer look at our patch. Rachel asked if we could fly over the Benjamin Mountain Cold War–era sonar tower as we headed back west.

"Not a problem, miss."

In a few minutes, the tower was straight ahead. The mountains around the tower were steep. We could see the remnants of old logging roads washed out from decades of erosion. After circling the tower once, Rachel instructed the pilot to fly northwest.

"Not a problem, miss. You'll get a kick out of what's just ahead. I flew this recently and saw these places a few months ago."

At first, it looked like green trees and rugged rock outcroppings were the only thing on the terrain for miles. Then standing out like a sore thumb was a massive industrial greenhouse perched like a herd of large, white-as-snow sleeping cows resting in a nest of green timbers. It was ours.

As Jarod's place came into view, I realized that we'd built the largest greenhouse we had seen at that time in northern Humboldt. "Wow, those are big," I said.

"Yes, they are," the pilot said. "I haven't seen this approach before this far out."

I was beginning to fidget. The pilot must have noticed.

"You know them?" he asked.

I was looking down at the exact greenhouses I had stood in front of at Jarod's the prior spring. We saw guys coming out of one of the structures, looking up as we did our third circle around the mountain.

"Got to be twenty-one or twenty-two greenhouses down on those few parcels," the pilot said clinically.

"Yep, looks like it. Let's head home," Rachel said, averting her eyes from our property below.

The rest of the flight was mostly silent, and we tipped the pilot well for his time.

"Good luck, kids. Be safe up there. Let's fly again next summer, huh!" he said as we walked down the tarmac.

We waved.

"Why does everyone call us kids?" I asked once we were out of earshot.

"I don't know, Ty, but he sure knows we have something to do with those greenhouses."

"I know. I wasn't expecting us to have the largest. There doesn't seem to be any safety in our numbers."

"Definitely not," she replied softly.

My encounter with the cops proved that. At the time, Sergeant Henderson said, "This is the luckiest day of your life," but I knew it was more than that. It was a reminder that our operation was big, remote, and under constant threat. It was a reminder that it wasn't our operation at all, but just mine for now. This was all on me.

. . .

When Rachel left for India, my cover story about going up north every weekend to see her was shot. Someone would put two and two together and figure out what I was really doing. I also knew it was going to be hard, if not impossible, for us to stay a couple from eight thousand miles away. The odds were stacked against us, as was the codependent and toxic dynamic we'd been developing over the last year. How could we possibly stay true to each other when we were continents away?

I didn't have class on Fridays that semester, so I started driving up north early Friday mornings. From early September to the first week in December, I made the trip up north nine out of ten weeks. Those trips weren't the carefree drives of last year. I was constantly worried—the crop growing in Anne this year was worth more than the cost of multiple homes. I worried about Rachel and a thousand other things. *Has someone stolen the plants? Is Rachel cheating on me on another continent? Can I find trustworthy people to help trim this season? How did I do on my thermodynamics test? Rick needs an oil change.* On and on, my thoughts circled into blossoming paranoia.

By the time I reached the first gate each Friday morning, my insides were on fire, and my sphincter was about to give out. Were I not utterly solitary, I would have been a comical spectacle to watch. I threw Rick into neutral at the first gate, kicked the parking brake, leaped out the driver's-side door, and ran full speed into the woods with a handful of paper towels in a frenzied ritual.

Once my gut was relieved and Rick was parked in his hiding spot, I walked to Anne. I was supposed to water and add nutrients to each plant "with love" as Rachel had, but there was no love in my heart. Gone were the naked days of dancing joyously. I'd never yell "Lunch!" or turn on the radio. It was silent except for the occasional crow's caw or the distant rumble of a jetliner overhead. The nearest humans were still miles away.

By Saturday, I was angry about how much fun I imagined Rachel had the night before and who she might have woken up with that morning. Whether she was up to what I worried about or not, I needed a scapegoat. I was a young, healthy, handsome, hardworking, and smart farmer caring for beautiful plants in a warm greenhouse sanctuary on a gorgeous, forested mountain with all of God's abundance. But I was also angry, jealous, and exhausted. I couldn't help it. I was a young and angry Scrooge, bitter with his self-created situation.

One Saturday in mid-October, I had planned to take all the equipment to Anne that I would need to harvest alone the following weekend. I could have stayed the night and caught up on some studying, but I had done that for the last twelve weekends, and that night the neighbors, Jarod and his crew, were throwing a Halloween party on the coast. I had been so lonely, even more so hearing about the fun times Rachel was having; I wanted to hold on to a slice of social life. I was going to go.

Thirty minutes into catching up with friends, acquaintances, and even last year's trim crew, a childhood friend who had also gotten into the weed industry placed a couple of drops of something into my drink and smiled. Ten minutes later, he informed me it was acid.

"And here's a couple of tabs for another time," he said. "Fire stuff, man. Will change your religion, bro, or make you a believer."

"In what?" I asked, not ever having taken the stuff. He rolled his fingers and smiled big, pretending to be the character he was dressed as: Jack Sparrow.

"In whatever your subconscious has been trying to tell you. Your ears have been too clogged, matey! Argh!"

"Right," I said. I paused.

A little later, I ran into Jarod, who I had only seen a couple of times since he gave me my starter plants and showed me his operation, both of which I appreciated greatly.

"How are you?" I asked. I thanked him again for his part in my success.

He was still so aggressive and intense about the industry; he was all about the dollars, the size of his operation, his control of his plants, and the development of the land. I was just a student with an itch.

The party host had transformed a boat in his yard into a pirate ship. A massive mound of cocaine sat on the dash. Head after head was dropping to the dash, followed by yelling "Argh!" into the sky.

"Want any of that?" Jarod asked.

"No, no thanks." I hadn't done cocaine before.

"Well, I'm going to get my nose glaciered 'cause I got my million."

"Your million?"

"Pirate ships and millions," he said. "This is the life."

This was a different side of him—careless and cocky. I watched it all unfold around me but wasn't really part of it. It reminded me of a weed bro frat party, which was OK. I loved to see people having a great time—celebrating the holiday and their recent harvests. And then it hit me. *I am on the clock; I am still in class; my time is too valuable; my job has not been completed; I am not in a place to be partying.* The chemical drops in my drink started to make my vision move in odd ways. I chose not to finish the drink.

I started talking to a girl dressed as a circus ringmaster. I was about to start making out with her when her face morphed into Rachel's and she said, "I missed you so much!"

"I have to get to our flock at Anne," I told her.

I leaped to my feet from our bench next to the bonfire, startling her. As I looked around, everyone at the party started transforming into circus characters and animals. I took off and ran down the dark, narrow gravel driveway past the lines of trucks to Rick.

Rick and I drove the winding, dangerous hour and fifteen minutes all the way out to the plants. As I shut the first gate, the red glow of Rick's taillights was shutting out the world. It was like all the aspects of life were on the other side of the gate, divided, calm, clear, and dual.

"They're just trying to eat too!" I yelled to myself as I drove over the culvert Tractor Frank had dug to block the police when they came by just months before. "They're not coming back for me!" I drove to the very top of the mountain so I could watch the sunrise in eight and a half hours. As I approached the top and my headlights shone on the seed plants, they began to shake, and pollen danced into the glow, swirling up into the darkness and falling slowly onto the surrounding kolas. The plants were mating. *Incredible*, I thought.

When I killed the engine, my brain caught up to my visual trip. The plants were moving. A mama bear and two cubs emerged from a small field of plants and wandered into the spotlight Rick provided. I turned off the headlights so only the glow of the running lights caught her yellow eyes. She turned and bounded into the woods.

I finally caught my breath. *My mouth is so damn dry.*

"I'm sorry, mama," I rasped.

I was talking to the bear, but I may have also been talking to my own mother and Mary, the mother of Jesus. I thought about how the mama bear was protecting her young. How I disrupted their security. How scared they must have been. Emotions swept over me. I put the truck in reverse and drove back down to Anne as I came down from my trip. I backed Rick into Anne through the front doors, crawled into the camper shell, and fell asleep with our flock of orphans. It was one week 'til harvest.

The next morning was chilly. Morning dew rose like diamonds. To keep the party going, I took the two little tabs of the acid my friend had given me. *These little tabs can't be so strong*, I thought. I had fooled around with mushrooms a few times in college and had taken a whole handful of those. One apple and some hot lemon ginger tea later, I found out I had underestimated the dime-size tablets.

The sky was purple and gray from the rising sun. I started Rick and drove to a lookout on the neighboring national forest land to watch. I saw a lot more than a sunrise.

As the mountains took form under the light, the old cedar stumps became grandparents from the 1800s with knit hats and wrinkled faces. They were crying as they whispered little statements of wisdom. Wisdom of the mountains. Wisdom of business. Though I couldn't hear what they said, I could feel each word in my body.

I watched the wind approach from the west and curl through the trees. The trees shook their used-up leaves and cones to the ground. I watched as the forest exhaled and oxygen raced toward my mouth, hanging open. The stumps cried as the living trees awoke, yawning and rubbing their eyes. As the Sun rose, the large rocks looked up from a game of poker and nodded to her as if to say, "Morning, ma'am," like she was walking into the diner to grab a cup of coffee before work.

Some moments later, I had a realization. *These trees are the real crop of the mountain.* At that moment, all the trees turned into strong, eyeless muscular figures, frowning at me until I was tossed to the ground by my thoughts. I had never felt anything like it. My knees felt like they were cuffed with heavy iron shackles.

The sunrise hit my face. I tore off my shirt—my body was warming too fast, but my lower half was completely paralyzed. I looked at my hands on the rocky ground. They were being swallowed by the earth. Layers of ancient geology and decomposing earth crawled up my forearms.

"Watch the creation," the Sun said.

Her voice reverberated with the depth of many female voices.

"Watch the creation," she repeated.

I tried to lift my head.

Three layers of earth tones appeared in my eyesight like a wall of Neapolitan ice cream as the cinema of the chemicals intensified within me. I watched the mountains form from dust and gazed as four seasons of a single year came and went in a blink. I watched simple rains create little flows of water that became canyons, tributaries, and river basins. I watched as snow fell and glaciers melted, as massive rocks crashed through the earth's surface and reached for the sky. The Sun was a hot ball, zipping around in a figure eight over and over and over again. I watched the hundreds of thousands of years pass in an impossibly real time-lapse.

After what felt like hours, animals started traversing the land. Birds circled my waist and built nests on my elbows. Squirrels appeared as each winter's snow melted. Deer danced in the meadows as fawns but left as doe grandmothers. Herds of elk battled outcrops with their molting antlers. The trees grew to impressive stature. Lightning struck them but never burned them whole.

At some point, I used my arms to pull myself across the earth to my pack and canteen of lemon water. Pains seared through my shins and calves. Blood ran down my legs as I dragged my bare skin across the sharp serpentine aggregate. Little beavers chewed at my open wounds. The hairs of my legs danced with the wind. The shackles were gone.

"Ohhhh!" I struggled to speak as I brought the canteen to my lips.

When the water hit the back of my throat, I saw the fluid flow through my body, allocating the perfect ratios to my internal organs. The hairs on my legs began swirling as the windstorm increased. I lifted my gaze, and my surroundings came into focus. I was surrounded by a fantasy forest and a panoramic mountain view. Spring wildflowers bloomed everywhere, even on clouds. Crystal rivers and creeks packed with fish flowed through a river canyon and across the sky like the wind. Eagles flew overhead and talked with the vultures.

I used my palm to turn my head. To my left, the mama bear and her cubs from the night before watched the sunrise with me. She looked at me. I apologized, and she nodded approvingly, and then the three of them faded into thin air. The trees, geology, natural eco-systems, mammals, birds, and insects were all in perfect geometrical balance. The elements relaxed and calmly did their jobs like individual gears on an incredibly elaborate watch—the Earth watch.

I'm not sure how long I watched the nirvana of the beautiful world around me before I passed out, but I woke to the feeling of large timber ants crawling on my face. I rose to my feet.

"I can stand," I heard myself say.

"Can you walk?" a soft male voice said. I looked at my bare feet, where seven three-inch-tall Native American men were climbing over them.

"We are on an elk hunt," one said, looking back up at me as they walked into the low bushes and disappeared. Forty feet ahead of me was an elk the size of an elephant.

A storm that was also a fountain for a river appeared from within one of the clouds. Darkness fell. I started to wheeze. I looked around for my canteen. It was just a few feet away. I grasped for it and caught hold just in time.

"Timberrrrrrrr!!!" someone yelled.

The massive trees started falling around me. Little trucks carried massive trees. Railroad tracks circled my ankles like bear traps. I began to vomit. Every time I rose from being sick, the earth was more and more scarred. Burning. Eroding. Animals dead. Brick buildings with smokestacks popped up in the fields of my leg hair. The smoke filled my nostrils.

I heard myself speak again. "That's why I'm suffocating."

I saw the mountain as it was after the western red cedars were cut in the late 1800s. All that grew from underneath the slashed and eroded hillside were little weed buds with smiling faces and dollar signs for eyes. Little tribal camps and reservations on the edges of my pools of vomit starved and became riddled with disease. I cried as they watched their children be taken away to schools.

I passed out again.

I woke what must have been hours later in my boxers and boots. The pools of vomit were dried and cracked from the day's heat, and the sun was dropping below the trees to the west. The mountain was closer to my recollection of reality. I guzzled the rest of my canteen, crawled to Rick, and drove to Anne to fill my body with spring water.

That evening, I parked Rick where I saw the hunter the year before and walked out to the western point to watch the sunset. As thick layers of fog rolled over the coastal range to my west, I recalled the words and feelings the elder stumps cast on me at dawn. Recalling their words was like remembering a particularly angry, vocal session of British parliament, and I was the prime minister. The old stumps, large puddles, and rock formations scolded me and told me it was up to them if my growing success would be granted. "It will only happen if you respect us," they chanted.

I thought about the near miss with the raid team months before. I thought about the first time I saw the neighbors' operation. Jarod's words played over in my head: *I got my million, bro.*

I realized I could only ever partially do this for the money. I had to tattoo my soul with the knowledge that I was growing for a temporary time, and needed to do it sustainably. I needed to do it for the earth, for nature, like Rachel taught me the first day she met the ladies and the mountain. I was finally able to understand Rachel's approach to the plants and the space. I finally understood why she never brought anger to our flock of orphans.

I looked at myself in a sunset's reflection on a puddle. I watched my raggedy shoulder-length hair transform into a short military crew cut, a sign of transformation.

Then I remembered the smiles on the little hunter men's faces and the pained frowns of the loggers. I promised the mountain I would never cut a tree down as I watched the last red dot of the sunset disappear below the western coastal ridge. "We can take it all away at any time; we can take you away, we can put you away," the massive old outcrop said.

After being in my boxers and boots all day, I put on some clothes and built a fire. I watched the flames. My body shivered, and my teeth chattered uncontrollably in my sleeping bag as I lay in the fetal position, waited for the fire to warm me, and watched my breath steam up from my mouth. As the three-hundred-year-old piece of stump burned into smoke that rose into the stars above in the clear night sky, I was struck by the temporary nature of everything.

I fell asleep in the camper shell with the back window wide open so I could watch shooting stars zip across the night. Sleep overtook me as I wondered what Rachel was doing on the other side of the globe. How would I explain all this to her? Would I ever explain it to anyone?

I walked through the garden and thanked every plant before I drove back to Santa Rosa the next morning. I thanked the spring that fed the grow. I looked up and thanked the trees.

I was still lonely but not as lonely anymore. The mountain, I now knew, was my best friend.

CHAPTER 18

First Trim Crew

FALL 2009

TWO DAYS AFTER MY TRIP, I walked into a Great Clips near campus and asked for the haircut I'd seen on my reflection in a puddle. A few weeks later, it was time to trim our first grow and harvest from the crops of the huge greenhouses. Rachel was still in India, so the burden of the harvest fell to me. Over the coming years, I'd learn everything there is to know about the historical flow and best practices of a trim crew.

At the peak, I would have people from thirteen countries camping on my land. It gave me the feeling of owning and managing an international youth hostel where the employees and the travelers were the same. It would have been an absolute human resources nightmare if it had been an actual business. It was a lot to deal with, and I learned on the job.

My first trim crew, however, consisted of just ten people, mostly from the San Francisco Bay Area, whom I had met through a friend. They came up for two weeks and lived in tents at the cabin, and we trimmed as much of the crop as we could afford to before I had to get back to class.

Why were all these people migrating to this small corner of Northern California? To trim weed, the pot, ganja, reefer, the marijuana—oh, and my favorite, Le Cannabis. These "trimmigrants" were the hands that handled this process. They were paid by the pound. That year, the going rate for the crew was $175 per pound. It was classic agricultural piecework. The experienced and skillful could do two to four pounds a day in about ten and a half working hours. That was anywhere from $35 to $60 net per hour. Yummy money.

It took only a few days for me to realize that running and managing a rural trim scene was an unexpected stew flavored with a splash of anxiety, a pinch of great wages, a dash of survival, and a sprinkle of Temptation Island. Being the one responsible for it was the oddest mixture of extreme fear, excitement, sexy danger, wild potential, and pure exhaustion. Mixed with substances, it created a vertigo-like numbness.

It was just me and all of them.

The crew rules were simple and applied to all of us:

1. No one dies. Not an option.
2. No fights or sexual assaults. Ever.
3. Don't bring anyone who is not directly invited.
4. Don't leave until everyone else leaves. We are here to work.
5. Never smoke outside the smoking area. No forest fires.

"The Barn" kitchen was unlocked at 6:25 a.m., the generator rumbled to life at 6:45, the first cups of coffee were poured by 6:55, the last of the bagels popped up in the toaster at 7:20, and work started at 7:30. Squirrels and Steller's jays started to yell and demand scraps at about 8:20 a.m. One fifteen-minute break was allowed in the morning, one thirty-minute lunch, and another afternoon break followed by clean-up at 6:30 in the evening. Paper plates were handed out at 7:00 p.m. sharp, followed by dinner. The local family of mountain lions slid through camp between 8:50 and 9:30 p.m., curious about the evening's events, always traveling to the north along the east side of the barn and cabin and back around the mountain to the south along the western side. At least, that was the only way we ever actually saw them traveling. There were nights we slept on the deck and heard them below, rummaging through the camp sink drainage for scents and flavors. Rattlesnakes were captured or killed on the daily. The war against the mice was relentless. Each day, over twenty traps were set, and at least fifteen mice were tossed in the garbage the next morning, to the rattlesnakes' dismay. Fire extinguishers put out near catastrophes, and drunken fistfights had to be broken up at times. No drug use was ever allowed. Well, at least not until after dinner.

We were to do nothing to bring any attention to us. Dealing with problems was the game board of running any kind of business; dealing with self-created problems was a fool's errand. That was especially true if any problem could lead the cats right to your mice, which was our exact scenario.

Each day, I gave them each an individual tote of dried branches. They sat in the main sunlit room and snipped away, placing the buds into brown paper bags. Each bag was labeled in thick black marker with a random, crew-created fake name, the strain, and its grow site. The workers created their own nicknames even in the first year: Bad Canada, Fake Chain, Piss Olympics, Whore Chata, Hot Coals, Valentino Stud, Humboldt Horror Show, Seattle's Secret, Cousin It's It, Dizzy Goth, Ojos Amarillos, Why You Call Yourself Simba, Melony Carmichael, Question Magic, Padrino Wrong Underwear, Virgin Pasta, Acid Astronomy, and Daisy Dukes It Out.

Due to the early and heavy fall rain and snow, the two highlights of my second season—and my first season with a crew—were enjoying the burn pile and the "cannibal pot" we built for evening soaks. The cannibal pot was a basic circular galvanized cattle trough propped up on cinderblocks. We lit a campfire underneath it in a short chimney stack. With a floating hot tub thermometer and a cold-water inlet, our tub contraption was a fun, sloppy place to gather on intoxicated evenings.

The burn pile was even better. Each damp evening, we dumped all the sticks and trimmings from the day's work in the burn pile just below the house. On top of that, we emptied about a gallon of gas. We didn't need any of the leftover evidence to stick around. It would only have increased our weight totals should a raid take place. Once the burn pile was soaked enough, I grabbed the compound bow we had hanging in the shed and duct-taped a wad of newspaper to an arrow tip, which I also soaked in gasoline. Whichever trimmer won the final rock, paper, scissors game of the day got the honors. I lit the arrow tip with my lighter, and they pulled back the bowstring (sometimes with my help) and released the flaming arrow into the pile. *Whoosh!* The burn pile erupted into a big ball of flames. Gas fumes and warm air flushed our cheeks, and the massive glow of fire was reflected in our eyes.

After smoking out the entire community, the burn pile dimmed to a small orange glow as the others made it back to their tents hidden in the trees around the cabin. One evening, as I was brushing my teeth at the outdoor sink, the day's flaming arrow winner walked up.

"That was so exciting. Thank you for the opportunity," she said.

"You're welcome."

"Want a blow job?" she whispered in my ear.

I spit out my toothpaste in shock. A rush of thoughts filled my exhausted and anxious mind. *What kind of college job have I created for myself? Running this crew is nuts. Am I a drug dealer or just a hustler that hustles a drug currently? No, I'll call myself an "unconventional entrepreneur." "An opportunist of a circumstance." Yeah. And this proposition is just icing on this crazy cake. Man, this mountain life keeps getting wilder,* I thought as I followed her inside.

I was becoming something unexpected, and I enjoyed it: a pot star. It was an unforeseen consequence of my success and power.

. . .

With all the trimming finished by the first week of November and the semester finished shortly after that, it was winter break. With the sales from the second season rolling in, I had some cash, and I wanted to see my girlfriend, however fraught our relationship was. Though she'd ripped herself out of the scene and off the mountain when she took off, Rachel didn't fully rip herself out of my life. We were still deeply entangled and exchanged messages daily and video calls when we could. Somehow, despite our own various flings over the last few months, we still considered ourselves boyfriend and girlfriend. Most days.

In December, I went to visit Rachel in India. Within the first thirty-six hours, we had a crazy blowup breakup fight in the middle of the streets in Mumbai.

"How could you have all those side flings but leave me love notes and texts?" she shouted.

"How could you go out all night with that guy and then call me the next day like nothing happened?" I lobbed back at her. I wasn't even sure she had done that, but the trust was paper-thin on both sides by now. Maybe what I really wanted to scream was, *How could you leave me all alone on that mountain?*

Our heated discussion and tear-filled eyes drew the attention of many people. By the climax, we were surrounded by an audience watching our bout from their fruit stands, CD booths, and knockoff clothing kiosks. We were a classic white American disastrous couple in a tragic romantic comedy. By the end of our row, we were screaming in the middle of an internet café. The management looked truly frightened.

As a result, Rachel took off traveling with another guy she had been dating, and I went to explore the Ivory Coast with her fun French female roommate. A few days later, I flew home and spent Christmas at JFK Airport.

I spent the first couple weeks of January up in the cabin with three girls, where the four of us enjoyed each other's company in front of the always-burning fireplace as we snipped away at the remaining barrels of the fall's harvest. It was a calm, blissful, and romantic couple of weeks, sipping hot toddies in the evening as we watched the sunset glow cast colorful hues across the snow-covered hills, but somehow, a girl all the way in India who I wasn't even sure I wanted anymore kept springing to my mind.

One evening, I got a phone call from a San Francisco number. It was Rachel.

"I'm sorry," she said. "I miss you. I'm at Heathrow Airport in London, and I'm flying home to see you."

Oh wow, she's coming home. She had borrowed a phone from a woman who was on the same flight. She would arrive in about sixteen hours. My ego was excited that she missed me, but my mind, the gorgeous winterscape around me, and my calm, enjoyable love circle didn't want any chaos. However, ghosting and blocking her after going in separate directions on the dirt streets of Mumbai hadn't worked. The chaos circus our relationship had turned into still had some trapeze artists ready to put on a show. Dang.

Five days later, Rachel was back on a flight from Humboldt to India. All the product had been trimmed but not before she tried to kick the other three ladies out of the house. She had come home to pee on her turf and then left.

. . .

That spring we hired Noah, our transient, God-loving friend, to keep the clones warm, fed, and showered. An acquaintance was coming out to California that May to be our first full-time hired help. But that was still two months away.

During the spring break in April the year before, we'd spent all week building a greenhouse for that season's starter plants, only to have it collapse and be crushed from heavy snowfall. After crawling commando-style for a day under snow-weighted plastic and hoop house framing, we were able to rescue our little frozen plants. We lost less than 10 percent of them.

"A miracle," I stated nervously.

"No, brother, this was another lesson literally falling from above," Noah had said. Losing only such a small number of those little plants during such a destructive collapse and series of harsh weather days, I knew the Universe or God or the mountain wanted me to grow them. It gave me comfort and a boost in confidence regarding my choice in entrepreneurial venture. This spring break, Rachel and I chose to meet secretively in the Netherlands for a week. I told my friends on campus and out in the hills that I would be hiking the Lost Coast Trail. We were becoming a little too free with our spending habits regarding travel, but we hadn't taken a moment in this offseason to create our financial plan or calendar for the year. We had been too busy fighting.

After a couple of days riding the magic mushroom school bus, walking through the parks, gently being escorted out of museums for excessive laughter and abnormally long gazes at centuries-old art, and getting stuck on the staircase in the lobby of our hotel for hours, we enjoyed our first ever legal weed experience at an Amsterdam café. It was calming to purchase a couple joints, but it was also so interesting and motivating to watch a simple cannabis transaction.

Some rested hours later, we got dressed up for a night of clubbing. At the coat check, we grabbed the name ticket and dropped a 180-euro tip for a hefty handful of colorful pills to enhance the sounds, sights, and touches of the evening of dancing together ahead. Forty-eight hours later, the handful of exotic chemicals were gone, as were the liberal handfuls of secrets we had each been keeping from each other over the previous couple of years.

A barrage of honesty flowed out of our souls like a cascading snowmelt in a hot afternoon sun. While rolling high on little pink-and-blue beans, it was a new and enjoyable feeling to spill the figurative beans in a nonconfrontational manner. While gazing into each other's exploding pupils, we told one another about sleeping with friends and roommates. We admitted to changing passwords to emails, Facebook, and voicemails. We calmly and passionately communicated to each other what hurt our feelings and how we could be better partners. We made plans to build a cabin on the mountain. We agreed that the garden was both of ours, and we decided that I would move in with her at Humboldt for her final year of school. I would have a single big season on the mountain without the added stresses of school and living five damn hours away.

It was a blissful high, and I was intoxicated by the idea of really making it work with her. Then, our bodies exhausted, we crashed. All was out in the open, and it felt liberating. However, it was all weaponry scattered in the field of our relationship, waiting for a later battle. We were nurturing and cultivating our now-toxic relationship just as well as we were nurturing and cultivating our plants. This was the pressure valve release that we so desperately needed, or so we thought.

CHAPTER 19

The Wrong Type of Smoke Signal

SUMMER 2010

I LIFTED THE BACK TIRES of the quad and pulled them toward the front porch. "It only needs to be over there for a couple of weeks. Once we finish planting and connecting and fortifying the water system, it will be brought back over here."

"But we use it here every day," Rachel said. "I like our rides up the road to The Rock to be with the sunset."

She was right. I loved our nightly sunset rides up to The Rock, a natural castle overlooking the incredible panoramic vistas of the ridge and valleys below.

"I know. I do too."

"We need to keep doing that every night. It's been good to us and for us."

"I hear you," I said.

I heard Rachel walk back into the cabin and slam the door. It was a Wednesday—her day to prepare lunches, clothes, soap, and towels for our workday at Anne on the mountain. She was in a mood. We'd made the trip for the last seven days straight, and the last three were spent filling thirty-five-gallon grow bags and mixing amendments by hand and shovel. We thought we might be able to finish filling bags that day.

It was 8:14 a.m. on June 18, 2010. Looking back at the chairs, I thought about how our evening trip to The Rock was twelve hours away, but it did feel like a daily reward.

Heading up on our nightly pilgrimage, she would drive the hippo, aka our four-wheeler, and I would ride Charlie, our '98 Honda 250 dirt bike. Each evening, sitting barefoot at The Rock in those stained and ripping folding chairs, eating cheese and Triscuits while sipping two buck chuck, was special. Though we'd made some hill money, we still liked simple pleasures. It was the grounding of our minds amid the chaos of daily crimes committed and capture once again averted. At the end of each day without getting the crop cut or facing a police bust, moments on The Rock were the post-game. It was also the reward for living with a lack of modern amenities. I believe that over time it was actually the lack of amenities that gave us better mental and physical health. It gave us healthy time every night to share our thoughts of the day, to have our relationship skirmishes, and to discuss our dreams for the future. We didn't have phone screens to stare at and let distract us from learning more about each other and ourselves.

Our times at The Rock felt like life in the pure, though it took some time each evening before our community quieted down enough for us to fully enjoy that purity. Dogs from the neighboring ranches barked, automatic gunfire sprayed through the valley, and the last few cuts from a Skilsaw whined through the brush.

Then the shift started: A couple of generators gurgled to their off positions, the last projectile emptied from its magazine, the last scoop from the backhoe was dumped into place, and the vultures began their descent from high in the skies. All the creatures and elements of the area's congregation showed respect to the natural church at the closing of the day. Silence and stillness knelt to the sun only minutes before she set. Even the easterly winds paused to look back at the mighty Pacific and pay their respect.

The birds sat as families, perched in the mighty oaks; trucks pulled over at turnouts, killing the loud diesel engines into a resting silence. From up at our rock fortress, we could overhear and oversee the silence as the day's light diminished. The routine was special and peaceful during an unstable illegal-*ish* summer college job; it was the piece that kept the peace.

Our nightly gaze at the shimmering Pacific swallowing the sun reminded us that we were where we were supposed to be. The "Almighty" wanted us up there, growing that plant for the people and for our future. I could feel it every time my bare feet stood on that rock. The pads of my feet absorbed the warmth that the rock had captured throughout the day, reminding me to try to at least stay a little bit grounded in this pot rodeo ride.

. . .

It was early morning, and we were preparing for the next trip up. I ratcheted the last strap as tight as a guitar string, holding the quad into Rick's bed. Taking a deep breath, I looked over at our two-room rural mansion and saw the cheap folding chairs leaning against a kindling box. We had retrieved them from the free pile at the dump. Beyond the chairs, through the window of the cabin, I saw Rachel working on the PB&Js for the day.

"Do you want to strap this back on?" she asked as she came out the front door.

I looked up. She was pointing to the fire extinguisher. As with everything on the mountain, we'd gotten into a rhythm, and this morning was no different.

"No, I want to leave it. I'd like to have two here. I'll strap the one we have at Anne to the Ranger when we get there."

"You sure, Ty?"

"Yeah, it's still June and pretty green out."

I had a five-gallon tank of gas in the bed with the hippo, but we would be at Anne soon, and we would have that extinguisher.

"Let's go. This morning has been a slow one."

"Don't be grumpy," she said. "We're doing fine."

Normally, there were two fire extinguishers Velcroed to the up-rights of the lumber rack. We were getting up to the gate a little later than usual that day, and we needed to finish creating a shower of some sort on the side of the cabin back home. It had been crunch time the past seven days, and we had made the daily round trip from Mule Mountain to our mountain on every one of them. Living at the cabin that summer made it a lot easier, bringing our door-to-door travel time down to just a half hour from over an hour. The hippo, with its fake authorized personal numbers on the fender, looked more like we were forestry personnel of some sort, as did the two neon work vests draped over the back seats and the yellow legal pads we carried with us.

I got out, and Rachel pulled the Ranger forward.

"Will you close the gate?" she asked.

"Sounds good."

Just as I snapped the gate lock, I heard a truck coming up the drive. I figured it could be the sheriff, so I just left it locked and got back into Rick.

"Who is it?" she asked.

It was another twenty seconds before I could get a visual. It was our neighbor Jerry—one of the "Alabama boys," as folks in Oak Creek called them.

"Looks like Jerry's truck," I replied. "Here, let me unlock the gate for him."

I walked back to the gate with my head mostly down. Jerry's

brakes screeched as he came to the gate. Just before the gate, I looked up to see a twelve-to-eighteen-inch flame jetting from underneath the center of Jerry's engine. I froze.

Jerry gave the truck a little bit of gas to roll forward. Another flame shot from underneath the truck. I kicked into gear immediately.

"Get out of the truck!" I yelled. "Get out of the truck! There's a fire! There's a fire!"

I could hear the bass from his music. He looked confused. I yelled again.

"A fire under your truck! Get out of your truck! Get out of your truck!" I panicked. My arms were flailing as I motioned for him to get out.

Then the flames started shooting two feet out with sounds of whooshing air. Jerry wasn't getting out. I leaped over the gate, yelling even more. He was taking his seat belt off but didn't get out. I picked up a rock and threw it at his truck.

"Get out of your truck. It's an emergency!"

Pointing to the flame flying out from underneath his truck, I saw that he was pulling a mini backhoe. I ran to his passenger-side door and opened it.

"Jerry, get out of the truck, man. There's a fire under it!"

"What?"

"Grab the dogs now!" I yelled, pointing at the two hounds in the back.

He finally understood and jumped out. Rachel was running to the gate. The inner tire on the right front side of the truck was melting from the flames.

"Back to our truck! Oh my God, oh my God! Is your weapon in there?" I screamed.

We got to the Ranger and looked back; the flames were everywhere.

"Where's the fire extinguisher, babe?!" Rachel yelled.

"It's at the generator!"

The closest fire extinguisher we knew of was at the top of the mountain two and a half miles away—at least eight minutes of driving. I jumped into the back of the Ranger, started loosening the latches for the quad, and dropped the tailgate.

"Hurry! Put these racks on the back of the truck! I'm driving up to the neighbors' now! Hurry! I'm sure Frank has a large fire extinguisher! He knows what to do!"

I rolled the quad backward and filled the gas tank as fast as I could. I knew it would take me at least twenty minutes to drive to the spot where I thought Frank would be that morning. The flames were getting bigger, about four feet wide and five feet long. The truck was a diesel, so Rachel and I didn't think it would blow too fast.

But I hadn't heard a diesel engine coming up when Jerry first approached. *Wait, is that truck diesel or gas?* Jerry's eyes were open wide, and the dogs were at his side. He was in shock.

"Jerry, is it diesel or gas?" I yelled.

"It's gas, dammit!" he yelled back.

I looked at Rachel. "Move the Ranger if you can, another hundred yards down the road, out of sight!"

"I'm calling it in! I'm calling it in! We have the radios here, Ty." She leaned over across the front seat, digging through the cab. "Here!" She tossed one to me and kept one.

The flames had started curling up the sides and poking slightly into the cab through the open windows.

"Give me two more for the neighbors!"

I stuffed two of the radios she gave me into my pockets and clipped the third to my left shoulder strap just above the gold clip of my torn and stained overalls.

We knew that calling in the fire over the radio would get interest from more than just the fire department. The sheriff's department and the forest rangers would definitely perk up hearing the location of the incident. There were no planned logging projects slated for that area all summer. They would recognize the road from the previous summer's warrants, and they would at least come to provide tactical support for the local volunteer fire department. It was a no-win situation. We had to call it in and pray for a "good boy" pass, that they would see we were doing the right thing even if we weren't doing the right thing behind the gates.

"Channel five. I'll be back soon, Jerry! Don't let anyone through that gate! Give me your key!"

"I can't give you my key! What if we need to do—"

"What if we start a forest fire?"

For ten long seconds, we were hypnotized by the flames whipping and curling up the sides of the truck.

"Don't let anyone through that gate, Jerry!" I sped off on the quad.

"I'm calling now!" Rachel yelled.

Shit. Over the next mile and a half, the quad got sideways like a rally car at every turn; with every bump, the four tires came off the ground; and on every straightaway, I had a moment of clarity as the thicket went by. It was as fast as I'd ever driven before. This was the worst thing that could happen at the worst time.

I had run into one of the neighbors the day before, so I believed I would find someone there first. It was a gamble since I didn't have cell service. Even if I did have cell service, what were the chances one of the neighbors would have service at the same time? I turned up to the neighbors' driveway and glanced back down the road. That driveway was the worst of the four properties, rivet after rivet, washout after washout, up to the top of the mountain.

The gate was locked.

Dammit. I looked quickly to both sides. Could I drive around it? It was impossible. I hopped off the quad and started running. I had been up here only once, two years before when Bob first brought me to the property. I could see the little cabin. It looked closed up, and no one seemed to be around.

I heard voices farther down. I came around the hill. Jarod and his crew were building a new greenhouse down in the flat. Grateful Dead music was blasting. There were five people there, and I knew them all. *Perfect.* I needed a break.

"Hey!" I yelled.

The new, bearded guy from Florida looked up and noticed me.

"Turn off that music!" he shouted. "Bookworm, what's on ya?"

The music turned off, and all of them looked at me. I came to a stop.

"What's going on?" one of them yelled.

"Jerry's truck is at the gate! It's on fire! Seriously on fire! He's towing a mini backhoe with the transfer tank! Rachel is calling it in to the fire department! The sheriff's department is coming to our gate right now!"

"What?"

The deep sound of a large helicopter abruptly caught our attention.

"I'm not kidding! We need a fire extinguisher!"

One of them leaped onto a quad. "I'm going to get Tractor Frank!"

Two others got onto their dirt bikes and zipped past me.

"Here!" I said, handing Jarod a radio. "Channel five!"

"You sure she called it in?" someone asked.

"She called it in," I yelled. "It needs to be called in. It's going to explode!"

"We got thousands of plants up here right now, and who knows how many they have over there!"

"I know, dude! I know, but it had to be called in. It's gonna start a forest fire!"

Static erupted on the radio, and I heard Tractor Frank yell,

"Goddammit, boy! We freakin' beat them at their own game, taking out the road last year. Now we just sent up a damn smoke signal calling them back. This is absolute bullshit!"

"Had to be done," I radioed back.

"Here, take this!" I shouted to one of the remaining guys, tossing him the last radio. "Channel five. I gotta go back down there. Don't say any names over the radio!"

I turned and jogged back to the quad.

"Ty!"

I turned back.

"Good job, man, good job!"

I paused, my heart still going, my mind still racing.

"Thank you!"

As I drove back to the Ranger, I heard a quad coming behind me.

"Move over!"

The quad ripped past me faster than I'd ever seen, with four industrial-size fire extinguishers strapped to the front. Coming around the bend, I saw massive flames. At that point, the truck was fully on fire but hadn't exploded yet. The trailer with the mini backhoe seemed to be on fire too. The wood planks burned right below the tractor and a transfer tank with 120 gallons of fuel in it.

I could see two of the guys jumping over the gate with the fire extinguishers. They let them rip, emptying them. Then they emptied the others. Nothing was changing. The fuel line spewed gas and flames as quickly as we put them out. It was impossible; we didn't stand a chance. I grabbed my extinguisher.

"Keep that extinguisher on the quad!" they yelled. "We need one!"

We were defeated. I turned back down the road, and Rachel was there running back toward me, cell phone in hand, wearing her flannel shirt, boots, and cutoff jeans.

"Did you call?" I asked.

"I called! Everyone's coming, dammit!"

We looked at Jerry.

"Jerry, this is on you. We'll be right around the corner, but this is on you."

Rachel jumped on the quad, and I jumped on the back. She drove quickly back to the Ranger. The other vehicles were following right behind us as we came around the bend to the west and found the Ranger there with the neighbors in a Chevy diesel. Tractor Frank was coming down the lane in his Jeep. We were covered in fire extinguisher dust.

We walked through the trees as the sound of helicopters and sirens surrounded us. And then there was an explosion—an incredible blast—the sound when a wave crashes on the sand . . . and then a crackle.

As we emerged from the overhead thicket and back onto the driveway, we could see that the entire truck was on fire. The flames shot almost twenty feet above the truck, and the mini backhoe was fully engulfed, the grease ripping smoke into the air. The surrounding trees were on fire and crackling, the first fire engine made it up over the crest, and then the sheriff's trucks followed into view.

And then the mountain started to roar. The California Department of Forestry's massive helicopter circled to assess the situation. We all stood silently, watching from behind the trees hidden in the thicket.

I looked at Rachel.

"If the sheriff's deputies come through that gate, I need you to run and hide. I need you to know that you will be OK, but you need to stay hidden until all goes quiet. You need to keep those Ranger keys on you; they won't tow the Ranger. And at the end of the night, you drive that Ranger out of here."

"OK."

She could tell I was serious. We were all serious. We could all own up to what we had created and what we were doing, but it was not fair to her. Rachel had never been in it for the money.

"You did the right thing by calling it in," Jarod said. "You did the right thing."

"I know," she replied.

The fire engines retreated. Jerry was talking with one of the deputies. The flames were still ripping, inching toward a mature madrone. The fire had spread to one hundred feet by one hundred feet. Then we heard the chopper overhead again. The trees around us swayed from the massive winds. The chopper got so close to the fire that we thought it was going to catch. Then it unleashed a massive foam bomb over the entire area. Two feet of foam coated everything—the gate, the truck, the mini backhoe, you name it—foam everywhere. The chopper sped off, and the firefighters unleashed all the water in their trucks on everything they could find to the south of the fire.

"I think they have this handled," Tractor Frank said. "Let's get out of here. We don't need to watch the spectacle. We need to get safe."

He was right.

When we reached the corner of our property where we could look down onto the mountains and valley below, we could see the helicopter circling and some smoke curling up a couple of miles to our south. The fire had at least slowed.

"Let's keep these radios on us. Jarod, in about a half hour, can you go down and tell us what it looks like? Walk back through the woods?"

We parted ways. Tractor Frank made it to the top first, where he sat on the hood of his Jeep, looking out over the skyline and watching the smoke fall through the sky toward the mountain towers to the south. It was a crystal-clear day; anyone for miles around would've noticed the massive amount of billowing black smoke. It looked like a volcano.

"Well, boys, that right there was a fire drill and one hell of a lucky situation," Tractor Frank said over the radio. "That could've been way worse if it would've happened a month and a half from now. We could've lost everything, and we could've created a situation where everyone around us would've lost everything. Jerry is now on my short list."

"Keep the radios for the rest of the day," I said. "I'll get them tomorrow. I don't see myself leaving this place 'til seven, and I want to make sure no one is sitting on the other end of that gate."

It was only 10:15 a.m. *What a hell of a way to start the day*, I thought. We pulled up to Anne and looked in quietly at all the plants in their gallon containers and their squares of one hundred. They looked so beautiful, and for the first time, I realized that place was dangerous. At any moment, everything could literally go up in smoke.

"I don't feel like planting anymore today," Rachel said, breaking the silence.

I couldn't have agreed with her more. The mountain was telling us she didn't want us working that day; she wanted us to reflect on how we would protect her.

We fixed the water spring and finished building our tables and summer camping area. It was another reminder to always listen to the mountain, for she knew best. And to always listen to the women of the mountain, for they could listen to her best.

CHAPTER 20

An Opportunity Cost

SUMMER 2010

IN THE SUMMER OF 2010, I turned down an internship. I'd been thinking about opportunity costs for years. I decided I was going to give this weed thing my all—at least for a couple of years. I had read the attorney general of California's remarks on medical cannabis. I bought *The Wall Street Journal* once a week, and I always listened to public radio. Even though I was far from everything half the time, I tried to stay up on current events to keep from fading too far into the woods. The years 2009 and 2011 would be the worst to graduate (due to the real estate crash in 2008 and the Wall Street crash in 2011). I graduated right in between with very few prospects for work. But I had a love for the mountains and an entrepreneurial spirit.

A couple of days after graduation, I told my parents everything. While they knew I was growing a little, they had no idea the magnitude that our second season had taken on. I told them what Rachel and I had agreed to in the Amsterdam hotel room—that I would move north full-time during Rachel's last year in college and grow weed for another year. I told them about the various greenhouses and gardens. Everything. They were shocked, but after my tell-all, it was better. I was better. Not totally free but freer than before.

They knew the status of job opportunities for recent graduates. They knew my entrepreneurial spirit. They understood my love for those hills and mountains, camping, and those plants. My parents knew how hard I worked and why I was doing it. The economy was shit, and academics had never come easy for me, but I'd made the dean's list while all that was going on and my natural skills were being cultivated.

I was still detached from the idea of becoming a "pot grower"—a term I'd never used once to describe myself. *If I don't believe it, it's not real, and I won't give in to the grower's mindset or consider this situation permanent,* I would tell myself.

From conversations I'd had, it seemed the majority of locals disliked the stereotypical actions and attitudes of growers, who were always living a fast-cash life—driving too fast on single-lane roads, taking up two parking spots at the grocery store, and getting loud, drunk, and cash-flashy at the fancy restaurants. The worst growers over-offered on real estate and then ruined the properties by trashing expensive vehicles, shooting guns day and night, running loud generators, and sometimes polluting and sucking nearby creeks dry. Their obnoxious lifestyles put them somewhere between rock-star hicks and fake hippies, overall making them unpopular in the community.

"Crazy, cocky pot growers," I said when reading about the weekly pot busts in the paper or listening to growers peacocking the size of their operations in loud conversations at the hardware store—not because I thought they were actually stupid or crazy but merely to constantly remind myself not to be blatant. *We are a business, that is all. We are doing this to make a great living—not to show off or compete in an unwinnable competition with the Johnsons of spiraling envy, money, and grandeur. The energy, time, labor, and risk we put into this is just too great and too hard to try to simultaneously fight our own egos. We will stay in harmony with that mountain and get weed out to the masses to enjoy. It is a timely opportunity and a temporary venture.*

"It's all temporary, Ty. Temporary," I would whisper to myself as I read the list of charges facing the operation and subject. Right next to these stories was always an advertisement for growing materials or legal services. That summed up the truth of the situation, the irony of the predicament that I and the community of Humboldt County found ourselves in.

Still, damned if we do, damned if we don't, right? my brain constantly tried to remind my heart.

Even though I wasn't raised to be a grower, and I still didn't consider myself one, my parents could see the value of what I'd built, and my dad even offered to come help harvest at the end of the season, when I would learn that he'd been a consumer for years. Of course, they were also completely terrified because of the legal ramifications and the distraction from my education and career path. Part of them didn't want me to succeed because they were afraid that I wouldn't leave the industry and that my younger brother might get involved. They were OK with weed, but they were less OK with growing and selling. They knew all the Humboldt stories just as well as I did.

"I don't know anyone that has or was able to make a career out of it, and I knew some very big players in that world," my father said as we sat in a park just off campus the day after graduation.

"I know," I said. "Trey from River's Garden Supply told me the same thing a few years ago."

"He would know. One year, son, then you two kids move away and have your relationship and start your career somewhere else— not up there."

"Yeah, OK." I knew subconsciously that I was lying to him and myself.

"Or you could break up with her now and go take that internship." He spoke quietly, probably aware that his son didn't have much chance for a future with Rachel.

"Wait 'til you see what this is first, Dad," I said. "Imagine running a secret super-high-dollar business in college while still being perceived as a college student just getting by. It's a once-in-a-generation opportunity."

"Unless you go to prison for a generation."

. . .

I moved up for the year to be with Rachel at Humboldt. The start of the 2010 summer season brought a new feeling of excitement. Not carrying the fear of having to leave the coming August created a heightened level of focus and drive in me to go big—to improve the land's use and create an infrastructure beyond some greenhouses and a tent. I would be able to focus on the harvest in mid-August, and in the fall ahead, I would be living on the mountain.

We also had our first employee starting. Nick was an engineer I met when I was still in construction through a friend in the electrical industry, and he was fascinated by the engineering side of growing. He had grown up on a rural property, so I hired him—somebody other than me was going to grow the weed. Nick had expressed interest in the Humboldt County weed scene when we met four years before. I didn't know anyone in the industry then, but a lot had changed in a few short years. When we needed help building and growing that summer, I reached out to him. He came on for eight months with lots of experience and a master's in electrical engineering. We were lucky to have him.

The goal for the summer of 2010 was to secure a bit more water storage. We built another large greenhouse at the top of the ridge and added a greenhouse next to Anne to do a light-deprivation grow, an agricultural technique that manipulates the amount and timing of light plants receive to mimic conditions in autumn.

It was becoming a popular method of growing. If you do it right, the plants can think it's time to flower or bud almost anytime during the year. During the winter and early spring months, grow operations did not produce revenue. Light-deprivation grows require precision and daily attention, but having extra grow time during the year could increase our operation's profitability. In the areas where multiple light-deprivation greenhouses would fire up their light at the same time, regional pilots could see their glow from the air. The flyboys started calling the lit-up greenhouses "glow bugs."

We also added four above-ground swimming pools to the operation. Two at Anne, one at the massive new "top spot" (which we nicknamed the Google Plex for its size), and one hidden in the trees. Fresh spring water trickled into Anne's pools, creating a wonderful cooling-off spot after a long workday. We hired Tractor Frank to clear another flat on the south side of the property and extend the road to the summit of the ridge, offering an incredible view of the Trinity Alps, with impeccable sunrises and snowcapped mountains.

We made a camp of a single, two-person dome tent for our sleeping bags and air mattress. Next to that, we had a four-person dome tent for our clothes, toiletries, a simple vanity, and a spit sink. Outside was a circular fire pit made of local rocks. We constructed a wind-block wall by sinking four snags into the ground and stacking and tying vertically placed gray logging slash to build a fence. Over the fence were a few layers of brush. It was remote, hidden in the foliage. You could be about forty feet from that camp, and if the fire wasn't burning, you could easily miss her. We named her Camp Camo. The summer before, we had our bohemian love nest of a cabin; this year, we had a thin layer of fabric between us and the elements.

On a cold morning in late May, I awoke before sunrise to an eerie silence surrounding our tent. As my eyes tried to adjust to the light-gray and dark-orange hues making it into the tent, I could see my breath and feel the wet and frozen pillow next to my cheek. I rolled over to gain warmth from Rachel. She was gone. I shot up like a bullet. I always woke up before her. Always. I grabbed the throwing axe beside my pillow.

Her boots were missing too. I zipped open the tent in a flurry of concern, desperate to find her. Up and over went the zippered flap and *bloop!* Into the tent poured a sheet of snow.

"You're awake, my sexy mountain man. Don't let the snow in the tent."

I heard her voice through the brush about a hundred feet down the hill east of our campsite. Stepping out into eight inches of thick, wet, fresh snowpack in my boots, I turned and quickly scooped out the snow that had fallen inside, took a T-shirt from the day before, and dried the last of the evidence from my blunder.

"Quick, come down here. The sunrise and stars are dancing together, and this view—this is it. This is the place."

About ten inches of wet spring snow had fallen during the night. Snow was common on the mountain from September through April, but May snow was unexpected—unexpected and beautiful. We had gone to sleep under gusty winds and a ring around the moon. The prior afternoon, the NOAA report coming through the hand crank emergency radio had called for light slush and heavy rains with clearing in the morning. Those heavy rains must have become silent flakes. Nick was camping in the trees about a mile away from our Camo Camp.

I tromped over the flattened spring grasses and weighted shrubbery. I ducked below the low-hanging branches of the black oaks holding up columns of snowpack and followed her foot imprints from her solo walk. *How long has she been down there? What does she want me to see so badly? How had I not heard her unzip the tent or break trail in the snow? What is this "it" she is referring to?*

As the branches and snow-covered foliage cleared, I saw her standing in the middle of a meadow-like clearing. Her back was to me. The orange dawn light outlined her silhouette in a burning aura of warmth. In front of her was what seemed like a sixty-mile view. The Trinity Alps' ridgeline was a perfect silhouette against the sun's glow. In the foreground of the mighty alpine range, different mountain ridges with ravines and valleys covered in snowy forests reflected gorgeous morning colors.

The scene in front of me looked like a mid-1800s French painting of an unspoiled landscape. The sun had not yet risen above the ridges of the Alps to the east. I felt grounded and frozen in that moment, like the sober version of my solo acid trip on the mountain the year before. But I had missed the incredible view, companionship, and authenticity.

After some moments, still not turning to look at me, she extended her hand out to her side.

"Come hold my hand," she said.

I walked through the snow to her, and I reached out to grasp her warm hand in mine. We locked fingers and stood in silence. We gazed forward, holding space. We were as still as the tall tree beside us in the meadow.

"She's about to grace us with Her magnificent powers today," Rachel whispered as her fingers coiled tighter around mine.

A few breaths later, an amazing crown-shaped display of light that looked like a pink, yellow, and white version of the crown atop the Statue of Liberty shot out across the top of the ridges, straight up over our heads, and into the last of the night sky behind us to the west. It was beautiful. It was church. As the moments passed, the brightness lowering in angles from the last of the faint stars above faded, and the Sun, the lifeblood to our existence, rose.

"She, the Sun, always first; may She never be still," Rachel whispered. It was a saying we had repeated many times before while watching the last quick moments of a sunset, but this was our first sunrise together.

"We will build our cabin right here," she proclaimed.

I was in awe of the location, the view, and the feeling but concerned about the incredible amount of work it would take to hike all the materials down to this spot, let alone build here. But my girlfriend, with whom things were either tremendous or tenuous, was having a harmonious idea, so I let it go.

"Make a mental mark in the snow below our hands," she said. "This is where the woodstove will be. Warmth lives in this spot naturally. We will call it the Chalet."

"I was just thinking this all looks like a French painting. Chalet. I like it."

She glanced down at our glowing, locked wrists.

"I know what I believe in," I said to my surprise.

She lightly squeezed my hand a few times, intrigued by what I had just said, and urged me to continue. I had never truly believed in any of the popular or conventional religions or belief systems. I had grown up with believers and followers on both sides of my family and had made it to Sunday Mass enough times to graduate from catechism school. Sure, bits and pieces seemed logical and morally good, though not all of them. I believed in breaking bread and helping thy neighbor. I respected the notion of the commandments but wasn't willing to give up my Sundays or limit my reading choices. At the time, I liked sex more than marriage and substances more than sobriety. I believed people should be able to love who they loved and that genders are equal and so are beliefs. Last, I found it wild to believe that something written so long ago was stark truth. Anyone who has played a game of telephone can attest to that.

"What do you believe in, sweet pea?" she asked, turning toward me.

"I believe in the Sun," I said with full conviction. "Not like the Son and the Holy Ghost but the Sun, the S.U.N."

I was excited about not having to figure out an answer to life's spiritual questions anymore.

"She sure is something else, isn't She?" Rachel said, turning back to the rays once more, closing her eyes and taking in the sun's morning medicine.

"She is, She is," I said as a liberated believer.

Some days earlier, I had been thinking about all the opportunities for failure in this weed-growing venture we were taking on—and in life, for that matter. I thought of the inconsistencies in my relationship with Rachel, how some days we were so up and other times we were so down and mean to each other. I thought of all the places I had lived in the last eight years, the good days, the bad days, the healthy days, the painful days.

"I have been contemplating just how unfair the start of life can be for different children of the world. The absolute massive differences in wealth and opportunity," I said. "I have thought about the big life-event days like graduations or the days friends and family pass away.

"Through all these thoughts and changes, one thing has been the same. Every day of my life, the most consistent thing is that gorgeous big ball of hot burning mass and gases. She is an absolute warming goddess of light and life right there. If She disappears, all other problems of ours just won't matter. All we will become shortly after She clocks out and turns off is a bunch of frozen matter sucked out into the holes of the universe.

"But not today, not yesterday or the day before that, nor tomorrow or the day after tomorrow. She will be as consistent and warm as She always has been in my lifetime. Right there."

"You know who else believes in the Sun as their God, my love?" Rachel said, snuggling up underneath my chin for a kiss good morning.

"Who?" I asked, thinking she was going to say herself.

"Our flock of orphan plants in Anne, in the top spot, in the woods, and in the greenhouse we built and named District 84. Their leaves perk up the moment the Sun appears and follow Her throughout the daily arc of the sky, praising Her, worshipping Her, and thanking Her for Her gift of life. These strong trees all around us worship Her too. And really, we should be worshipping them—not some patriarchal character in an ancient story—for literally creating the air we breathe to live." She spoke softly but sharply and clearly.

On that snow-covered mountain during that spectacular sunrise, I unknowingly followed my shepherd to the meadow and vista, found what I believed in, and trusted in Her consistency, no matter the circumstance. And we decided where to build our place of worship—the Chalet.

Toward the end of July, construction on the framing of the Chalet began. We had spent two and a half years putting the plants first. It was nice to finally build a structure for myself. I joked that I had built over a hundred homes for others in my life; this was the first where my bed would be placed—like Odysseus. We got the frame and sheeting done that season and covered the roof with the thick black tarp from that season's light deprivation. We planned to complete the project the following spring and summer with more help, funds, and time. Our plywood shack would have to survive one harvest season and a brutal mountaintop winter.

· · ·

"This canned chicken and romaine salad is incredible," Nick said to Rachel.

The three of us were eating lunch as we did every day at 12:20, sitting on plank-and-cinder-block benches around the weathered coffee table. It was the middle of July. She didn't answer and seemed to be staring into space.

"Hon, did you hear Nick?" I rested my palm on her shoulder.

"Yes, glad you like it," she said quietly, glancing at us both. "Shhh."

Her intuition and awareness of her surroundings had been

batting a thousand since the first day she stood on that mountain. She was our "alpha sense" on the mountain, while "the itch" created a distraction for us.

"I heard a helicopter moments ago while I was squatting before lunch. It seemed to be down by the woods grow."

"The woods" was a guerrilla grow we'd planted near the strongest spring on the property, where a grow had once been in the 1990s. It was down a steep, overgrown, almost half-mile trail to a location on the southeastern corner of the property. We had rigged it on irrigation and only needed to make the hike once a week to feed nutrients to almost four hundred plants—a little something extra we hoped for in the fall.

"The hum of the chopper was faint, but it was getting a bit louder for the last few minutes, and now nothing." She broke her blank stare.

Our forks stopped moving and our jaws halted chewing.

"It probably went in a different direction," Nick replied, going back in for another ravenous bite.

"No, no, it doesn't work like that!"

She slammed her fork against her thigh and then paused to stretch her ears, startling us both with her severity.

"When the sound goes silent, it means it is coming right at you," she said. "I learned that when I worked on the military base."

She was annoyed at our skepticism, but before I could answer her with something of comfort, we heard it. *Woosh, woosh, woosh, woosh, woosh, rum, rum, rum.* The trees to our south began dancing aggressively, and the sound deafened our thoughts. Directly above us was a chopper no more than thirty feet above the trees. We all yelled profanities as we dropped our lunches.

Commando-like, we rolled off our benches and crawled to an inside corner of Camp Camo, grabbing strong holds onto the large camo tarp and trying to keep it from sailing off the frame and exposing our camouflaged home and us as frightened human insects. For a long fifty seconds, the chopper hovered directly above us. The chopper pilot must have been staring at the American flag in hurricane mode from the propeller's propulsion. Rick was surely in their view as well. If they had had a clear bottom in the chopper, they would have seen us too. Then the chopper started flying due north toward the top spot, our biggest greenhouse that year.

The trees stopped dancing, and the tarp seemed to be stationary.

"I'm heading to Zeus!" Rachel shouted. Zeus was our newer, bigger truck—charcoal gray, loud as thunder, and freaking big. We kept it hidden down by the gate. Nick and I took off running through the woods in a horseshoe trajectory toward the top spot. This was our plan should we ever be raided, which seemed to be the case in that moment. As we crossed a section of the dirt road that led to the top spot, Nick yelled, "hot dish!" and leaped into the air and to the right, falling flat on the ground.

From the sight of it, I thought he had been shot. Then I saw it right in front of me, coiled up and ready to strike—a large rattlesnake. I leaped up and dove to my left like I was stealing home base in a baseball game. I frantically clawed at the air before I slammed into the rocky ground. After rolling twice, I jumped to my feet, my eyes searching for the camouflaged snake I assumed was in pursuit. My mind was trying to differentiate the pain of a potential bite from the many pains of broken skin. I noticed movement on the ground just across the road. After striking toward me, the snake was now moving in the direction of Nick, who got to his feet just in time to run away.

We met behind an old fallen tree, trying to catch our breath and seeing how much blood was soaking our shirts and pants. The sound of the helicopter was again deafening, about 150 feet to our right. The top of the greenhouse shook violently, and the frame danced along.

"That was absolute fuckery, mate," Nick said. "I swear that thing bit the heel of me boot as I jumped like a bullfrog!" He often joked with a fake Australian accent, which he tended to bring out when he was super sauced or anxious.

"Not as much fuckery as this might turn out to be," I said, pointing toward the helicopter as it began to descend. It was about thirty feet above the ground in a faceoff with the gable end of the greenhouse.

"Are they dropping guys off?" I asked as he looked through his binoculars.

"The ground is a cloud of dust. I can't really tell."

"If so, we better get comfortable. We'll be hiding behind this log for hours."

"No way those guys' boots hit that earth over there. We got to just chance our luck and start running like gazelles in heat, due east, deep into the Sierra Pacific property. We are way too close for them not to find us."

If he was running, I was running.

A moment later, the chopper began to gain altitude. When it was about fifty feet above the greenhouse, it flew right overhead, covering us with large fir branches and needles. Peering through our cover, I noticed five passengers and a pilot. The side doors were open, and a man dressed in full air fatigues wearing a helmet and a harness hung out of the chopper holding what looked like a small camcorder. It was one of the same choppers I had had hovering over me almost a year before, when the officers had stood over the pit that blocked their continued travel on our driveway. I recognized the short-haired blond officer belted in the back seat of the chopper. *Back for more*, I thought as the chopper banked due west and flew down the ravine toward Anne, surely to get her mugshots too.

After a half hour without helicopter sounds, we all reconvened at Camp Camo. Our lunches were spoiled, pillaged by the resident chipmunks, but it didn't matter. None of us were hungry anymore.

CHAPTER 21

Mountain Weird

SUMMER – FALL 2010

OUR "EARLY CROP" turned out wonderfully. We dried it on wires deep in the woods in the middle of August. We trimmed it ourselves with the help of a few who had camped several nights on the mountain. We got twenty-eight pounds, and donations were received for all of it within a couple of days.

Nick was growing homesick and becoming "mountain weird." Loneliness and isolation can be a devil if you're not careful. He had passed his electrical engineering license exam and had been going to the library in town to apply and interview for jobs back near the Twin Cities. In late August, he landed a job and had to leave earlier than we had agreed upon and before the hardest part: harvest. Rachel and I reluctantly understood, as we had imagined growing as only a temporary stepping stone to our future careers. However, our stepping-stone had become larger than we had imagined just two years before.

In mid-August, we still had four gardens starting to bloom vibrantly, which equated to 9,700 square feet of greenhouses and one guerrilla grow of about four hundred plants I would harvest with Rachel's help on Fridays through Sundays. It was all to be dried in a 320-square-foot plywood Chalet with no insulation, no wood stove, a two-thousand-watt generator, two propane burners, and a tarp roof. The small Chalet didn't seem adequate, but there were no other real options. We did, however, have funds in the company account for the harvest and trimming season due to our successful light-deprivation garden.

Jesse, who helped us build Anne and had become a close friend, returned from fishing in Alaska in August. So Rachel and I hired him along with a fellow fishing buddy of his, Matt, to help frame the Chalet. This luxury was a first. I showed Jesse around the farm on the day he arrived.

"Man, this place has come a long way since those wild days working with Daniel."

"Sure has," I said, having a flashback from my acid trip.

I hadn't shown Matt around yet. He needed to earn his keep first. I hadn't told them our helicopter story either. After a few weeks of framing the Chalet, we would have to wait until the following spring to complete it. I needed their help bucketing the last nutrients for the plants prior to their harvest. It was the first of October. Clear, dry days had graced us throughout September. The crop was the largest I had ever seen. *Knocked it out of the park*, I thought.

"Let's load up all the tools, tents, and sleeping stuff. We'll head down to town and your trucks after watering. Grab all food items too. Bears have been everywhere the last month," I told the boys as we sipped our coffees around the campfire just after sunrise.

"Man, it gets cold up here at night in the fall," Matt said.

"It seems to get cold up here every night but August," Jesse said.

The past three weeks felt colder to me, not because of the weather but because Rachel had gone back to school in town. Though she was only a seventy-five-minute drive away, the tent was many degrees cooler each night, and the feeling of being alone was creeping in and causing anxiety.

Jesse and I gave Matt the "blood brother oath" after he agreed to the rules for seeing the gardens. We walked over to the top spot.

The next hour and a half was spent with each of us lugging two five-gallon buckets of nutrient mix from the cattle trough by the pool to each orphan plant for her last feeding of the season.

Driving down to Anne a half hour later was bittersweet. The end was coming. The crew that had helped frame our plywood shack that would someday resemble a Chalet was heading off the mountain for the year. The leaves of the black oaks were all yellow and barely hanging on. The nights were frigid, the days noticeably shorter, and the sun lower in the southern sky. As Zeus slowly made his way down the dirt road toward town, I told the guys of the eventful summer. I told them Rachel and I were to do the operation one more time after she graduated in the following spring, the same semester Jesse was to graduate.

"I don't know how you two do it. It's like you are soulmates, but you both have different trajectories. She's type A, and you're a Tasmanian loose cannon drinking ADHD tea."

"I appreciate your evaluation, dick," I said, both of us laughing at the truth of it all.

"Come on, dude," Jesse said. He was sitting in the back seat. "I mean, you two support each other so strongly in these wild goals and ambitions, but at the same time, we are all witnessing the most toxic resentment and jealousy-fueled explosions of retaliation any of us have ever seen. It's wild, brah."

"Well," I said, "we are now living together in an actual home with electricity, running water, and an easy walk from nice dates in town. We are trying to start back where and how we met. A reset."

As we turned onto the highway west toward the coast, Matt let out a long deep breath. "I only spent eight hours at weed camp, and I tell you what, it's crazy out there. Seems like every day must be some kind of up-and-down rodeo of crazy hard labor and a blizzard of inescapable emotions and wild events."

"Sure is," Jesse said. "You going to be OK out there by yourself all next week?"

"I'm going to have to be. You saw all that weed up there. Doesn't harvest and dry itself."

. . .

Seven days later, Rachel and I were three days into the hardest labor we had experienced so far in our weed venture.

Tractor Frank brought us some gas and checked on our condition. "This mountain can't hold any more water," he said. "She is saturated and just sheeting water in every direction now. You kids still sleeping up there under Camp Camo in those tents during this storm?"

"Yes, sir," Rachel yelled out the partially lowered window of the truck.

"It's looking like another ten straight days of solid rain and possibly snow in a week. It's just the two of you over there now?" he asked, exhaling a cloud of cigarette smoke into the pouring rain.

"Yes, sir, we'll get'r done," Rachel shouted.

"Warm up your jaw muscles, kids," Tractor Frank yelled, smiling.

"What?" I asked, looking up from my frozen, wet hands.

"'Cause I think you two might have bit off more than you can chew."

Tractor Frank always liked to leave with a little joke.

"Ha, ha, happy harvest," Rachel said.

We had been harvesting Anne for three days straight in the pouring rain. We cut the plants and loaded them into Ranger Rick to drive them to the new plywood shack Chalet. Rick sloshed through the muddy ruts the whole way. Once we got as close to the shed as possible, we unloaded the plants into a wheelbarrow. Because of the rain, we had to bungee-cord a tarp over the wheelbarrow and push the wobbly, heavy load of plant matter over the 150 feet of trail to the shack. It was grueling, time-consuming, and not an efficient process in the slightest.

After rolling the wheelbarrow up a ramp and into the shack, Rachel quickly shut the door. Our shoulders burned and cramped, and our cold, wet jeans stuck to our skin with every bend of our bodies. We lifted the heavy plants up and over and onto the wires. Once a full camper-shell load was hung, we changed our clothes before we drove the mile back down to the greenhouse for another load.

There was no need to imagine how much better our neighbors had it—we knew. They loaded their harvests into fully insulated barns equipped with woodstoves, and four or five people harvested and hung the plants no more than a hundred feet from the greenhouses. When they were done, they went back to their cabins for a hot meal beside a fireplace.

"Why even take up space in your mind thinking about that?" Rachel said when I made a faint complaint about the neighbors' operation. "We have what we can afford and what the Universe has given us. We are doing the best we can with what we have. That is all we can hope for and hold on to."

"My hands are literally too cold to hold on to anything," I replied, moving my hands back and forth between the steering wheel and the heater vents on Rick's dash.

Sometime around 1:00 a.m. that night, Rachel rolled over in her sleeping bag and nudged my back. Whispering in my ear, she said, "Ty, don't move. Something is outside the tent."

My dreamy mind quickly defogged, and my eyes shot open. My first thought was to figure out how close to my pillow the hatchet and the Rambo knife were. We lay in silence. For a moment, there was nothing but the sound of raindrops softly beating against the tent's top tarp. No wind seemed to be rustling the trees, and after a while, I thought it was a false alarm. Then I heard two footfalls just outside our tent, no more than three feet away.

I took a gulp of fresh air. The faint sound of my lips parting had been enough for the intruder to notice me. I heard a single step forward. Then a large paw landed at the base of the tent, and the dome slunk down just a hair. My arm instantly clenched the axe. I swung it by whipping my wrist around. It was a wild flick aimed in the direction where I figured the creature was. The flat end of my axe head landed on muscle and skipped off a solid mass.

The intruder leaped forward shortly, seemed to turn, and pounced back. Its retreat knocked over the plastic mixing bowl intended for our eggs in the morning.

"Good job, sweetie," Rachel said.

"That was a mountain lion."

We noticed that the generator had died down at the shack, but I wasn't going to go out and be midnight bait. Starting the machine would have to wait until morning. I sat up, pulled the blankets over our sleeping bags, and fell back asleep. You know you're exhausted when you can immediately sleep after a mountain lion leans against your tent.

Rachel went back to the coast the following afternoon for the school week. Even though she had wanted me to call her every day at 4:00 p.m. to check in, that wouldn't work because there wasn't even cell service in the nearest town. I was once again all alone.

The following six days were some of the most physically and psychologically challenging of my life. On top of the workload, the days were getting shorter and colder. The rain never let up once. I could have gone mad had it not been for the morning news crackling through the radio and the recognizable voices calling baseball games over staticky AM channels.

The shack was packed with plants from Anne. The harvest from the woods had to be hung on wires between trees and covered by a tarp. Not to keep the buds from getting wet—they were soaked like sponges living in a sink—but to keep sunlight from reaching them if it ever stopped raining. Sun plus wet buds equals mold growth.

I was starting to show signs of fraying around the edges. My morning coffee had become hot water with whiskey, a teaspoon of salt, and half a squeezed orange. My midmorning coffee, my beverage for lunch, and all my fluid intake became the same. Rachel had bought five fifths of the brown warming sauce in May—none of which had been opened until that week. By the time all the plants were harvested, a bottle and a half were left.

One morning, I sat on a cinder-block bench, hovering my hands and face over the small campfire. I watched the space outside Camp Camo like it was the morning news. The rain turned to slush when it started snowing. I sat and watched the slushy snow increase in intensity until I decided that it was snowing hard. The sound of flapping tarps was loud but only familiar white noise at that point. I hadn't washed my face, brushed my teeth, or had a bite to eat. I just grabbed the opened bottle of cold brown warming sauce and guzzled a good eight ounces in one pull.

As the brown liquid warmed my stomach, I had a realization. *It sure is a lot easier to grow a ton of this shit than it is to harvest and dry it. We're screwed, and I'm a drunk now.*

I gave the large pink spray-painted pruning shears that hung in Camp Camo a nice kiss on the blades and walked out into the snow to start the generator and light the propane burners down at the shack.

CHAPTER 22

Green Buckets

FALL 2010

I CALLED IN A PANIC as soon as I knew Rachel's school day had finished. It would have been a perfect occasion for a little dinner out and a couple of drinks to celebrate her finishing a school project—but not today. I needed help. The lack of a proper drying environment was destroying our crop by the hour. I hiked out to a point about a mile from the cabin and got a single bar of cell service. I hadn't talked to anyone in days. I practiced talking before I called her to make sure I remembered how to speak.

"Oh, thank goodness, you're alive," Rachel said across the choppy service.

"Hello, yes, I'm alive," I said.

"Are you hurt? Are you still on the mountain? I finished my presentation this afternoon and was going to call Bob so both of us could look for you. I haven't heard from you. I've been sick going to bed thinking about it all. Are you under the tent? It sounds like it's pouring. Only a light drizzle here on the coast today. Oh my gosh, your voice is comforting."

"Honey, honey, slow down," I tried to say in a reassuring tone.

"How are our ladies? How is the Chalet?"

"Not good, and not working. I'm way out at Sky Point," I yelled over the sound of rain pelting my green rain poncho. "I'm not good either. I'm hungry, my bones ache, and I think we are losing the whole crop to mold."

Hundreds of pounds of fresh product hung in the new shack of a cabin. The generator and dehumidifier had been off for sixteen hours now. The propane heaters were running, but there was no air movement or moisture reduction in the new cabin. The situation was wrecked. We were losing dollars fast.

"No, no, no, our ladies, my man," she said.

I had to drop the other shoe. "It's worse than bad, and more snow is in the forecast."

We agreed to meet later that afternoon down where the county road met the highway. She was going to go pick up a couple of generators and more food.

"Hey, remember the sun and stars. I love you," Rachel said.

"I haven't seen either in six days. I love you too," I croaked back.

"We can still chew our way out of this. I know it."

I laughed at her attempt to motivate me. She hadn't seen the dire situation we were in. I flipped the phone closed and stayed in that spot for a long while, crying. I had been standing inside a cloud of pouring rain, snowy slush, and wind-whipped mist for longer than my feet preferred. On a clear day, you could see sixty miles in every direction. The vast views and endless constellations of stars gave a sense of power, opportunity, and clarity. I'd gotten used to those feelings for the last hundred days. The last eight days without those feelings, coupled with the state of the crops, were about to break me.

I wasn't mature enough yet to respect that I might be changing. As snot poured out of my nose and I cried in the low-hanging clouds, I blamed the mountain. Somehow the mountain had changed. The mountain had trapped me. Mountain-sized problems can't be solved by calmly asking, "What do I do now?" No, the mountain and the weather conspired to kill the itch inside me.

Somehow, I pulled myself together enough to meet Rachel down the mountain. She went over the list of supplies she'd gathered and showed off a new generator she had bought. We tried to load the new generator in my vehicle, and *bang!* The generator hit the wet, muddy ground behind the car.

"Shit, that almost got my toes, and now my shoes are dirty," Rachel said.

The brand-new generator was lying on its side in the wet gravel. It didn't matter. And I had little sympathy for Rachel's dirty shoes. For the first time in a long time, I had to turn off the worry of what others might think we were up to. That lack of concern even extended to Rachel. She was still in her school clothes and slid into the back seat of the car.

"Hurry, shut the door," she said as I opened a bag containing her mountain outfit. She was taking off her blazer and heels and trying to take off her pencil skirt. It was like a superhero changing—going from business work attire straight to dirty country work clothes and boots. I shut the door and walked back to Zeus. I looked back at the brand-new generator on its side. There was a tag around the gas cap reminding the new owner to put oil in before using it.

Dammit. I remembered we would need to swing by the gas station again and buy a few quarts of oil. *Whatever. She could use a coffee, I'm sure.*

Turning the truck around, I finally admitted to myself that my emotions were shot. Even with the hellish days behind me, it looked like at least thirty workdays were ahead to wrap all this up. With guests living in tents around the cabin for weeks. My first fall out of college, and this was what I chose for my career. I could have been in a warm office all day and heading out for a steak dinner right now.

Stop, I told myself, simultaneously stepping on Zeus's brake pedal and putting him in park. All the what-ifs, could haves, should haves, would haves, the damned if you dos—none of them mattered.

The task on the mountain still needed to be completed, no matter the octane levels I had left in me.

We finished loading the gear and headed back to town for oil and coffee. During the drive up, I tried not to show Rachel how bad I was feeling. I asked her questions about her presentation and made suggestions about celebrating over the weekend. It was Thursday evening, and she only had one class on Fridays at 1:00 p.m. She'd be home and rested with plenty of time tonight . . . *we thought.*

When we finally got back up the mountain, I pulled our rain gear from the back seat and instructed Rachel to put it on. We ran out to a lean-to and surveyed the situation.

"This is bad," Rachel said.

"I know. It's really bad. I didn't want to tell you how bad on the phone and panic you before the wet drive over the hill. Please grab the wheeled cart from down at the Chalet, and I will put oil and gas in the generator. We'll put the generator in the small tent."

"What? Really? Why?"

"It's too wet under the Chalet. The fuse will pop. It was happening with the other one."

The generator roared to a start after the third pull. The loud industrial sound of the engine was comforting. I reckoned we had been without power for at least eighteen hours, and the propane had petered out five hours before.

"If it's really bad in there, we are going to have to move all this stuff to my uncle's cabin even if my aunt doesn't want us to," I said. "It's too valuable. What's in that shed could buy his property and build him a new cabin ten times over."

"I didn't look in yet. I figured I'd wait for you," Rachel said.

"We will take the pain together."

"Don't say that. We don't know anything yet. It could be fine. It has been very cold. That's better than warm rain."

We fired up the generator before walking into the drying tent.

I could tell from the sound that at least some of the machinery in the dry shed had come to life. She unlocked the shed's door, and we walked in. The six-by-four-foot entry was the only area in which we could stand. The rest of the building had metal wires running every three feet, loaded with hanging branches of weed. The one box fan and the two dehumidifiers were running. It was an upgrade and a small success.

"Oh my God," Rachel said, "the tops are molding on the bottom lines closest to the plastic. Shit." She was almost in tears. I could see it in the glow of the shop light and our headlamps. "We have to take this to Bob's cabin, babe. I know we can't do it tonight. It's too dangerous. I'll do it tomorrow afternoon. I'll prepare the cabin in the morning."

The realization that all the product had to be packed up, carried up to the truck, secured, hidden, driven thirty minutes away, and hung up in another location was deathly. It was lucky Rachel was there when I realized that every bit of work I had done over the past eight days would have to be redone. Had she not been, I probably would have poured gas everywhere, shot a flaming arrow through the front door, and sat in Camp Camo dusting off the last bottle of brown warming sauce while I watched it all burn.

Shaking off the destructive fantasy, I said, "I got to get this propane heater running."

Rachel passed me a full propane tank, and I switched out the empty one. I grabbed a long lighter and tried to fire up the heater—nothing. I ran gas into the system for a few seconds and tried lighting the heater on the heating coils. I even tried lighting pieces of paper towels to light the heater. Attempt after attempt played out, and the heater wouldn't light. My heart ached. My mind raced with the thought of how perfect all these buds were less than a week ago. I brought the flame to the heater again and pressed the fuel knob.

"This damn thing won't light, dammit! Why?" I burst into tears.

I threw the lighter across the room and doubled over to punch the wood floor. With every punch, I visualized more and more molding branches. I hadn't heard Rachel crawling to me, but she embraced me and lifted me back to my knees. She hugged my whole body with hers. I was having a full meltdown, and I couldn't stop.

"It is really bad now, but we are OK. We will fix this. I love you. I love you. It's OK," Rachel kept saying.

We knelt on the floor, rocking like a mother and her crying toddler. I was defeated.

"We're screwed," I said.

"This is a lesson we don't understand yet. Let's pray and meditate for a minute."

"What?" I wiped what were hopefully the last tears of the night from my eyes.

"Come on," she said. "Sit up and cross your legs. Hold my hand."

I obeyed. She was right. After all the tough times we'd had on the mountain, in loud nightclubs, on dirt streets of third-world cities, and after arguments, we would stop and meditate. We sat surrounded by the hanging plants and breathed in deep and slow. She asked the Universe to give us strength and protection. We reminded ourselves of how much we appreciated our plants and the life we had. Then we were silent again. Warmth and sweat had formed in our embraced hands. My heartbeat had slowed noticeably, and I felt lighter, as if the tears had been the weight I had been carrying for months, probably years, and I was finally freed from their burden.

"May you please allow us clarity and warmth that we may give to our plants tonight," Rachel said, breaking the silence. "Take one more large breath in and out and open your eyes, sweet pea."

As I opened my eyes, she was already crawling over to the lighter I had thrown across the room. She grabbed it and shimmied over to the paper towels.

"I'm sorry for yelling at you earlier and for cussing and for truly losing it," I said as she returned to my side.

"I know you are. I'm actually glad you broke down. You needed to. I'm going to light Mr. Heater."

I liked how Rachel didn't say she would try to or hope to, but she was *going to*. Her small fingers clicked the lighter's trigger in rapid succession before a flame emerged at the bent tip. With her left hand, she moved the paper towel wick to the flame. An orange glow filled our surroundings once more. The whistle of the gas began to race through the cylinder. She held the pilot button on for what seemed like an almost dangerous twelve seconds and placed the flame in the ignition hole. Just before another piece of failed paper towel ash was about to break free from the wick, it caught and ignited the heater.

"You did it!"

Rachel did not reply. And then the load whistle began to howl. The sound filled the room like a battle cry of victory as the red glow continued to move across the heating coils. She sat looking at Mr. Heater with her button nose and puffy cheeks, blushing from the warmth. "Thank you," she said. "We appreciate you a lot."

I was amazed. I looked up at the ceiling and quietly said, "Thank you." Then I slowly looked at her and said, "Thank you."

We decided on the treacherous and dark drive down from the mountain. Eating at the nearest Mexican restaurant and grabbing some more groceries wouldn't be a terrible thing. Staying the night at Mule Mountain to get a good night's rest tonight would make setting up the drying system in the morning easier. Rachel was going to skip her Friday class and help out. We would bag and tote up all the product and drive it over with the generator and heaters late the following afternoon. It wasn't ideal, but we would devise a plan and alibi like we always did.

"We smell like weed," Rachel whispered. "I can taste it falling off my hair."

Though the restaurant was nice and warm, we ordered quickly and headed back outside and up the wet sidewalk to the only grocery store in town. We got supplies to make a hearty breakfast and lunch, and a couple other things. The cabin wouldn't have the generator tonight or a Mr. Heater. We would be living by candlelight and woodstove heat, which was what we preferred and all we knew for the most part.

I came out of the restaurant with our dinner. She transferred her things from Sally, her little sedan, into the truck.

"You want to leave it here for the night?" I asked.

"No. Too many break-ins and vandalism here lately."

"I know, but the roads are treacherous." She was right, but I knew it would be a tough drive up to the cabin if it was slushing, and near impossible if it started snowing.

"I just saw Buddy's Towing go by with a busted-up Subaru and minivan on the back. The fire department was right behind them."

"That's not a real great comeback to you not wanting to leave the car here for the night," I said and laughed.

"Let's go, I'm getting hangry."

So was I. I drove in front to keep her from going too fast, and it made good tracks along the highway for her. She kept a healthy distance behind, so much so that I would slow before entering a turn in the roadway to ensure I could see her headlights in the rearview mirror.

It's fourteen dangerous miles between Oak Creek and the summit. The country radio station went in and out as Zeus climbed the road. It was dark. Coming around a hairpin right turn, I cut hard into the rocky hillside, jutting out. I saw a small Civic barely pulled over on the opposite side of the road with one blinker going. *Shit.* I realized the situation just a second too late. The boulders and debris must have damaged the tiny car.

A boulder about the size of a La-Z-Boy recliner was in the opposite lane, and a few boulders ranging from basketball-size to softball-size were in my lane. I swerved to the right, and my tires sank into the drainage ditch. However, my undercarriage clearance was enough to startle the softball-sized aggregate and smash through the freshly fallen mud. I accelerated hard, pulling the right side of the truck up and out of the ditch and back onto the roadway. I sped a hundred feet past the potential of more falling rocks and debris, and pulled over.

My heart raced as I slammed my thumb into the hazard button on the dash. Rachel would be coming around that turn in the next twenty seconds. I grabbed my headlamp and pocketknife from the cup holder as I leaped out of the truck, never turning it off. The rain was intense. I could see that the dome light was on in the Civic, and I could make out the figures of women inside. I was still another sixty feet from being visible to those in the line of cars coming into the turn and into treachery when Sally's lights appeared—Rachel's car. Through the windshield, I could see that her face was processing the scene, but she wasn't slowing.

Rachel braked about ten feet before the boulders, but it was too late. There was a *bang!* And a *riiiipppp!* She skidded straight and hard for forty feet with a rock the height of a five-gallon bucket wedged underneath the engine. Oil splashed behind the car and flowed down the highway from the hard rains.

"Oh my God!" someone yelled. "No!" I looked back at the Civic. A woman was standing outside it, drenched, with her hands over her face, while another woman still sat inside, watching Rachel's car grind to a halt.

"Grab your stuff and head to my truck now, ma'am," I said. "This hill is still moving!"

I could see little rocks bouncing across the oil streaks through the red glow of Sally's brake lights. My body must have floated to Rachel in the car because I don't remember moving toward it. I had her out of the car, cradled in my arms, and running up to Zeus in seconds.

"I'm OK, not hurt, just in shock." She looked ahead at the women just getting to Zeus. "Are they OK?"

"I don't know yet."

I propped her in the now-soaked driver's seat and told the women to get in the passenger seat. I tossed all our grocery bags in the back of the truck and our clothes on the women's laps.

"What are you doing?" Rachel asked.

"I have lights, flares, and vests under the back seat. Someone comes down this hill in a truck like mine or a semi, and they are dead on impact or swerving off the edge."

"It smells like weed in here," one of the women said.

"Shut up," I said to her, then, checking again, asked Rachel if she was OK physically.

"Yes, I think so."

"Good. I'll be back."

I went running up the road to set flares. After setting flares on the uphill and downhill side of the road and putting a vest on the top of a massive rock, I saw a couple in a new Ford Super Duty had stopped on the uphill side. A second truck approached.

"I'm going to head to the summit and call this in," the driver yelled over the diesel gargle as he made the three-point turn to head back up the hill. "Any injuries?" he yelled out again.

"No, let them know full road closure when you call."

"Roger!"

The pickup sprinted up and out of sight. More debris came down and moved the Civic off the edge of the roadway. The women stayed with the firefighters and CHP officers when they arrived. We told the local tow company to grab Sally when they could and get her to a mechanic on the coast sometime by Monday. I didn't care to check the damage. We were safe.

"Nice work," one of the CHP officers said quietly. "Glad you two are safe. Heading home from work late tonight, I see." There was a glimmer of a smirk behind the large blue hooded rain parka he wore. I had sat by him many times before at the Mexican restaurant, and we played ball against each other in high school. He knew my character over my profession—a small-town understanding.

When we finally made the remaining fifteen-minute drive to Uncle Bob's cabin, the truck slid and sloshed through the fresh wet few inches of snow. It was almost midnight. We bathed in the kiddie pool in the living room. My body was covered in bruises.

"It'll buff," I told her.

"All right, tough guy. We'll see if you can light the heater tomorrow."

. . .

As the French press was brewing on the small kitchen counter before breakfast the following morning, we had to think about how we were going to fit more than four hundred soaking-wet plants into one fourteen-by-twenty-four-foot room and one twelve-by-eighteen-foot room. The twelve-to-sixteen-foot ceilings would be our saving grace. It seemed impossible, but it was our only choice. We had dried in this room before, but in stages and with smaller crops. Earlier in the summer, we had scored a free roll of five-foot-tall deer fencing. That was the answer.

At the beginning of spring, we determined that we could dry all the product for the price of one pound of product, or $2,200, so that's what we budgeted. Since we did not allow for vehicle repairs and the like, we had already overshot our budget by the $1,200 we would have to pay for a car repair after this disaster.

After breakfast, we created a wire grid throughout the cabin with the deer fencing. We figured our creation could hold forty pounds of buds on each shelf when dried, so that was a start. Before we left to pick up the buds, we hung black plastic over the windows. In a few hours, we'd transformed the cabin into a dry barn.

"It will work," I said.

"No damn doubt," Rachel replied.

The cabin-turned-dry-barn looked like it was going to be our best setup to date. We left the warmth of the cabin and trekked up the mountain late that afternoon. It was still raining, and slushy snow was falling hard at the tops of the mountains. We surveyed our mountaintop setup.

"I'm happy this is happening," I said. "It's better we dry over there anyway."

"Yeah, it's closer to home. It feels safer once the rain comes," she said. "I'm scared out here, Ty. And after the other night in the tent with the mountain lion, I think the mountain was telling us we've overstayed our welcome."

I felt like this might be the last time we would be up on the unforgiving ridgetop. As we were about to embark on our fifth trip of moving all the product, I glanced back at the shack with its plywood walls and tarp roof. It looked like the bones of a structure from *Sleepy Hollow*. My shoulders ached from carrying two full propane tanks as I looked at it in the light glow of my headlamp, rain pouring down still.

I spoke to the cabin as I turned to walk toward the weed-filled truck. "I will turn you into something beautiful and weatherproofed if you can please make it through this winter. A true Chalet, I promise. I'll be up in a month or so and do a final clean before the snow melts. I love you."

Two pieces of plywood, an extension ladder, and a tarp were the only things hiding around a hundred pounds of marijuana from onlookers—a felony carrying a five-year minimum sentence—as we drove to our improvised dry barn and back to the cabin four times that afternoon. Finally, we had just one last run to make, our fifth and final trip of moving one hundred pounds of product that day, and the sun was setting.

"We're going to make it just fine," I said. "It's pouring rain, and our deputy from last night is working the section. A hundred bucks says he's parked at the runner station under the eve, chatting between windows with the sheriff's deputy."

"I hope you're right, and I hope you're not," Rachel said. "I'd rather not see them."

"Well, look on the bright side. As we turn onto the highway, we both wave and mouth, 'Thank you.' They will think we are talking about last night, not the free pass."

Unlike last night, it was great that it was dark and dangerous and pouring rain. It was reasonable for us to be on the road at the same time and with a tarp over whatever might be underneath. And if I had Rachel with me, they would assume I wouldn't be moving anything.

Rachel cut me off with a kiss. "We're going to make it. I prayed and visualized the whole thing while you were down there talking to the cabin." She never seemed to fear anything. Sure as could be, when the headlights reached the intersection of the two highways, parked under a gas station's roof was the CHP from the night before and the regional county sheriff.

She chuckled. "Smile, breathe, and mouth, 'Thank you.'"

Both cops subtly waved and nodded.

"Oh, Sally!" was all either of us said for the remainder of the drive to the cabin. We had to make the trip back and forth to the mountain five times that day, which meant nine trips past the spot where the huge boulder had been the night before. Muddy water cascaded down every drainage ditch, washout, and tributary in every direction we looked. Tractor Frank wasn't wrong: The mountains couldn't hold an ounce more water.

We got back to Uncle Bob's cabin without incident. We both tapped Zeus's dash. "Five for five successful trips, that a boy, at ease, Zeus," I said to him as we jumped down out of the truck and into the mud. It was still raining. The fumes from the fresh scent-covering gasoline on the black contractor bags burned our throats and nostrils as we poured the bucketed buds into totes covering the cabin's front porch. The fire was ripping inside, and we worried that the fumes would catch and burn the place down if we were to carry one of the bags inside, so we let everything air out on the porch as best we could in the pouring rain.

We took a little break to eat a burrito, and then we got to hanging. By 1:15 a.m., we were punch drunk, but our buds were all resting on nets. We got all of six warm, dry hours of sleep before one of the generators ran out of gas and needed to be filled. I unzipped the window of our tent to see what the weather was like. It was cloudy and looked like it could be the first rainless start to the day in the last thirteen.

· · ·

The drying buds smelled great and looked royal that morning in Uncle Bob's cabin. We were proud of all the hard work, danger, and stress it took to grow them and get them to that point. Drying the product was a major step closer to getting the product transformed into greenbacks. We felt so close. Yet as we had just learned, we were still far away from turning those buds into currency. I could smell the shift happening by the hour. As the buds got drier, I could almost hear the voices in the wind of the fans and the hum of dehumidifiers asking, "Got any green?" My own mind replied, "Got any greenbacks?"

We had a lucrative product that, at the time, was in high demand and low supply. It didn't take a Harvard business degree to know that the reward shattered the risk potential. It was mighty valuable because it was illegal, required very hard work to create in mass, and was even harder to move where it needed to go. I had that feeling of knowing I had made it one hurdle closer to a fiscal reward. My mind was shifting from that of a hardworking farmer to a smooth-operating hustler. The buds patiently waited to be manicured by a callused set of fingers, which would get them another step closer to those stacks of greenbacks dancing in my mind.

"The green buckets are on the back deck," Rachel said. "When you cut open the plastic, can you bring a few inside?"

"Yeah, thanks," I said, coming back into the dry room after dumping out the last reservoir from the dehumidifiers. It was a good sign that we had taken out over four and a half gallons of water over night. The dry room was at extremely low humidity and 85 degrees Fahrenheit. The conditions were a little extreme, but we needed to stop the spread of mold immediately. Aside from regulating climate, we had to cut out the moldy buds to kill the infection at the source.

Plunk, plop, bop, plunk, thud. That tragic sound of beautiful buds hitting the bottoms of the buckets was deadly and frequent. I tried not to think about it as I cut the mold out of buds that were perfect twelve days ago. We pruned out forty-six pounds of moldy weed that morning. In the last forty-eight hours, we had lost at least $450,000 worth of product.

"If it gets cloudy and drizzly this afternoon, we are bombing that burn pile," I said. "I can't spend the next few weeks looking at all the product."

"We should get high tonight on treats," Rachel said.

"Really? Tonight?"

"Yeah, all we have to do now is keep the generator and the fire going all night. Maybe we should just go all night too."

It was Saturday, she was all caught up on work, and we didn't have trimmers showing up until the following Friday. This would be our last little hurrah before the madness of guests for the next four weeks. It was a perfect time. The mountain was soft, cold, and quiet. We finished our work that afternoon and took the treats.

I placed the flame from the lighter to the tip of the arrow. It was the same cracked lighter I had tried to light the shack's heater with when I had my meltdown. I'd wrapped the arrowhead in gasoline-soaked linen. The arrowhead burst into a small flame, and Rachel pulled back the compound bow's string. With a dead eye, Rachel aimed through the glow of the fire at the brush pile thirty yards away.

"Rest in peace," she whispered and released the bowstring. The arrow smashed into some tanoak slash of moldy buds and burst into forty-foot-tall flames. The warmth covered our bodies and ignited "the treats." Our faces, lips, hair, and hands felt amazing—ecstasy amid tragedy.

"Send that smoke back to heaven and the lesson to the back of our brains, forever," I sang to the stars above.

It was my fault that we didn't have a good enough dry room. We knew what we needed. We hadn't allocated enough resources or planned correctly, and that misstep lost us about 70 percent of the crop. *I've got to do this all again next year*, I thought as we watched the funeral pyre blaze.

CHAPTER 23

Percentages

SPRING AND SUMMER 2011

THE GREAT MOLD OF 2010 was disastrous, but the ironic truth was that one shining light had come in the form of our first successful full light-deprivation attempt.

In early 2011, Jesse approached me and said, "Once I graduate, I want to work the farm for the summer. I'm not going to go to Alaska to fish this year."

It was wonderful having Jesse back on the team when he returned the following spring. It was like I finally had my twin working with me. We both understood the risk, the amount of labor and devotion to the task required in order to justify and receive the reward. It created a nice sense of comfort. I presented him with the light-deprivation plan. He presented *me* with eight able young men who could help us set up and harvest. The fishing season fit perfectly inside the light-deprivation season. Harvesting on clear, warm, and dry alpine August nights sounded glorious to him.

If we did that, we could be off the mountain two months earlier than the October harvest season. The crop would be cleaned up before most raids. August was a dry month, and we'd have funds in hand for trimming the full-term crops should we choose to plant a traditional grow. It almost seemed too good to be true. No mold. No green buckets.

We planned to plant full-term plants in some sixty-gallon containers we had around the light-deprivation locations and move them into the greenhouses once *all* the light-deprivation process was completed. They would have plenty of space for airflow, and we would have a conditioned cabin completed to dry them come October.

We developed business expense estimates and potential outcome sheets. We weren't finance majors, but we worked out a transparent plan for expenses and profits. Many of the problems we heard about from other operations were related to confusion in pay once harvest and drying time came. Some growers made up false costs throughout the grow season to short any profit-based incentives for their partners or workers. I wasn't that type of person. Estimates of all our expenses would be itemized before the season even started. By my calculations, we'd get a net profit of almost 78 percent, an amazing return in the agricultural industry.

Once Jesse and I agreed on our reasons and goals for taking on the summer's risks, we wrote everything down and signed it. The document wasn't necessarily a legal contract but more of an accountability agreement. We shook hands with eye contact that dried the ink. Our mottos were "Get'r done with tunnel focus" and "It'll buff." We even agreed on a song of the season: "In the Air Tonight" by Phil Collins.

The method for keeping revenue and expenses straight was about as low-tech as it gets. We purchased sturdy pink blouse boxes and labeled them with who or what the money would go toward and the percentage each person got. Every time we made a transaction, we split the percentages and put the cash in the box. Except for what we were putting aside for next season's operation, we paid everything out right then. Everyone got to see everything out in the open.

Now that all the financial systems were in place, the next step was to build a light-deprivation system one person could operate on their own. Jesse and Rachel were still in school, and I'd be on my own for the first part of the grow, so whatever system we had in place had to be as simple and low-labor as possible. We also decided that part of the light-deprivation plan included forking out the big bucks to put a translucent woven-poly privacy top over Anne. The top cost almost the same amount as the structure had years before. But I had just survived the scare of being visited by Sergeant Dwight Henderson and narrowly saved by road construction, and I knew that we were about to triple the plant count inside the building. It was paramount that nobody could see inside, and now that we were more funded, we could afford privacy tops for the greenhouses. We didn't have the option to fake another construction scene.

Anne couldn't house everything, so we turned to hoop houses as an economical solution. Hoop houses have a metal frame that's staked into the ground. The tunnellike structure is covered in heavy plastic to keep out the elements. Hoop houses aren't permanent structures, but they're cheap and can be put up relatively quickly. The garden required approximately 3,200 thirty-five-gallon grow bags for our light-deprivation-only operation and 238 massive 1.5-yard-deep holes in the ground. Filling those by hand would have required an army of weed-farming Olympians working like ancient Egyptians for months. I gave our tractor operator an extremely generous tip to never talk about the thousands of plants or show any of the other farms how we did it.

Preparing for a light-deprivation operation is extensive. Before building the frame inside the structure, we hung shop lights in a grid throughout Anne. The plants were brought in late April. I camped up there most nights. Rachel and Jesse were in school for three more weeks, so I was pretty much running the light-deprivation show solo. Everything had to be done in an incredibly precise and timely manner for the process to work.

The one-man method we came up with to deprive the plants of a light source was pretty ingenious. For Anne, we used one large poly film, nicknamed panda film, to pull over the interior frame and black out the sunlight during the day. At the hoop houses, we ran ropes over each hoop and connected them to tennis balls wrapped in the panda film. We sank tall poles in the ground between the hoop houses, and we hung pulleys where the tennis balls and rope were pulled up to. Then we released the tarps, and they fell gently over the hoop houses. One person could walk down the center of the two hoop houses and pull the ropes to pull the film up and over the hoops. Sandbags secured the film on the ground to prevent wind from lifting the blanket and letting any light in. Light leaks were an absolute no-no. A light leak could lead to the plant getting confused about what time of year it was, which might make them seed out. The marketplace would not purchase product with seeds.

Each evening, I turned on the lights from about 7:00 p.m. to 11:30 p.m. That low light level kept the plants from flowering too soon. If the outside temperature got too low, I ran a propane burner to keep the plants warm enough. I was able to pull off everything on my own until Rachel graduated in May and joined me on the mountain in early June.

. . .

Once we were all at the grow for the summer, our typical day started at 3:45 a.m. Jesse and I got up and drove down past the hoop houses and then down to Anne. As the truck descended, we turned the headlights off and drove slowly with just the green glow of our headlamps leading the way. We used green lights because it did not activate the chlorophyll in plants like all the other wavelengths of visible light. Normal headlights could trick the plants into thinking the sun was up, and we didn't want that. We went as far as parking a hundred feet from Anne to make sure we didn't kick up any dust. Moist dust could lead to mold on the leaves. This time around, we weren't leaving anything to chance.

Every night, we watched the clear sky of stars turn to gray over the eastern mountains and then to a red glow, then an orange glow. Finally, the sky emerged again, and a beam of yellow would pierce our faces as the sun rose over the Trinity Alps to our east. Rachel got up at 6:30 a.m. Her job was to manage the setup and the planting, so her schedule wasn't quite as strict as ours. At 9:15 a.m., the tarps were pulled off, and watering and nutrients began. The workday with the plants was done, for the most part, by 11:30 a.m. For the specific strains we were growing, Double Blackberry Kush and Sour Diesel, it took about ten and a half weeks or seventy-five nights of pulling the tarps at the exact times, never missing a single day.

We had harvested about thirty-seven pounds of premium buds in mid-August the prior year. That year, we harvested close to twenty times that number, and we had cleaned and found a home for it all by the first week of September. We dried the plants by hanging them in a shaded section of the forest away from our living area. The warm, dry days made the drying process infinitely easier and cheaper to manage than what we'd gone through the previous year. Free power, no generator, no propane tanks. Just Zephyrus, the Greek god of the western winds. The location also had a phenomenal updraft and made all the large fan leaves lightly dance in the wind.

Doing a light-deprivation grow was an eye-opener. The production per square foot was incredible for the amount of work we put in. We had a few technical problems to work out, but we had all winter and spring to focus on and prepare for the next light-deprivation grow. We would have done anything to avoid being defeated once more by mold. It seemed that at this point nothing could stand in our way.

. . .

We would become even more successful than we had dreamed with our choice to go 100 percent light deprivation. Flashing forward, by the next year we would develop a smooth operation for pulling the tarps. We only needed one person to pull each plot of six greenhouses for a twenty-five-minute period. All the neighbors around us at both mountains had operations that required about three guys to do half of the same square footage.

In 2012, even by Humboldt standards, we would have a very aggressive number and size of greenhouses for one parcel. Our production included eight hoop houses that were sixteen feet by one hundred feet and three cold frames at thirty feet by one hundred feet. We had truly started to combine our construction experiences, fishing and boating rope and pully knowledge, and scholastic engineering skill sets into a modern farming technique for optimized and profitable efficiencies. The itch had us good, so good that I think I was so passionate about the farming, building, and business side that I was becoming somewhat numb to the fact that it was all for weed.

"Looks like you're really going for it," a friend who had flown over our grow in his helicopter said. But when Jesse first came back, all that success was still to come.

CHAPTER 24

Meeting Mountain Royalty

LATE SPRING 2011

I MADE THE LAST TIGHTENING TWIST with a flathead screwdriver on the hose clamp as the newly installed water main valve and plumbing to the cabin sink were installed. That was a massive accomplishment three and a half years in the making. Little by little, we brought bits up to finish the 320-square-foot cabin—everything from decorations to plywood and electrical outlets to drywall. We'd even fitted out the drying house with a roof, insulated and sheet-rocked walls, a woodstove, and proper outlets for fans and dehumidifiers. With the light-deprivation grow done, I focused on the one thing the cabin was lacking: decent plumbing.

On the surface, Rachel and I were doing good at that moment in our unhealthy and codependent relationship; hints of happiness past were shining through each day. We had forgiven each other for the infidelities, the fights, the lies, and the chaos. We were no longer in a long-distance relationship or in school; we were just trying to finish our homestead and "save some money one last time." Spring had been beautiful with daily romance. The snow lasted on the ground until mid-May. We had snow and rain many times, even in June. Vibrant wildflowers and buzzing bees surrounded the cabin and mimicked our relationship.

On the mountain, we had to walk up the final 150 yards each day as the snow still glaciered the last section of the driveway for some three weeks. It had been daunting, but we had made a temporary camp halfway between the greenhouses and the cabin to wait out the melt. We blasted through the snow one abnormally warm afternoon using Jesse's early 1990s Toyota pickup truck, blasting "In the Air Tonight" and cheering to shots of whiskey. Our thighs and backs felt blessed because the daily hike up to camp was over.

Jesse was helping me hook everything up when I looked up toward the parking area. He was connecting hose bibs into a fifty-gallon drum—our water supply to the house and outdoor shower. Before that, we had to carry water by the gallon from the spring to the Chalet every day by hand. It was exhausting and backbreaking work after we had already done exhausting and backbreaking work.

As such, completing the cabin's water system was more symbolic than convenient. Rachel and I were growing. We were improving our situation, homesteading and green rushing. Our living standards were about to include running water for the first time. No more heating up pans of water to bathe. No more carrying seven-gallon jugs down the trail to the house every day. We were safe from the outside elements and could sleep without fear of a mountain lion leaning on our tent. No anxiousness, no fear—only bliss and happiness seemed to surround me in those days and moments. I looked around.

Jesse signaled that he'd finished his bit, so I turned the newly installed valve to the *on* position and heard water rush through the line. There were a few gurgling air pockets escaping back up the hill, but there were no visible leaks.

"It'll buff, baby!" I yelled up the hill to Jesse.

"She's singing," he yelled back. Bubbles escaped the top of the fifty-gallon barrel.

"Got'r done!" I said.

"So done!" His California surfer dude's voice came through loud and clear.

A feeling of accomplishment, love, and "doing wrong right" filled my body and mind. I practically skipped to the cabin to try our new outdoor water spigot and wash my hands before our tuna sandwich lunch. My legs bounced in freedom. However, my eyes focused on what I initially thought was a large yellow dog that had jumped out of the brush some sixteen feet in front of me. *Whose dog is this?* I thought. We found two dogs the year before, but this wasn't one of those. The massive animal abruptly stopped, bent its front legs, and leaned down to where its jawline was a foot from the ground. It looked right at me. We were less than twelve feet from each other and no more than six feet from the corner of the cabin. Rachel was moving about in the kitchen, oblivious to the drama unfolding feet away.

"Oh my God! Oh my God!" I yell-whispered twice.

My lower lip began to quiver, and my wrist joints cracked as I traded the screwdriver in my left hand with the pliers in my right. The animal couldn't have been a pound under two hundred. Its face was the size of a volleyball. Gray and charcoal hairs were mixed at the beast's bulging jawline. I was astonished at how large the thick whiskers were. The hair was dense and straight, reminding me of porcupine quills. The paws were larger than I had expected, similar to the size of a horse hoof. Both of us were statues. I didn't dare blink. I was afraid if I did, he would have me by the neck.

"Stand and breathe," the wind spoke to me as I felt a draft of gentle air race into the back of my tank top.

I must have looked like Notre Dame's mascot in a fighting Irish pose. I stood still and strong, but I stood no chance should a bout begin. Obviously, I was the prey—not the predator. The muscular male mountain lion took in a long, full, deep breath. The outline of muscles began to appear throughout his whole body. The cleanliness of his fur became vibrantly noticeable.

"Oh my God! Oh my God!" I whispered again and finally let my lungs exhale.

Was he as shocked and startled as I was? No, he must have been casing us with curiosity. He must have been hiding beside me as I installed the house plumbing. He was waiting for the right time to pounce, which should have been right then. Rachel was opening cans of tuna, and the smell found its way through the window screens. That must have tantalized the mountain lion too much, and he had to investigate the possibility of an easier meal. I must have startled him with my confident jump to my feet.

Was this the mountain lion that had leaned into our tent that wet, cold night last fall? Mountain lions are territorial, so there was a good chance this was the same one that I had hit with the butt end of my axe. The more I thought about it, the more I knew it had to be the same one. Did he remember me? Was he out for revenge?

"Jesse," I whispered as both a call for help and a reminder to myself that he was just up the trail.

"Jesse," I said again, louder.

Jesse's boots stomped around behind me. He was strolling in my direction.

"Jesse, oh my God." My voice was finally closer to a normal level.

"Ty, what are you doing?" Rachel asked through the window screen. She finally saw me standing like a statue, holding a six-inch screwdriver in a stabbing stance.

The mountain lion turned slightly and looked up at Rachel. The movement caught Rachel's eye, and it dawned on her what was happening. She let out the scream we all needed. Jesse yelled from behind me as he began to pound faster and closer to me. Rachel yelled again and pounded a pan against the glass part of the window, breaking a pane. Shattered glass rained on the ground below.

The mountain lion got spooked, broke his stance, and leaped almost twenty feet from the house.

"It's a mountain lion!" Jesse yelled.

My body collapsed to the ground in a complete surrender of my useless battle stance. My knees were numb. The lion disappeared behind a rock outcropping away from the cabin. Jesse pulled me to my feet and almost dragged me into the cabin. Rachel was in the kitchen crying, her fist still locked on the cast-iron frying pan. The tuna salad sandwiches were on the counter.

We gathered ourselves. Jesse grabbed the rifle and a pack of rounds from above the armoire. He loaded the rifle, and we all walked out front to fire a few warning shots down into the clearing below the house. Maybe that would let the mountain lion know not to come back. Jesse fired three shots. I reloaded and fired twice. After the second splitting bullet echoed across the land, the inevitable silence returned to the mountaintop. Everyone was satisfied that we'd scared the big cat away.

That was a mistake. The mountain lion emerged from the edge of the clearing and walked right into the line of fire fifty yards away from us.

"What the—" Jesse said.

I lowered the barrel, flipped on the safety, and positioned myself to get a better look. Rachel looked back to make sure the front door was still open. The mountain lion took three more steps to the exact center of the clearing, where five bullets had flown seconds before. It turned its head and looked at the three of us. There was a gaze of wisdom, old age, strength, and ownership in the mountain lion's eyes. He was the real king of the mountains. He had been there before us growers and would outlive this green rush.

I sat the rifle on the ground and watched as the mountain lion turned and walked gracefully away from us. The cat's massive tail danced upright as he disappeared into the brush. I'm not sure how long the three of us stood there watching the bushes at the edge of the clearing. I knew he had had his chance to take me out twice and didn't. That knowledge carried me through many more days on that mountain. I needed to make sure I didn't disrupt his kingdom too much. Strike three, and I knew I would be out.

· · ·

We spent the days during the offseason figuring out the best techniques for the least amount of labor. When paying for labor by a percentage of profits, efficiency is the secret weapon to success and happiness. The irrigation systems were one of the biggest examples of efficiency we designed. How could we water all these plants with the least amount of personnel and time? Massive vats of nutrients were made at each greenhouse site according to the amount of water in the doughboy swimming pool. Our pools held about twelve thousand gallons of water when 85 percent full. In the past, they were just for backup water; at that point, they were our mixing tanks. We developed a plan to mix in nine days' worth of nutrients in these pools. Why mix during every watering when you could mix once every nine days?

To achieve that, we needed a massive supply of items on hand. We purchased pallets of soluble granular salt-based nutrients, tarps, greenhouse tops, and industrial mixing pumps from an agricultural supplier in Iowa. Buying in bulk saved us at least 70 percent on our nutrients and kept our faces out of the grow stores, but I still liked to keep some of our business local. Our grow bags and soil amendments were still purchased from the trusty garden center I'd used my first year.

The look on the older woman's face who ran the register when I ordered the bags was a spectacle.

"Kid, how many did you buy a few years ago on that first day?"

"Forty, I think, but only needed thirty-eight," I said.

"Well, how many of these thirty-six hundred are you going to need?"

"About thirty-four hundred so far."

"Wow, giving zero fucks now, I see." She grabbed the large wad of twenty-dollar bills. I was shocked at her response.

"Well, I still choose to spend my dollars and load up my truck here," I said.

"Oh, hon, I was referring to the number of plants you're growing. You're getting ballsy."

My jaw dropped, and I burst into laughter at hearing those words from a sweet seventy-something-year-old lady. Our projection was to get a third of a pound per plant and have a thousand pounds of light-dep product ready by September first.

CHAPTER 25
Monticello Madness
SUMMER 2011

AT THE END OF JULY, Rachel was accepted into an internship program. There was a four-week orientation near the Central Coast of California, and she would spend the following four months out east. It was happening again. Distance.

Sitting in the truck facing west on the eve of her drive south, we watched the sunset—just above Anne at the same location we had first camped some four summers before. An unspoken feeling hung in the air as the sun disappeared below the western ridges. Rachel wouldn't be returning to the mountain for at least six months. Our partnership was fractured, and our relationship was a mess.

Six weeks later, between our harvest and the start of trimming, I left the mountain for three days to fly out to Washington, DC. After I arrived, we took a short drive for a night to Virginia. We had talked about getting engaged, so when we went to see Thomas Jefferson's house at Monticello, I pulled out a ring and asked, "Well, do you want to get engaged?"

Rachel blinked in shock. "You know I do, but I have somebody coming to see me."

"Oh God," I said—my turn to be completely shocked. The man from a couple of years before in India was coming to see her in DC.

We started to fight in the gardens of Monticello. After hours of tears and yelling, I hate yous, I love yous, I'm sorrys, and never will I ever see you agains, we were escorted out of the park.

It was finally the end to the end. Our relationship had been fraught with pain for years. Whatever healthy was, we were the opposite. So when we arrived at Reagan National Airport in the short-term parking, I told her that everything in my carry-on in her apartment could be thrown away. We had one last toxic naked tumble in the back seat of the rental car. Then I got out, slammed the door, and walked in to buy a plane ticket home. I was walking to security when she appeared at the top of an escalator sobbing uncontrollably.

"This can't be the last time we see each other!" she sobbed.

"You have another man coming who, I'm guessing, knows very little about my existence," I said through a snotty nose and streaks of tears running down my cheeks. "How did we get like this?"

"You fired the first shot, you asshole. You cheated on me! That blonde bitch with frizzled hair and stupid rodeo belts. You did that!" I think she knew this was pointless, but she pleaded louder. "Stop growing weed and start a new life with me!" She was right. I had fired the first shot that penetrated the heart and started the leaking of love. But she was also wrong. I couldn't start a new life with her or us. Neither could she.

Passersby in the terminal looked at us awkwardly. She knew my insecurity about being stuck on that hill for the rest of my life, how the stress-riddled and dysfunctional rat race of being a grower lingered and kept me depressed. Late-summer thunderheads cut streaks of light through the terminal's massive walls of windows. The colors were analogous to our entire relationship. We had started with a bright, warm, opportunistic sky. We painted a colorful skyline of all the love languages. Then I threw splatters of black, blue, and gray paint all over the masterpiece. She followed suit in retaliation, and then I followed—back and forth. In that terminal that day, we accepted what we always knew: Trying to make a relationship out of distrust won't work.

I grasped her hand just as I had in the snow that morning years before. As flight numbers and boarding statuses were called over the loudspeaker, I wiped my face on my sleeve and repeated what she'd told me time and time again out on the land. "Remember to always look up at the stars. She, the Sun, always first; may She never be still, may you never be as well."

As I leaned in to kiss her one last time, Rachel slapped me twice hard across the face. Then she grabbed my head with both hands and planted a firm kiss on my lips.

She stepped back and said, "I had to do both. Goodbye, Mister Man."

"Goodbye," I said.

I knew I would never see Rachel again.

· · ·

Two days later, my post-Rachel weed life began. Even though she was no longer on the mountain, her presence remained. The mountain remembered her, and so did the plants—and the bright pink tools she'd spray-painted for herself were often the only ones we could find. Regardless of our history, it was time to move on from the thousand toxic reasons that kept us from doing so for entirely too long.

I picked up three gal friends of Jesse's from his college days to trim. Jesse called while I was away, saying it looked like we would need a good twenty-five trimmers for the second phase of our very successful, even larger light-deprivation harvest. Twenty-five people plus Jesse and I camped in tents around Camp Camo for the next month. *Let the reality show begin*, I thought.

"How long have you been growing?" Keli asked. She was the gal Jesse was most excited to see arriving at weed camp later that day. I gave Keli the quick, sanitized version of my story.

"What would you do if you were to get pulled over?" she asked.

"Same thing you always do: Have all your paperwork and calmly smile and say a lot of yes ma'ams and yes sirs."

"Is it true we might have to trim topless?" a softspoken gal with shy eyes asked from the back seat.

"Who told you that?" I chuckled. Jesse had joked with me about it, and I heard from a friend that it happened. "No, that's not real. Not out here, at least."

"Are you single?" Shy Eyes asked, no longer shy.

"I am now, finally," I said, partially lying about my actual feelings.

The gals peppered me with questions about my recent breakup and rolled their eyes over the incidents at Jefferson's residence and in the airport terminal.

"So you're not gay?" Keli asked abruptly.

"No, ma'am, I'm not. What made you think that?" Confused, I giggled.

"You're just dressed too nice for a grower. It smells like expensive cologne here too. Figured you were a gay cowboy." She seemed a bit too honest.

I explained that we preferred the least amount of direct profiling from our friends in cop uniforms. The cologne helped distract from the stenches of weed and mountain life.

"I guess it takes a little more than yes ma'ams and yes sirs," I joked. "I'm a builder, developer, and mountain enthusiast who has become a grower. I always have a gecko look and an alibi—always."

"I think it's hot," Shy Eyes said from the back seat.

Keli glanced at me and raised her eyebrow like a sister, disapproving. I could tell that Keli and I would be great friends—and just friends. After settling their fears of mean drunks, misogynistic growers, scary dogs, guns, and topless work, we made the final climb to Camp Camo near the Chalet.

"You're so full of it," Keli said abruptly.

I was taken aback, still trying to focus on crawling the large truck gingerly up the hill.

She slapped my arm. "They're naked!"

"What? Who?" I was still trying to pay attention to driving.

"Look at those gals. How would a gentleman cowboy describe this, huh?" she said, pointing toward the clearing at the top of the ridge.

"Oh geez!" both gals in the back seat chimed in as they noticed what was happening.

Our two actually gay employees, whose real jobs were as photographers for prominent fashion advertisements in New York and Los Angeles, had chosen to turn lunch into a full photo shoot. There were cameras on tripods, and the Persian knockoff rug from the Chalet had been laid on the ground. Three gals, fully nude, stood barefoot on the rug. They were reenacting Adam and Eve-like scenes with their breasts and private areas covered only by large weed leaves. Jesse and Matt, who should have been weighing and calculating that morning's trimmings, were behind the camera operators doing pushups in the sun, getting ready for their pot-star shot. The rest of the crew sat in the sun around the photo shoot finishing their lunch.

"Just head on over there and introduce yourselves," I said. "They can explain themselves. Maybe you can make next year's calendar, Keli," I taunted, grabbing their sleeping bags and other belongings out of the truck.

The not-so-shy gal became demanding. "You can put my bags in the cabin down there. I'll be staying in there."

"Ah . . . that's . . . ah, my house," I stuttered.

She looked over her shoulder as she skipped in her cowgirl boots down to meet the rest of the team. "Well, isn't it a good thing you aren't engaged after all, cowboy?" she said.

"Where's the bathroom?" another asked.

"There isn't one," Jesse said, pointing to the shovel. "Always put the shovel back and the roll of TP onto the handle."

"What? Really?"

"You can hold it or bury it—your call."

"Shit, man."

"Yep. And always shit on the eastern side of the mountain, that way." He pointed toward the Trinity Alps on the horizon. "Our drinking water comes from the western side."

Then I turned 180 degrees and pointed toward the ocean on the horizon.

"Just remember, don't shit on the ocean side. That's the water side. Ocean side equals drinking water—easy to remember."

In seasons one, two, three, and four, someone was taking a walk toward the east with Ol' Digger Ames, our shovel, every hour. There's a lot of shit on the east side out there; I'm guessing about six to eight hundred little buried treasures, natural wonders composting daily.

"Welcome back to weed camp," I said as I lugged the two gals' belongings down to the Chalet with the constant pain still clamped on my heart from breaking up with Rachel.

However, immediately after she left, we started extracting more from the mountain. We built the three large reservoirs the month after, and we started pumping from all the springs on the mountain. We received donations so fast that year that we wanted to expand that fall for the following spring and summer seasons. It was like I was now playing the game without a referee.

CHAPTER 26
The Rush Becomes a Stampede

SUMMER 2013

THE START OF 2013 was the industrial year. Large logging companies started selling their land to weed growers, which exploded the northern Humboldt industry. My business skyrocketed. Large tracts of timberland and long-held family ranches were being split into new communities of "grow properties." The land they sold was "sixty-plus lands," which meant there would be no viable timber on that land for at least sixty years.

When the logging industry dried up, it left a lot of abandoned mills that sat empty for decades. But now, with the shift in the weed industry, soil-manufacturing companies bought them up and started making high-quality and nutrient-rich soil there. Many locals began to change their minds when they saw the physical change from graffiti-covered old mills to having people working them again. Granted, they were not making two-by-fours or timbers, but they were mixing soil. It was bringing jobs back to the town. The companies needed people who could operate heavy equipment and drive big trucks that used to haul logs. Only now, they were hauling cubic yards of soil.

Grow stores were popping up everywhere; soil trucks filled the highways instead of logging trucks. Excavator operators were getting harder and harder to schedule. The bars and nightclubs were packed with twenty- and hundred-dollar bills flying across the cash registers. Families in the community who had been against it were now involved. The local weekly publications, blogs, billboards, and classifieds were filled with ads for nutrients, greenhouses, irrigation supplies, trimming supplies, trailers, trucks, water tanks, and a full catalog for the new "green rush." It was taking over. The "safety in numbers" odds kept increasing in my favor as the business grew.

We were going big already, but we would soon begin running generators at each greenhouse location and running lights all the time to get the plants started. We even hired a full-time excavator.

We needed water reserves, so we built two-hundred-thousand-gallon snowmelt reservoirs. However, before we did that or any other major project, I always read up, then did everything to code and took photos. We printed everything out and displayed it on a plywood sign like at construction sites in case we got raided. The authorities were starting to raid not because weed was illegal, but to collect environmental fines and enforce construction permits.

On August 1, 2012, a blog post was published online that included many aerial pictures of several grow sites in the county that the public wasn't aware of, although the police were. It showed the whole local community just how many grow sites there were and that the growers had found a legal loophole to maintain those greenhouses. That new knowledge spread like wildfire. People with long-held family ranches started selling or became willing to sell their property to cash in on the cash crop. Grandparents were more willing to have their grandkids build a greenhouse on the old ranch. People who had been forever against weed were starting to change their minds.

And after reviewing the comments from that blog post, I realized that law enforcement was starting to take a new approach. It might not have been a clear-cut case to bust a weed operation, but it would be a slam dunk if they could bust growers on environmental infractions. And there were plenty of people breaking timber laws and illegally pulling water from protected sources. Still, to this day I consider that blog post and TV news stories from the time the first snowballs that began to roll down the hill to become the avalanche of what would be the green rush in Humboldt and the greater Emerald Triangle. It showed the community and nation how the industry was changing. No longer did weed have to be grown hidden under bushes or in trees or even in underground bunkers. It could be grown in a greenhouse or flat orchard-like field out in the open. The floodgates were opening fast. *Cut, clear, build, plant, grow, harvest, dry, and process* became the equation of the hills. Money was the answer. Environmental destruction was, sadly, the by-product.

Since I genuinely cared about the land, I had always wanted to do everything to code and be as sustainable as possible. And thanks to my construction background and a few environmental law classes I'd taken in college, I had always made sure I had permits for everything I did or at least did things as close to permittable as possible had there been codes. In 2012, I made maps and blueprints based on whole packets I found online for farms growing non-weed crops. We created everything as if we were growing tomatoes, and I created a whole package.

Then, a few weeks after the blog post in late August of 2012, I walked into the Department of Fish and Wildlife in Eureka, California. At the time, our community of four properties on the mountain contained a combined twenty-eight industrial greenhouses. There had been maybe six active operations when we built Anne, and now I guessed there were as many as three thousand across the county.

I knew that law enforcement could only take down a small percentage of that three thousand every year, and they were increasingly selective about busts. It was no longer about the size of the operations, but whether the growers had been creating environmental damage—clear-cutting, stealing water from a salmon spawning tributary, felling timber without a permit. There were so many bad apples. I was going to show the powers that be that we were possibly one of the best apples out there. But we were walking a fine line between self-incrimination and proactivity.

I gave them everything anyway. It even had all the plant counts, though I didn't identify the species. While there was no law for weed, there were laws for the construction process, so I showed them I was following the process and constructing to code.

They couldn't stamp it because they didn't have a code for cannabis grows. And I never had to say I was in the weed business because it was obvious. It was the only reason I would have all these greenhouses in the middle of nowhere. Either way, I walked in and asked for the director of that office, which is one of the top offices in California.

"Yeah, how can I help you?"

"I will just take five minutes of your time to go over my application so you can see the maps and stuff. I know we are at the start of a California drought, and this is my water-saving catchment and dispersant plan. We won't be pulling anything from springs after the thirty-first of May."

She looked at the package. She looked at the satellite imagery. She looked at me.

"Are you serious? It's all here. OK, come to the conference room. I'll be right back."

She's going to get law enforcement, and I'm just incriminating myself, I thought.

I sat there for ten to fifteen minutes, having second thoughts. Then she came in with a couple of the enforcement officers who most often went out on busts charging fines, and they introduced themselves.

"Do you mind if we take a look at this?"

"Yeah, please."

"This is incredible. Who did you hire to do this?"

"Well, I consulted with a local environmental engineer firm. I told them I would keep their name private."

"This is a great job. This is incredible. We know your property. We've flown over. We know you guys."

"Oh."

"Can we photocopy this to help make the codes?"

"Yeah, can you just take off the APN number so that nobody other than you guys knows where it's at?"

"Yeah. Great job!"

Then they handed me laminated pieces of paper.

"Hang these on your gates."

They were the codes stating their reviews of the operation. We were the first ones. I did this for the same reason I always wanted the hoses rolled up perfectly, flew an American flag, and wanted everything to look beautiful from the air. I told the crew that I knew that the only people who would see this other than us were up in a helicopter. Our whole mentality of farming as cleanly and normally as possible ended up helping everyone. We were farmers—it's just that what was inside our buildings happened to be weed.

CHAPTER 27

Fire in the Sky

FALL 2013

AFTER I HAD WALKED in and submitted our package to the wide-eyed and disbelieving staff at the Department of Fish and Wildlife in Eureka, I knew it would be the golden ticket if there were any fires later in the summer and fall—or anytime for that matter. I planned to drop the paperwork off with Brenda at Kinko's and have laminated copies made while I went on another supper date to break up with another temporary girlfriend. I had an unfortunate feeling the paperwork would be needed. Looking up from the map, I noticed the two fire extinguishers on the floor next to the kitchen island and grabbed them. I wasn't about to head up to the mountain again questioning whether to have one on me after what had happened some years before.

Looking back around the home I had recently moved to, I thought, *Hell, if this shoddy wiring burns this place down over the next couple days, I don't really care.*

All my important papers, photos, and a small amount of life's physical treasures were hidden out in the hills. There wasn't much in this place I would miss if it turned to ash.

It wasn't that I wanted more income or greenhouses; I just wanted my life to be less chaotic, to have structure and a schedule.

A busy, hardworking life I could handle. It was having a time to clock out that I missed. I was always on, and it seemed inevitable and almost unavoidable that my business would die. I had checked off every one of the precautions from Trey's original list of what to avoid and fear.

I stood in the doorway for a moment on the threshold of the below-standard housing I owned and didn't even care to spend the night in. I walked over to the open driver's door of the truck that would just take me back out to the highway and up to the mountain for the second time that day—out to start another green rush deployment.

My shoulders were low from the weight of my duties on the horizon over the coming months. My soul was bummed, my heart only in it enough to fulfill my monthly necessities of food, shelter, and bills—no longer for dreams of empire building—even with all the Pelican cases of cash, the vacation house rented for fun times, and the overload of female attention. I didn't see how I could get to the life I wanted. I thought of how a close friend described harvest and trim season. The season we question our lives and all the choices and decisions we've ever made.

One would think my bones should have been shaking with excitement at the mere thought of all the dollars coming into my possession, adding to the secured savings I'd stockpiled over recent years. All that hunger built up over the last five months was about to be satisfied from the great harvest some days before. That beautiful harvest was now curing in totes, waiting for manicuring to start the following day.

But I was not excited or even relieved—not at all. *Maybe I'll get lucky and get busted this season. Something needs to push me out of this place*, I thought. I locked the door. The house sitting there in that field must have sighed each time it felt me lock the door and back down the driveway, leaving for another unforeseeable length of time.

. . .

The day before the next trim season started, I was busy preparing all the items I'd need. "Man, that's a lot of propane and gas cans," my college pal Ryan said. "How long will that last?"

"The gas about three days, the propane closer to a week. I brought up thirty gallons of fuel this morning and four propane tanks."

"Wow."

"This should be enough to get the mountain through for a week and a half."

"How much will be up there?"

"Ah, eighteen five-gallon cans of unleaded and forty gallons of propane, or eight tanks. Couple more of those trips, and that should be the last of it for the year."

"You show up to the gas station at dawn with twenty-five five-gallon gas tanks and twelve propane tanks?"

"Yes, sir, gimme the black to burn," I said and laughed.

"Shit, I remember when you would put four bucks in your tank just to make it to the job site on Friday."

"I think about that kind of stuff every time I do this. Hell, it costs closer to $450 to fill up and make it to the job site now."

We both laughed.

"Your truck could start one big-ass highway explosion in an accident."

"I know. I think about it. Got a couple extinguishers in the cab."

"That won't do shit with the bomb you're driving around in."

"I know, but to be honest, it's not my truck I'm worried about today—it's those," I said, pointing toward the massive, dark thunderheads rolling slowly across the sky toward the hills.

A man filling up on the other side of the tank chimed in. "Heard it's expected to be a real bad one this evening, real bad."

I recognized him. He was an older gentleman—cattle farmer—and he planted an annual pumpkin patch across the highway. He wore faded jeans, a gray T-shirt with grease and sweat stains, and a John Deere ball cap with pieces of grass stuck to the netting. His weathered boots were caked with gray silt from the creek bed that ran through his pasture.

He was a true weathered, opinionated, and green-chain local like most of the men I grew up with around these logging and mill towns. Some of those men were unsavory characters, but this man, on the few times I had met him, was a good one. He rented a small, old farmhouse to the mother of a good friend of mine who had passed away unexpectedly. I heard he had always helped her in the tough months. Even in a rush, he deserved my attention.

"Cutting down a little early this year?" he asked in a smokey voice.

He smiled, pointing toward the little box on the center console of my truck. *Damn, old men always snooping 'round here.* The box he pointed to had been cut in half and was filled with five-hundred-foot rolls of rebar wire, three boxes of latex gloves, and some thirty Fiskars scissors. There were also six gallons of rubbing alcohol visible in the back seat. I had left my driver's door open.

I turned to my buddy. "All ready, bro?" I said, trying to send another signal that I didn't want to talk.

"Yes, sir."

"Good, let's go. You should get a head start. We will meet at the highway intersection in Oak Creek, in front of the bank. I drive fast."

"Roger that," said Nick to me. "Have a good night, sir," he said to the old man.

"Might want to toss that box in the bed. Out of sight, out of mind," said the old man, glaring right at me. We both replaced our green nozzles. He leaned against the pump toward me and spoke in a quiet voice. "Now, son, I know you're a good kid. I also know a lot of folks don't like all this growing and such that's going on in those hills, and you're a part of it, so they don't like the extravagant grower life you're living. They don't like how much money you just spent in there when they're trying to buy a couple gallons to get to work."

He pointed at the convenience store in the gas station.

"I don't think anyone in that store cares?" I answered, annoyed.

"Well, duh. The Tribal Council sure don't mind. But the customer in line behind you, they're the ones bitter at it all."

As I had countless times in conversations like this, I stood there giving the man his time on his soapbox and feeding him with nods of affirmation.

"Son, no matter how big you get doing this and what you build from it, you will always be known here as an outlaw. A target's on your back, not just from the illegal aspect but more from your success at it. Only paid retirement from that farm is behind bars. You good with that?"

"It is what it is," I said.

"Shit. All right. Get up on the hill. Looks like you're going to be driving a firebomb through an electric storm. Better get ahead of it."

"Yes, sir. It's now my get-out-of-jail card too. Good seeing ya." I thought about how I could have been twelve miles farther up the highway had he not said hello.

I turned the ignition key, and the truck roared to life. I could see him coming back to my window to say something else, and just as the window made it down, he put his hand on the frame and looked directly at the clouds ahead. We both watched a streak of lightning splinter across the dark thunderheads.

It was not advisable to drive a three-quarter-ton iron horse full of thirty gallons of propane, twenty-five gallons of gasoline, and six gallons of 90 percent rubbing alcohol through a lightning storm up over two summits and to the very top of a third. But that's what the day demanded. Times of chaos like this drive were calming in an odd way. The choice to move forward through the risks had been evaluated, and the decision had been made to continue with the task—the task of living by the sword. But a schedule was a schedule, and I wanted the trim season over before it had even begun.

From the moments of being naked with the bear to watching the mountain breathe while on acid, driving through lightning with the metal building, and weighing-in the face-to-face with a mountain lion, I truly believed that if I respected Mother Nature and tended to her gorgeous cloak, she would give me shelter against the laws of the old white Nixon men of DC, from the DEA's marijuana department to my local sheriff's department. Moments like this drive through a gorgeous and potentially destructive lightning storm gave me solace during my odyssey through this place, odd as it was for a person like me to be wrapped up in such a venture.

The fear was real beneath my skin. Fear of the karmic repercussions for scarring Mother Nature, retaliation from the matriarch of Terra for slashing down trees, leveling flats, damming creeks, and digging up artesian springs. Fortunately, I recognized the strong presence in my heart of her karmic powers. I knew not to tempt her anger or be tempted by her siren's song. I knew that such actions would cause her trade winds to shift sides in the battle; the locks on my gates and the stalks of my plants would both be cut. Gone would be my profitable livelihood. My operation was the sword I was living by, and if I upset Mother Nature, she would grow a root in my path to trip me right onto her own sword.

The drive was a spectacular display. Zeus and I witnessed the real Zeus's sheer anger. Most of the strikes were on the north side of the highway, right in my path—a natural Russian roulette analogous to my life's choices.

· · ·

We woke to the sound of an infrared heat-mapping jet circling the house very low, shaking the windows. My college buddy thought we were getting raided, so he jumped in his truck and left. The pilot came so close to the house that we could see his face. He began pointing frantically down the hill toward the first gate. I splashed myself with cold water, jumped on a dirt bike, and rode fast over the three miles down to the first gate. Just before I reached it, I noticed a Forest Service fire ranger walking up the road.

"Do you have the little cabin with the red roof?"

"Yes, sir. I do."

"There is currently an active fifteen-acre fire about a half mile below your house and other structures."

I immediately unlocked the gates. He followed me up to the house and barn. As my breaths came loud over the dirt bike's engine, I thought, *This is the reverse of the scenario with Jerry's truck. Then the fire was on top of the mountain, and we had locked them out. Now we need them in.* My heart fluttered, and my brain spiraled over what to do.

I heard the mountain and trees speak to me again as they had that wild acid-filled morning. "Your success in all this is up to us. Protect us first, and you shall be protected in return."

Confidence and clarity suppressed my hangover and anxiety. Smoke was beginning to appear from the blaze, and the sun exposed herself over the Trinity Alps mountain ridges to our east.

I grabbed all the information I could for the ranger. "Here are all the maps of the property and water sources. We will move the pumps to the reservoirs for trucks to be filled."

"How much plant material is in the barn?"

We had harvested four days before, and the trimmers were supposed to be coming the next day. It was a slam dunk for law enforcement. Helicopter and airplane sounds reverberated in every direction. My chest pounded, reminding my mouth to synchronize with my lungs.

"I'm not sure, but if you glance through that window, you might have a sense."

I pointed to the window next to the front door, as the other windows had been blacked out to prevent light penetration to the drying plants. He walked over and glanced through the glass.

"The whole thing filled like that?"

"Yes, sir. I believe so."

"Let me connect with dispatch on an update."

He walked fifty yards to the clearing, where he could see the fires to the east. It felt like twenty minutes but was probably less than five before he returned.

"Listen, this fire is smack on the corner of your property, national forest, and Sierra Pacific Logging Company. USFS is planning on sending a full ground strike team and rangers plus an air attack. That is a great thing for the safety of yourselves and this property. I appreciate all these maps and your cooperation. I suggest that whatever you have hanging in the barn finds its way deep into the woods where only the flames might find it for the next week or so. Understand?"

"Yes, sir."

He was a local Forest Service sergeant who worked at the station in Oak Creek and said he only focused on fire issues but rode and managed the clean-ups of illegal grows in the springtime. At least he was nice and gave us a heads-up.

"This place might be the cleanest and most organized I've ever been to."

"Thank you, we care deeply about this timberland and the watersheds."

My stomach growled aggressively, and my mouth was like cotton despite my quick rinse after a deep and hungover sleep.

"Out-of-the-area rangers will be stationed at the gate. They'll be turning the clearing at the gate into the satellite command center. They don't like you—not you exactly, but what you are and look like. They know what's here. I will do my best to keep them off the land. Get this cleaned up so if they arrive to assess structures, it's just quaint, cute, and clean. Copy?"

"Roger."

He walked back to his truck. As he opened the door, he looked at one of our work quads.

"'This timber property managed by Mountain Resources Group,'" he read off the decal on the side of the four-wheeler. "My oldest daughter goes to middle school, and she went on that class trip last year. That's a really great thing you support—great for the youth to get out and learn and see. I'll let the gate guards know."

I couldn't believe it. I had funded three nights each at a learning center for three different grades' school trips the year before because I felt it was the right thing to do and to pass along the funds to a good cause. I subconsciously did it for good karma but never thought it would be direct karma.

We started trimming a couple days later, after driving all the trimmers past the firemen. Each evening we watched hundred-foot-tall trees burning like candles on the ridges to our east.

It was still frustrating that the brand-new two-story, 3,200-square-foot drying barn we had saved for and had hired a contractor to build and that we were so excited to use was only used for three and a half days. We had to empty the barn, tote up the product, load it onto trucks, drive it deeper into the woods, unload it, and hang it from wires in the trees.

"Why does this keep happening?" I yelled at the old rock outcropping. At least it wasn't raining.

CHAPTER 28

Trim Town Green Stampede

FALL 2013-FALL 2014

I GOT MY EXPERIENCE with the trimmigrants thanks to fate and friendly pressure. In August 2013, we needed a way to go from fifteen to twenty trimmers to twenty-five to forty during trimming season. Enter the Armada. They consisted of five ladies and one man from Spain and Italy who were on vacation in California at the right time. They came at a time I least expected and were exactly what I needed.

A close friend I grew up with was visiting his family vacation home along the Trinity River, and he reached out to me while he was in town to invite me over. Needing a break, I went.

"How is it going out there?" he asked. He lived in Miami but was fascinated by the turn he knew my life had taken even though I did my best to hide it. "I know you are doing this new-age weed stuff."

In his mind, what I was doing was different from what we saw growing up.

"Well, it's doing all right, yeah."

"Shut up. I can tell. I know what's going on. I want to introduce you to these people that are staying at the vacation home next door."

"I don't know, you know. I don't want to meet many people."

225

"I know, I know, you're Mr. Elusive now," he teased. "Mr. Out of the Country or Mr. Out in the Country Without Cell Service. Mr. Thousands of Unread Text Messages."

"Come on, man. Take it easy on me."

"Well, hey, at least you're not Mr. Locked Up or Mr. Out on Bail. No, you are going to want to meet these people. Come over." He made a batch of margaritas in two blenders. "We are going."

I caved.

"This is not work," he pressed. "We are going to go have fun, and it's vacation for the afternoon. You could use it, I'm sure."

With a blender in my hands, not dressed for swimming, we both went to the big vacation home next door. It was a nice party house overlooking the river. Out at the pool in the back, we met seven gals and one guy. All of them were pretty much naked, and they were all speaking Spanish.

"Jackson," I said, "what in the world is going on here? What are you getting me into?"

"Wowzers, right? These people want to trim. They are from Spain."

"OK?"

"Ah, *hola vaquero, qué guapo*," one gal said as she grabbed the blender from my hands.

"Vaquero?" I asked the Spanish man at the table rolling a tobacco cigarette.

"Your boots, she says you are cutey American cowboy. My name is Emiliano."

I turned back to her as she salted the rim of her glass.

"Ah, *tu señora peligrosa, tu problema con esos ojos, muy bonita e intrigante*," I said. You're a dangerous lady; you're trouble with those eyes, very pretty and intriguing.

"Ha, *buena suerte*, American boy," she said, looking up with only her eyes. Good luck, American boy.

"You speak Spanish now?" Jackson asked. He was shocked.

"I can when I drink, and I can in times like this. Four months in Costa Rica, lots of drinking, dancing, and eyes like those."

Emiliano was a filmmaker, and they had just finished filming Yosemite, Mount Shasta, and Death Valley in California. They all introduced themselves.

"Am I being set up?" I asked Jackson.

"No. They want to trim the weed in California and experience it."

"Experience it, huh? Any of them willing to take my job?" I joked.

A couple of them were Spanish TV stars. One was the assistant on *The Tonight Show* in Spain. They were all fun, interesting, and beautiful. They wanted to see California, had heard about weed trimming, and were fascinated by it. And they just happened to rent a house next to my friend's family.

"Well, it's tedious," I said. "It's not like a fun job. It's trimming weed all day and just talking."

"Oh, it's fascinating. We want to see the weed and go up. *Sí, vamos al rancho de la mota y vemos la mota!*" the most animated gal yelled at the top of her lungs.

"Welp, they sure don't seem discreet," I told Jackson.

"They know when and how to be," Emiliano said.

Emiliano spoke pretty good English, a couple of the gals spoke a little, and others spoke none.

"How about we go up there for two nights and no filming?" I offered. "You can film the cabin if you want and the woods, but nothing with the weed, and you can experience it and get paid."

They agreed. And they soon gave themselves nicknames: the Niña, Pinta, and Santa Maria. And one lady who refused to participate in the glorification of Christopher Columbus named herself Smallpox.

"I'll come get you in the next couple of days."

"Oh, thank you," said the woman I found most attractive. She kissed me on the cheek with a smile.

Oh gosh, this is going to lead to trouble, I thought.

Over the next few days leading up to the trim, the Armada and I became friends. One night, I met friends at an event called Bigfoot Days, which is like an annual fair. A local homeless man we called the Bicycle Cowboy was selling a litter of puppies at the front gate.

"I never look at puppies," I said. I excitedly picked one up and buried my face in her puppy fur. Though they were mutts, she looked like a mini German shepherd puppy—black, brown, and fuzzy. Puppies were not puppies forever, though, and I already had enough going on, so I put her back. A few hours later, a local acquaintance walked over, and I started to laugh. The fuzzy black-and-brown pup was walking next to him. He'd bought her to impress his date.

By the end of the night, however, he was so drunk that he couldn't even hold on to her. My new friends and I made the executive decision (which our drunk acquaintance agreed with) to take the puppy back to our hotel and decide what to do with her from there.

My friends told me I had to take care of her until they could find her a home, that I could probably handle her even with my time constraints.

"If she wants to basically live in a truck, I guess," I said.

A few days later, I, the puppy, and the Armada drove up to the trim scene. The crews that were already working the trim and grow scenes quickly fell in love with the puppy *and* the Armada. The pup was sweet and brave even though she wasn't more than six weeks old. The Armada were animated actresses from Spain.

"Oh, it's dinnertime!" the Armada would sing out like a chorus.

"We are having this and this, and would you like some wine?"

"Yes, let's have some wine!"

"Good morning, sunshine!"

To them, it was a kind of a vacation. It was like a game. It was the polar opposite of what was going on in my brain, but it was fun.

They would go to thrift stores to get art supplies, then do arts and crafts in the evening and play games.

The pup acclimated to everyone so quickly. *I'm not going to name her,* I said to myself. *If I name her, she's mine. And I'm going to find her a home. My life is not meant for a puppy.*

One night as I drove out through the gate, I realized the puppy wasn't in the truck. I thought I'd put her in the back seat, but she wasn't there. Panic began to consume me.

Did I run her over? My heart was pounding. I was almost in tears. I couldn't find her, and I couldn't even call her name. I got back in the truck, turned around, and drove up the road super slow so I wouldn't run over her if she'd fallen out or followed me. As the gravel crunched beneath the tires, I heard a little yip. It was from *inside* my truck.

I stopped immediately and swung the door open. *Where is she?*

Relief flooded my body. She had gone under the back seat and was sleeping the whole time. *Dammit. I'm keeping this dog.*

A day or so after that, a friend who was trimming was listening to *The Hunger Games* through earphones. Suddenly, she shouted, "No! They killed Rue! Oh no, she didn't make it!"

I looked down at the puppy, who did make it despite my full-blown panic attack.

"I'm going to name you Rue," I decided.

• • •

The Armada stayed for a few days until there was a break in our schedule. It would be about a week, and I wasn't sure if they would be back or not.

"Oh, can we take a picture with you at the cabin or something?" asked Bella, one of the Armada gals.

"Sure," I said. Then she kissed me.

During the break, Bella and I started a relationship, and the group did decide to return to the mountain. Within a few weeks, we were serious. She met my parents, who both spoke Spanish. Before the group left for Spain, Bella asked me to meet her in San Francisco so we could spend time together before they went back home. I was in.

After one of the scariest flights I've ever been on, with a wheels-up emergency landing and another passenger being arrested for smuggling weed, I finally got to Bella at the hotel. We were having a great time when I asked if she'd like a drink.

"I can't drink. I want to talk to you." Her brows furrowed.

"OK, why can't you drink?"

Oh, she can't drink because she wants to talk to me. Shit.

"I need to get Plan B or something here," she said. She sounded a little panicky.

"Are you pregnant?"

"Yeah."

"Me?"

"Of course you. I need your help. I need to go to a clinic. I need help," she pleaded.

"Whoa, OK. Yes. OK."

We got her the correct medicine and went through the whole process in a matter of hours. She would fly out the next morning.

It was heavy. It all happened so fast. It went from being a goodbye afternoon to another very unexpected ending. I would see her again, but only for limited periods because of her tourist visa. We both agreed it would be best if she worked for someone else in the following years.

Often during that time, I felt like I couldn't get away from the heaviness. Every day of my life was a major thing. It was constant. The threat of a major felony arrest was constant. I knew I was putting myself in these situations, but I didn't know exactly what to do. However, when things like the Armada and Rue happened, I remembered that sometimes slivers of life were still good.

CHAPTER 29

Trim Town, USA

FALL 2014

TRIM SEASON was always the most dangerous time for a few reasons.

1. Farms brought outsiders behind the gates and into the scene and gave them some level of knowledge of the happenings.
2. Farmers carried the faint scent of fresh-cut weed on their clothes, in their trucks, in their hair, and on their pillows.
3. Farms become an easier public target for law enforcement—we were the fish during the run, and chances were higher that they would catch us.
4. When twenty-five to thirty people stayed on a piece of property for two months, it was a reality show. Being the jefe was just reality.

The woman held her arms above her head, moving them out and in as if she were a cheerleader saying, "Go, Team, go!" She wasn't. Instead, she was yelling, "Work scissors, work scissors!" while standing on the edge of a parking lot in town, looking for harvest work. Her sign was shaped like a giant pair of scissors with a lush green branch between the blades.

In my best Western narration, I spoke aloud to my dog in the back seat. "Ha, look at that; that sign is brilliant. Yeehaw, pup! Welcome to Trim Town, where anything can happen with a Sharpie, some cardboard, and a hundred and fifty bucks. Work scissors, work!"

Her cardboard sign—the whole scene, for that matter—was the most creative approach for seeking trim work I had seen in Oak Creek so far that year—and maybe the most attractive, which, in a modern gold rush town, mattered, just like it had 130 years ago in China Flat, Union City, Junction City, Weaverville, and, of course, San Francisco.

Welcome to Trim Town, USA, I thought.

"Yeehaw," I yelled once more as her cardboard blades connected.

The caffeine in my system was alive. I had awoken alone in the house and drove over the hill and into Oak Creek. Arriving that morning looked like a scene from an old Western movie. I went into town on an iron horse, the main street bustling with wagon trains, cowboys, railroad workers, miners, merchants, and women—some taken with rings, some available for considerations and propositions.

My attention drifted back to Queen Scissor Legs. She was slim and blessed in the regions of the upper chest and below the back. Even leaning over and dancing with her scissors prop, she seemed to be at least five feet nine. She wore an off-white tank top with the word *Milan* scrawled across it over a black bra paired with a short black miniskirt sporting ripped back pockets. Her legs were longer than those of most supermodels, and she wore black leather sandals laced all the way up her calves and tied in a bow just below her knees. We locked eyes and smiled.

I would allow her to control my life with a pair of cardboard scissors, I thought and laughed. Her smile held in a vanity pose, holding my full focus. It could have for eternity. It was such a beautifully out-of-place scene in the small rural wooded disarray of a mountain town.

In every direction, the whole small town was overrun with hints of the booming industry that filled the surrounding hills. Truck beds were stacked high with growing supplies. Contractors pulled trailers covered in mud and dust from remote job sites. Shopping carts were packed with bulk foods.

The industry had become so blatant, and the town was more and more reliant on it. Cash was everywhere. It was a politician's wet dream and nightmare all at once. The economy was booming, perfect for communicating the bounty to constituents. At the same time, the environment was being destroyed, trimmigrants were sleeping and defecating in the parks, and the non-growers were feeling overrun and outpriced on almost everything. It was a boom-town conundrum. A conundrum I felt like I was representing, sympathetic to both sides. I spent my workdays within the industry and around its characters and my days off around many people who had grudges and reasonable fits about it all. Outside of the gates, we just never admitted what we did. If someone asked, we said we worked in construction or real estate and left it at that.

There was now an official annual migration of these young trimmigrant folks from all over Europe, Central and South America, and portions of the eastern United States. They descended on the Emerald Triangle from late August to early October looking for trim work. They came by the thousands from over thirty different countries. It was like the miners of the 1840s, the Chinese railroad workers after them, and the loggers of the 1920s to the 1970s.

I looked past the dumpsters, the giant sixty-foot-tall Bigfoot, and the museum to the front of the Mexican restaurant. There were about six vans parked outside and about thirty-five "workers" sitting in the grass along the walkway to the front door.

"This isn't normal," I said out loud. "This won't last." It was a mantra that Jesse and I had started telling ourselves long ago. I used it to remind myself to do a reality check.

It was only four fall seasons earlier that Rachel and I tried desperately not to give any hint about our connection to the weed industry, and the town didn't want the connection out in the open. In three short years, people looking for work brought the industry out for all to see. I was still in the same parking lot, though, and Rachel was traveling around the globe on a productive trajectory.

Don't go down that rabbit hole, I warned myself.

I grabbed my yellow pad to reread the items the crew had requested that day as they sat around tables in the second story of the new barn, brainstorming their demands and requests. I scribbled it all down on the pad as fast as I could.

"It's a minimal list," they had said.

Kinda, I thought. I had gone to Safeway the day before, so groceries were good for the most part. But today's items were important, and they still needed a fair number. Trim season had become the most expensive ledger in the business accounting journal, accounting for over 70 percent of the annual overhead. It cost thousands a day for labor, trimming, food, fuel, the stipend for whoever made dinner, tons of toiletries, and any manner of miscellaneous requests and personal necessities. The crew was, however, required to reimburse the company for alcohol, tobacco, and concert tickets. They were responsible for any Peruvian marching powder—aka cocaine.

During the second work break, I often took the crew to some secondhand stores and gave them each eighty dollars to get a couple sweatshirts, a jacket, some long-sleeve shirts, and warm work pants. Then we headed into Big Five or Kmart to buy waterproof(ish) boots, long johns, a warm pair of work gloves, and a beanie for each. It was guaranteed that winter would show her fury long before fall would say his goodbyes. On one of those trips, I ran into Khloe, a girl I dated in my early twenties, and her boyfriend.

"Who are all these people with you?" she asked.

I brought her up to date on my life in sixty seconds. She turned and walked over to a few of the gals and began speaking Spanish, as she was fluent. Moments later, she returned, grabbed me by the arms, and looked straight into my face. "You don't look healthy. This has gotten too big and out of hand. Take a break."

"What?" I snapped. "A break? I'll take a break in three months." It was like we were a couple again, some twelve years later.

"This isn't going to end well. This isn't you. What does your girlfriend think of all this?"

I stumbled through an explanation she didn't buy, and we parted.

I had a timeline and a workload that demanded a full assembly line of folks. I needed quiet people full of fear of being caught, but driven, with strong work ethics and hustle. People fearful of the surroundings but able to tend to themselves in a tidy and clean manner. People fearful of the language barrier but kind and appreciative. People capable of traveling the world with only a backpack and without transportation. Young Europeans and South Americans were capable and perfect candidates. There were new characters every season. Most came, went, and never returned. It was hard. It was necessary.

It took about forty eleven-hour workdays to trim. Every tenth day, they stopped work at 2:00 p.m. and had two days off. It was time for laundry, resupply, real showers, a meal at the Mexican restaurant, beverages, floaties at the river, and a party at my vacation home, where I could now take them to unwind. Even so, we pinched pennies from year to year. We had to have enough left over to get the product trimmed and packaged and to make sure we could pay on time, which went a long way with the crews, as they had options. We wanted to give them every reason not to consider those options, so reimbursing them and showing them a good time was a great start.

. . .

As I entered the only small grocery store in town, my thoughts were interrupted by the voice of a young boy. He was holding on to the front of his mother's shopping cart as they exited the store.

"What did you say, honey?" she asked, glancing over her receipt.

"Who are all these people, Mom?"

"They come to visit each year, honey, like the salmon in the river."

"Why do they not have a home, Mom?"

"Huh, why do you think that?" she asked, puzzled, trying to keep his eyes on her and not on the scene.

"Because her sign says, 'I need a home.'"

The boy pointed to a gal sitting in the open back of a dusty early 1990s Ford Windstar minivan with a sign that read *I need a home!* and featured a drawing of a pair of scissors with a little green oval drawn between the blades.

"Oh geez, this is getting out of control," the mother said.

She glanced at me directly in the eyes and raised her brow in disgust. I nodded back in solidarity with my own partial creation. I was glad we had passed carts while mine was still empty. I understood her reasoning. I had walked out of this same grocery store many times as a child with my mother. I never remembered seeing anything like this.

An hour later, I unlocked the second gate, still thinking about the questions the little boy had been asking his mother. I got back in the truck and drove through the gate, threw the truck in park, turned off the ignition, and jumped out to lock the gate.

I didn't want to go up to the barn. Not yet. I wasn't ready to put on that face and step onto the stage of that play as the character of weed boss. Not yet. The dogs had already run up the road. The crew would know I'd be arriving soon. The feeling that happened every year at that time was boiling over in my soul once more. My emotions and my itch, all growing so exhausted from the daily possibility of being arrested for daily felony after daily felony.

I walked to the front of the truck and gazed up the road at the steep hill ahead—the section Jesse and I had charged up all those years before in Rick in a lightning and rainstorm, sober with the itch. It had been years since he left for other paths in his life.

"Damned. Yep, still damned," I whispered, flipping off the dirt road ahead. I stepped up onto the old fallen tree that lay perpendicular to the road. I stood there in silence—only the sound of cooling iron from the undercarriage of Zeus *clicked* and *clacked* in the air.

It was year seven of this same summer camp shit and the emotional roller coaster of no seat belts and little sleep. I was over the rock-star, outlaw, fake-weed-CEO life in so many ways. I was a moment's notice away from complete disaster or jail time. Tired and bored of the tiny empire I had created would have been a generous description of my feelings that afternoon.

Trim season was the most dangerous time, but in so many other ways, I loved it. More than workers, my crew were my friends, and more than friends, they were family. The bonds of trust and coexistence, the flow of the workplace, were carved in the old fir that shaded the barn. The meal planning, the toiletry needs, the alcohol and substance preferences, and even the debauchery were accepted if not encouraged. It was a seesaw, summer camp, real-life reality show.

Our parcel and farm was the only operation left up that dirt road. The only operation still in business, not locked up, with no deaths, and no one was fully strung out yet. But we were alone, the last target, the elusive big-horned buck during an open hunting season. The burden of responsibility and the potential for disastrous mistakes or injuries had all become overwhelming. Handling this all sober wasn't possible.

Chech, check, chech. The squirrel taunting me overhead broke up my philosophical thoughts. As I turned around from the gate and looked down the dirt road to the bend, I climbed the same hill where, years before, my itch was so pure and had some meaning. When my companions in this venture were my companions in life. It felt so long ago and so distant. I didn't know why I was still doing it all. I no longer had a choice. I had completely stopped saying "I love you" to the plants. The last time I had looked at the stars, I was so high that they became the faces of skulls frowning down on me. For years, none of the greenhouses had been named—only numbered, like ego-driven trophies to display my pot-star status to the world via Google Earth.

I had stopped walking the land naked. I had stopped praising the Sun. The greenbacks had become the priority. I was losing the game. I had lost myself.

In a few moments, I would see my friends, the workers from over nine different countries, trimming away, smiling, laughing, arguing, listening to music—it was all work. For them, a consistent grind in a constant place for a constant price. I never let them know the full picture. The full picture was a lot harder to keep together. It began to feel like a sports game each time I went to one of the trim scenes. I needed to be aware but fun, safe, scary, a friend, a boss, a lover, and, of course, the keeper of the money.

I looked down from the log at the large piece of bark broken off and lying flat on the mountain earth.

"Ah, hell," I said and jumped down, flipped it over, and grabbed the plastic salsa container from its little hole. I walked back to the truck, opened the back door, grabbed the *Best of Merle Haggard* CD out of the front seat pocket, placed it on the back seat, pulled out my driver's license, and sat it next to the CD.

I popped open the lid of the salsa, grabbed the baggie, and poured out a couple of white compressed pebbles of powder from the half-ounce supply, then proceeded to break them up into mounds of powder with my ID. I was literally face-to-face with substance dependence. One mound went into a little folded piece of an envelope; I made the other into three healthy lines. Within two minutes, only a white powdery residue was left on the plastic covering Mr. Haggard's beard. A comforting numb feeling began running down the back of my throat and through my mind.

"Cha, chaaaa," I said softly to the squirrel, now silently watching with bulging eyes from the madrone limb above.

I closed the baggie, the salsa container, and the back door of the truck, and a moment later, I closed the large piece of bark back over the salsa lid. I jumped back onto the log, splintering some rotting bark off and down onto the dirt road as small puffs of dust ballooned around my boots. I thought about what waited for me up on the mountain.

Sex had become another substance and comforting distraction from the potential daily felonies and farming dramas. It was a casual, fun way to release some of the constant anxiety and pressure I felt. Nothing was serious, but I also knew that whatever love triangle I was dabbling in with my different harvest-site flings would collide in time. I didn't and couldn't care. This wasn't the life, and these weren't the relationships, that I wanted anymore. Maybe I never actually had, but it was too late now. I didn't even know how I could get out.

The latch clicked as I locked the gate. It was quiet—no wind, no road noise, only the chatter of the squirrel high in the madrone-covered signs saying *No Trespassing* and who to call in an emergency. It would have been a battle to determine who had the wider eyes, the squirrel or me.

"Stay out of that salsa rodeo, little buddy," I said.

Then I drove up to the trim scene, ready to play the part of weed boss.

. . .

There was one large kitchen sink with gallons of Dr. Bronner's soap and new sponges always available. On the east wall, perpendicular to the sink, were two industrial shelving racks packed with dry goods, canned goods, sodas, beers, tea, and coffee. There was always enough coffee. Pots, pans, mugs, and ladles hung from wooden pegs and large nails. In the main area, near the woodstove, strings of Christmas lights hung from bent nails that crisscrossed the joists above and gave a warm glow around the fire. An assortment of out-of-tune instruments leaned against the wall and were played on most nights after dinner.

Then season five brought the classic crescent moon outhouse. It was dug and built right over the former location of Camp Camo, where Rachel's and my pillows used to rest. The irony. It lasted one summer season. Then it was lifted by chains and a tractor and sat back down over a new hole. The old hole was covered in a couple of feet of concrete and compost.

"Yeah, right there will be perfect," I said to our hero in the backhoe as he started to dig a proper pit. I had to yell over the machine's roar. "Maybe add a second over there too. We can just pick up the house and drop it on that hole when this one fills. Turn this one into a nice concrete pad. Happy days."

"Roger that, kid," he said. The excavator dug a deep pit, and we built a nice six-by-six-foot poop house over it with a national park–grade toilet seat and wash station. Even painted the inside and laid down some plastic mats—massive game change.

The upstairs of the new barn was just one big room with a vaulted ceiling and a nice sliding glass door and deck that looked out to the east. A big rectangle of folding tables was in the center—three tables long on each side with two tables as the cap. There were nineteen chairs of various shapes and sizes with an odd assortment of pillows, cushions, rolled-up towels, and pieces of pool noodles, all trying to add lasting support and comfort around the table. A rectangle of floor pads pieced together like a puzzle paralleled the perimeter of the tables. Many folks preferred to stand while they worked.

An indescribable smell, a mix of dried weed, plywood, perspiration, rotting compost, coffee grounds, and cedar kindling, created a light earthy funk—the trim barn smell.

Stacked along the whole north wall were black totes with yellow lids, only twelve at any given time. Pieces of tan masking tape read *SFVOG Anne* (San Fernando Valley OG—from greenhouse Anne), *SD Heli* (Sour Diesel from greenhouse Helicopter Pad), and *BBK10F* (Blackberry Kush—from 2010 Flat). That separated the types of strains, or varieties, which is how the customers preferred it. The greenhouse allowed us to keep track of our production per location and per strain on the ranch.

I was only able to keep up in my life with fewer cares thanks to a little "behind the gate" help from various substances. It was my seventh year of hosting a months-long summer camp for more than twenty-five people on the property. I wanted to spend the money made on the mountain off the mountain—not on the mountain. The dollar value of the work at the mountain would never be higher than it was right now, not anytime in the next forty years. But my body and mind were asking, *Who cares about money in forty years? We are living in your skin and skull not sure if we will make it four more years or even four more months.*

My subconscious and soul were beginning to see a blurry jumble of writings on the wall. I couldn't make out the words, but I was starting to admit my fear. I didn't want those writings to be an obituary or a news clip or a ticket to the loopy hospital or rehab. I knew I couldn't stay on top of the mountain—figuratively or literally. I just wanted to be able to get to the base of a new mountain to climb.

But how could I get there without tripping? The weed industry had brought me the exact opposite state it brought our customers. They received laughter, joy, relaxation, pain relief, mental relief, and in some cases neurological stability. I was the farmer, caretaker, processor, and distributor of the catalyst to these feelings, but I was truly living as their antonym.

Now what?

CHAPTER 30

The Art of Pot Supply

MANY ATTEMPTED SALES over the previous few years only fell through with a "No," "Nope," "Not it," or "Nah, won't work." That wasn't a surprise, really; no-gos were just part of business. It was like when a salesperson had a lead but didn't close—just part of the game. However, most salespeople were not driving five hours up north, hiking a mile through the snow to the pickle barrels hidden deep in the woods, strapping pounds of weed to a sled, hiking a mile back, and driving an hour into town only to be told, "Nope, not what I was thinking of or looking for" or "Someone else got here sooner."

Bummed and annoyed, I took a deep breath in and rubbed my index fingers with my thumbs whenever I felt like smashing a hammer across someone's jaw. I exhaled and softly said to myself, "Don't feel defeated; get educated." It happened often during our first few seasons, when we had the fewest number of connections and needed funds the most. I didn't want to be known for having weed, and I dealt with people who wanted small amounts, so they wanted to make sure it was exactly what their customers were looking for—all of which made it harder.

Eventually, I started asking questions almost incessantly.

If I could grow exactly what your customers want, what would that be? When do you need it most and what do you need the most of? What is the price difference that beats out the quality and type difference? I

wanted to know where the lines for quality, price, quantity, and no-
toriety intersected on the graph. I was OK with cutting myself a
little short if we were the first choice—we could always grow more.

Our connections started with Rachel's friends from college who
shipped to Hawaii and our neighbors in the hills. However, as time
passed, our connections grew, as did the methodology of transporting the product our ladies gave us. The fruits of our labor may
have started in Humboldt County—we kept all our transactions in
state—but they traveled to be rolled into beautiful little joints and
smoked in a thousand different ways by every kind of person imag-
inable, from shop owners in San Diego and Rastas from Brooklyn to
saltwater fishermen from Charleston and Mormons from Salt Lake
City—at least according to the secondhand accounts I heard over
too many beers at the local honky-tonk.

In those days, our motto in all transactions, no matter who was
running it, was "We don't want to know." Donations weren't my
world; I was just the supply. My world stopped once the buds got to
the trailer, the plane, under the boat cover, or stuffed into large fuel
tanks, and we said, "Bon voyage. Good luck!"

Clients whose real names we didn't know often said, "We are
taking it back east."

"Oh, OK, Redding, sounds good," I joked, signaling how little
information I wanted, as Redding is three hours east of Humboldt.

The less we knew, the better. However, some stories just stood out.

One retired couple took loads of illegal product across the
country repeatedly. They picked up eight hundred pounds of weed,
camped while zigzagging across the country, didn't give anyone
anything to ask questions about, and made close to six figures every
few weeks. If law enforcement started tracking their vehicle, which
wouldn't have been common, the police would find an elderly couple who'd spent three nights at the senior campground in Phoenix,
went and saw Redwood National Park, and made several more stops

on a cross-country trip. No judge was going to sign a warrant to bother retirees who had worked their whole lives and never missed a tax payment. It was always the least stereotypical sellers who made the most money.

I heard stories of coordinated deals between producers and car dealerships using tow trucks—stories told to me by amped-up and verbally animated growers while in line at supply houses waiting for lumber to be loaded onto my work trailer. They broke the front left axle of almost-new white contractor's trucks, which were loaded with pounds of product in every nook and cranny—lock boxes, a false floor, everything—which were then loaded onto a tow truck and driven to a dealership six hours south. The drivers knew nothing, but the puppeteers knew that the California Highway Patrol did not pull over tow trucks.

Sometimes sellers got their money via a piece of art.

"A million dollars' worth of hundred-dollar bills can be stored in the back of an expensive painting and sent through an art dealer," said a young man with a Jersey accent and four empty shot glasses on the bar.

"What?" I said.

"Right wild, huh?" He picked up another wedge of lime and the last shot in the line.

Huge, organized groups existed because of the marijuana economy. The logistics of some of the transactions never ceased to amaze me.

That isn't to say that we didn't have to be creative with the logistics of our own supply runs. After trimming each day, while the crew cleaned up, our main crew (Jesse, Nick, Matt, and I) separated, weighed, and vacuum-sealed our product in Seal-a-Meal bags by the pound and coded the labels for the strain. We wiped the sealed product with rubbing alcohol and fresh paper towels, then sprayed them with Windex and stacked them inside black trash bags, which we drove into the woods on the quads. We never wanted the trimmers to know where product was kept.

During our years of hefty production, I separated clients of the county's world-renowned cash crop into three categories: micro side hustlers, medium-sized brokers, and life changers. I was a local kid, and many of my childhood schoolmates were "in the hill game." Sometimes, the local growers needed a specific strain of marijuana to fill an order, or they might not have the supply on hand, so they needed to buy from another grower. Sometimes I was the grower who needed supply. It was important to know who needed, wanted, or could help with what.

The micro side hustler wanted five to fifteen pounds per month, max. I guessed they were shipping it somewhere far away because payments usually came in bank or Western Union envelopes. Those folks usually had full-time jobs, were students, and so on. Those clients were great for keeping the lights on because they were consistent even in the offseason.

I only worked with a few of those folks. They adhered to the medical guidelines and always showed their "scrip" from the doctor. They rented homes on the edges of town, where I would quietly deliver their product in a toolbox during low-traffic daylight hours.

Medium-size brokers ordered twenty to forty pounds every other month in batches of ten pounds for each flavor. For the most part, they lived in the area or had recently migrated from another metropolitan area where they had friends and buyers. We fronted forty pounds to them for a day and night and were compensated for the transaction the next day. They never wanted us to know who they were connected to, and vice versa.

We met at a local brewery, where I called in my order ahead of time. Then I loaded up the product in contractor bags that included ten Seal-a-Meal bags each, threw those into the bed of the truck, and locked the camper shell. Usually, about thirty minutes after sunset, I backed the truck into a parking spot next to a large dumpster, cracked the back windows for the dogs, grabbed my to-go food, and came out to the client, who backed in on the other side of the dumpster.

I placed the food on the front passenger seat of the truck and told the dogs to be quiet, which they did because they thought they might get a treat of the steaming food if they behaved. I shut the door, walked around the back of the truck, and dropped the tailgate without opening the camper shell window. I grabbed the four contractor bags, placed them behind the dumpster, got in my truck, and drove off, after which the buyers grabbed the bags. The next day, we met at a vista point along the highway, looking out over the Pacific around four o'clock in the afternoon on my way home from work. I cracked the back cab passenger window, then got out of the truck with my pup, Rue, and a pair of binoculars and walked away, still in view but gazing out at the ocean.

They pulled in and dropped a folded sweatshirt with a plastic bag full of banded currency through the window onto the back seat and left. We caught up during "non-work hours" about the next deal, but there was never a need for small talk during the transactions. Smooth, quick, discreet, professional, accurate, public, and within the normal flow of life was the code.

There were also folks at the same magnitude and velocity as medium brokers who were local friends I'd known my whole life. For those friends, I didn't mind going to their houses or having them come to mine. However, that group of people was extremely small, and we all knew where we came from, respected small-town discreetness, and wanted the best for each other's successes in the game and life.

The life changers were the big-timers and ordered between 240 and 1,840 pounds every few months. These big buyers came in from out of town, had no local brokers, and were only willing to work directly with growers. We called them the life changers or "the rewards" because if we managed and allocated our funds correctly from the other two types of clients, a transaction with one of the big groups could change our lives. It was the reward we all thought about when the itch took hold of us.

When I worked with people like that, I only supplemented my loads with product grown by close local friends or their immediate family members—never an out-of-town grower or transplant. I wanted to help, and I loved seeing the joy and relief when they received their reward. I enjoyed getting points off the deal too, of course. However, partnering with them was safe, and it went both ways.

The Emerald Triangle was not easy to get to by car or boat, and at times, the fog was too dense even to land a plane. That was actually the reason an airport was there in the first place. It had originally been a military airport for training pilots to land in dense fog and harsh Pacific Ocean storms. It was now a municipal airport. There were two other small airports around the county for private planes and a couple of other landing strips. The county was rich with beauty and people, but it was not very prosperous outside of resource-intense industries.

Regardless of who I was meeting, when it was time to deliver, I dressed in nice contractor clothes and boots with lumber, cut pieces of plywood, ladders, and a roll of Tyvek vapor barrier in the truck. I also carried a couple of boxes of nail gun nails, as well as a large contractor box in the bed of the truck with the camper shell off to look like I had nothing to conceal. I'd meet the quad with the black bag of product and load up fifty-six pounds of product mixed in with the rest of my "construction work supplies." Five trips every week to town for a couple of months was a lot of pounds and, in turn, a lot of "donations" for members of the community.

Over the years, we received donations from all kinds of people. While perfecting our growing process was the foundation of our business, concurrently working to perfect our donation process was just as important. The law was written such that we couldn't act as a for-profit entity, so we always spoke in terms of donations, just like Jarod had on the first day I met him and just like all the other growers. We could grow all we wanted, but if we didn't have "donors," if we did get caught, or worst of all, if we got robbed, we'd have no business at all.

CHAPTER 31

The Last Supper of Gross Domestic Product

WINTER 2014-15

THE SMALL FLIP PHONE in my cup holder vibrated. The caller ID read, *Hanes*. I had named him in my phone after the three packs of new white Hanes T-shirts he and his partner always had with them. This pair of guys from "out east" each would go through three shirts during a sealing and weighing session. Then each took a long shower, shaved clean, gelled their hair, dressed in black slacks and pressed collared shirts, grabbed their Church of Latter-Day Saints Bibles and their leather briefcases full of church stuff, and shook my hand. It was like we were all on a business trip in Salt Lake City, not Trinidad, California.

That was their alibi, but they had grown up in that faith, canvassed the streets for a year, and knew what the heck they were talking about should anyone ever question their faith. They always brought food and bags of greenbacks and had a couple of ladies make all three meals during their stay. One told me that the only store or building he had ever been in other than the vacation house was the Chevron in Trinidad.

"I buy gas and a newspaper with cash," he once said. "I'm never here, only passing through." In those days, we met every few weeks for a good couple of years. We worked thousands of pounds of product. To this day, we don't know each other's real names.

The vacation house was booked on the calendar but never with a name or credit card—simply a shaded block of days on the calendar marked *unavailable*. I would be occupying it the following morning. I was parked at an overlook near the airport, watching the last of the light disappear into the swells on the horizon of the Pacific, having a moment and waiting for this call.

"Yo."

"Three and a half cans of paint, same colors," Hanes said. "The paint sprayer can be picked up from Don's Rent-All at the same time."

"Thursday at 4:00 p.m.?"

"Yep."

"Over and out," I replied, flipping the phone closed.

We were to meet the following morning at 6:00 a.m., a Monday. They would be long out of town by Thursday at 4:00 p.m. Each time we had a "painting job," "dinner date," or "tee time," we always confirmed it in person ahead of the phone call. The call was only to confirm the quantity and to provide a green light for go. I strongly preferred these types of engagements over the small, in-town, go-or-no-go deals of years before. These sales of the county's most lucrative product increased the annual GDP by seven figures at a time every three weeks for years.

Grabbing an old receipt from the center console, I wrote down the phone number with the first four numbers in reverse and the last three correct. Then reaching into the back seat, I grabbed the little DeWalt bits box out of my tool bag, opened it, popped the plastic casing that held the bits, and put the receipt next to the remainder of the 8-ball I had gotten some days before. I closed it all back up and tossed it in my tool bag under a utility knife and screwdriver, then grabbed the phone and deleted the call. If I was raided and the phone found, I wanted no numbers to have been called or contacts saved.

Some would say this was over the top. But awareness and preparedness for the worst gave me an odd level of comfort. Working with big-timers was what I preferred. The risks were higher, but the concentration and respect for reality was present for both parties. If they had gotten to that level of smuggling and had sustained it, they ran a tight ship. And on the flip side, if I could deliver "two to five gallons of paint" (two hundred to five hundred pounds) every twenty-one days, they knew I must be connected to the local sources.

· · ·

The sun had set into the sea, and the skyline was beautiful, with its orange, pink, and purple hues lighting up the far-off fog bank. Normally I would have been heading home to cook dinner with my girlfriend, but we were not together at the time. It was for the best; she didn't know the deal was happening, even amid my longing and mourning our breakup. My business and life had merged into a love-hate relationship. Love existed each year until harvest. Then breakup and unhappiness finished out each year.

I had showered and was without my dog, Rue, who was my closest friend then. Fierce and scrappy, she had already survived being bitten by a rattlesnake, falling into a river, being picked up by a hawk, jumping on the back of a bear, and holding a standoff with a mountain lion.

It was to be a late night and very early morning getting the package ready, a perfect time to take myself out for a couple of drinks and a nice dinner at a fancy restaurant overlooking the sea a mile from my simple little home. I wasn't into new this or that. I liked a good meal. My feelings were telling me I had finally become dammed—not in the "damned if you do and damned if you don't" sense as during all those years before. Actually dammed. Dammed, like a massive wall of water and potential energy and ability blocked from any opportunities to become kinetic energy.

These dinners were an inside joke I had with myself. It was a reference to the "last supper." If I were to go to jail the next day and have the whole enterprise shuttered, I wanted to have had a nice last supper. If I accomplished a sale, I went out to dinner that night too, celebrating the fact that I didn't go to jail and that I got a last supper. Those dinners kept me grounded and aware of how fortunate I was. What they taught me most was where I wanted to be someday, which wasn't where I was. Dammed.

Most of the patrons in that restaurant on a Sunday evening were tourists between the ages of fifty and eighty. They were retired and seemed financially content. I used my time at the bar with the incredible view to observe the older people, make small talk with them, and learn from them. How did they get to this bar and to the area? What was their profession? Where did they serve in the military? What kind of losses had they suffered? Did they sell a business? Hardest times in life? Best accomplishments? Kids or no kids?

Those strangers were my professors of the outside world and the therapists I was unwilling to admit I needed. Those travelers, unlike many of their local professional counterparts, my significant others, and the nagging people on local blogs, never fully disapproved of my profession of choice. They listened to my reasons for being involved, they gawked at the possible lucrative return, and they agreed that there was space in the gray areas of the law for what I was doing, that it was possible to beat the odds if I kept my head down.

They were able to see it from the outside, looking in at the county and its circumstances. Those folks could see the opportunity, how it was potentially lucrative, and how the rest of the country was doing while rising out of the recession. They knew it wasn't normal for kids in their twenties to be able to afford $50,000 trucks and $400 dinners and to invest in stocks, real estate, and lackadaisical purchases of nonsensical luxuries.

It gave me balance, being informed by their macro insights into my micro hustle. They asked questions and gave solid insight into how I should plan for the future, where to invest, how to mend the mind during tough times, who not to marry, what sights to see on this earth before I died, which drugs to try and which ones to never try, what the most important parts of contracts are, how to choose an attorney, how to fly fish, what the international steel trade is, and how to write a book and "be true to the story you have to tell."

I met some of those individuals for a drink or small bite to eat in later years. We worked on my five-year plan and caught up on each other's lives. There were romantic encounters with women who escaped from their busy Los Angeles or Denver lives. There were trades with successful tech entrepreneurs—a quarter pound of fresh weed in exchange for some tips on good startups worth watching.

My solo last suppers were my secret evening staycations away from my inner circles, my dates with myself, my moments away from my family, my relationship, my employees, and my daily grind. In the end, those conversations made me feel less dammed up.

At the end of each last supper, I always felt empowered and full of clarity about where I was in life. Each night, I walked out of the restaurant into the cold, salty mist. My gut nervously reminded my conscious mind what was at stake the next morning. It also got me motivated and focused on how to achieve financial security and keep the *Open* sign on the business illuminated. I needed to find a way to always have last suppers, and someday I hoped to be retired and able to sit with a young person and watch them feel empowered and understood.

This particular night, the craziness of my morning consumed me. The payload was big, the risk bigger, and the dealers had been getting "hotter," it seemed, on the radar of enforcement. I had been told six months before that over $1.5 million worth of product was "lost in transit" with the individuals I was scheduled to meet in the morning. I needed to change the rate at which nervousness seemed to be taking over my enjoyable evening.

My tipsy mind and full stomach told me it was too early to go back to the house and start packing for the morning transaction. Instead, I chose to quickly slide into the back cab of the truck and took a couple of bumps of false confidence and distraction. Then I walked below the restaurant along the sand over to the caves at the north end of the beach. The sand was dry and still warm from the sun rays earlier that day even as mist hung in the air.

Tucked up against the largest rock face just around the tree line near the parking lot was a nice driftwood campfire glowing up the side of the rock and bleaching the misty night sky. Five people sat around the fire on large, old, weathered logs, all in jeans, wool socks, sweaters, and beanies. One set of arms danced in shadow against the rock face as each hand landed on the bongos lodged between his knees, and I saw a silhouette of a woman and her guitar through the flames. The other three passed around a Hydro Flask. They all watched one young man practice his fire stick routine some fifteen feet away. It was a beautiful California Humboldt Sunday night beach spectacle.

Gazing at the fire stick spin into a circle in the sky, I had an overwhelming admiration for them, and I longed to be able to do something like that. My social life outside of my now ex-girlfriend and coworkers trapped behind a gate for two and a half months was nonexistent. I spent most of my time with my dog, working on projects I couldn't tell anyone about, or going on trips I felt uncomfortable describing to friends due to the lavish, expensive, and erotic foreign experiences. I wanted to be more social, to have moments like that with people. I doubted that any of them sitting around the campfire would be going to pick up over a few hundred bands of cash at 6:30 the next morning and disperse it throughout the county. But who knows, maybe they brought it with them.

The thought brought me a satisfying itch but more sadness from realizing how much I had been working and hiding from healthier aspects of a life well lived. Would I still have friends later? Would I ever be able to talk about how my day went? It had been over four years since I graduated from college and left that double life I had been living, but I was still very much living it, unwilling to admit it, and aggressively cultivating it with unhealthy precision.

· · ·

Back at my little coastal bungalow an hour later, I placed the nozzle of a household vacuum into the fifteenth bag and pushed the *on* button, and the black contractor bag immediately started to mold around the twenty pounds of fresh product. Within a second, the bag took the shape of twenty-five solid black plastic rectangular cubes. After tying the top in a tight knot, I sprayed the top with Windex and the sides with Febreze, then took it to the guest room closet, lifted and stacked it atop the other fourteen, shut the closet door, opened the ironing board, and stuck it in front of the closet with a wrinkled collared dress shirt and the iron. It helped me sleep, not being able to see the units on the nights before a "surfing session."

Product is never stored at home, ever. Well, except for the night before.

Next, it was out into the night sky and over to Zeus into the driveway. I opened the driver's back cab door, hung the nicely pressed work shirt and jeans on the hook, placed my cowboy boots on the back seat, leaned over, and pulled my firefighting bag toward the middle of the back seat. Everything would be nicely visible for an officer looking in the passenger window were I to be pulled over in the early hours with three hundred cans of paint in the back of the truck. Every time, everything had to be thought through. On the floorboard was my DeWalt tool bag.

"Shit," I muttered. "Why not? Might help me calm down and sleep." I was getting dangerously used to the enjoyable, unusual effect cocaine had on my hyperactive brain; it calmed and relaxed me.

Grabbing the hard plastic yellow drill bit case, I locked Zeus for the night and walked to the little redwood carriage shed behind the house. It was dark, wet, and rotting with redwood mold. I loved the smell, though; it was the smell of my childhood.

In the dark, shutting the rolling barn door and meandering across the rooted floor to the workbench, I pulled the light cord. The spiders, mice, and other critters scurried to their hiding coves. I grabbed the small, old framed antique California citrus farming poster, set it on the counter, poured out the contents, chalked up a huge sidewalk, and railed it up into my nose. The flavor was instant and, sadly, comforting.

My breath slowed as my tongue meandered around the roof of my mouth. I immediately chalked up another, then brushed the better half of a gram into a small brown lunch bag. I then turned off the light and opened the barn door. I walked over to the garden hose, opened the brown bag, filled it with water, then poured it on the misty lawn. I already wanted more. When it came to my increasing coke habit, my isolation was leading to a loss of traction on my fragile self-control. But I knew how to deal with this shit, and I knew that on a night like this, two monster lines were all I got. Water on the rest would secure my self-control.

The cool, wet coastal night air felt great on my cheeks and wrists. I was calm, content, and almost done with the cycle of turning "clones," baby plants, into cash with this load. It was mid-September, and I had made these clones back in January out at the river.

Back in the barn with the light glowing once more, I grabbed the long surfboard I hadn't used in years and carried it to the grass behind the truck. Then I did the same with the open Rubbermaid tote that held my wetsuit, booties, gloves, and the chewed-up Frisbee that Rue enjoyed when we went to the beach. I placed it on top of the surfboard.

When I yanked the cord, the light went out overhead in the barn. The only light left was a glow from the open cell phone sitting atop the *One Way* sign that had been turned into a shelf. On the shelf sat a couple of antelope skulls. I stood there with only the soft sound of droplets of cumulated mist falling from the eve and landing on the planks in front of the doorway. My mind was calm, but my heart raced as I leaned over, placed the cut piece of straw to my left nostril, and vacuumed up the other rail I had left waiting for my return.

I took the rag that hung from the horn of the antelope skull hanging on the wall above the workbench and wiped off the Peruvian residue and just stood there in stillness, staring at the old California citrus advertisement behind the glass.

It had been Rachel's, an original she hung in the Chalet when the paint had finally dried. I wondered where Rachel was at that moment while I was in an old, wet, moldy redwood shed at 11:30 at night, railing coke lines and preparing for a drug deal in the morning. It had been many years since the evening we watched our last sunset on the mountain together—the sunset of our partnership, our relationship, and friendship. She was probably somewhere in Europe, in a classroom or office that Monday morning, living a life there, I presumed, on her way to getting a great job and fulfilling her goals. Not here in this cold, wet barn or growing weed in those crazy hills of a confused and bitter county. Clearly, all those I had started with had made the right choice. Gotten "out of the game."

"Don't go there," I told myself in a whisper.

In the immediate aftermath of the breakup, my thoughts about our relationship were of its tribulations—unfaithful nights, yelling, making up, being inseparable, long distances, and chaos. Those thoughts were fed with anger, lust, sadness, and comparison. Ah, the addiction of the toxic tincture of the mind as it spirals, trying to find a reason for an unreasonable reality. "Oops, I went there," I whispered to my mind louder.

A loud diesel truck drove on the street in the distance, and the sloshing of wet tires whined up the lane. The white glow from the aftermarket headlights lit up the houses under the redwood canopies for a few seconds. The sound and light yanked me from my emotional rabbit hole of memories.

"You're tired," I said.

I wondered if cute agriculture ads for California weed would ever become antiques hung on people's walls above conversations where onlookers discussed how odd it must have been when that was illegal.

I laughed, thinking about an antique image of the twenty-five cubes wrapped in black plastic and stacked in an old, funky closet. But the morning would hopefully prove to be another successful transaction. It was time to head to bed.

. . .

The rattling of the alarm chimes woke me at 4:14 a.m. I felt surprisingly rested from the nice last supper and a couple of bumps for dessert the night before. It was still early. Dark, heavy, cold mist hung in the air, and tinsel crystals reflected the beauty of the towering redwoods.

The cold floor permeated my socks as I walked over to the small kitchen stovetop and turned the flame on to start warming a kettle of water to a boil. Over in the fireplace, small, slow flames were emerging from under the last log, silently requesting an injection of oxygen to bring new life to her red coals. After tossing some two-by-four scraps and fanning the logs with a paper plate, I got her ripping and brought light and warmth to the room. I walked back to the stove, grabbed the kettle, and poured the water onto the grounds in a French press. It was time to work out the options.

Option 1: It could be a pleasant Humboldt-County-GDP type of day. A nice chunk of the funds was for me. The remaining chunk would go to a good friend and his wife, with everyone paid and everything wrapped up by 8:30.

Option 2: Unavoidable and unbeatable legal woes.

Option 3: Maybe this time I would get robbed by these gangsters.

A log fell in the woodstove and cut off the thought process.

"Let's rodeo," I said out loud as I aggressively pushed the strainer in the French press through the hot water and into the grounds, making the coffee as dark as the night.

I turned on a little flashlight, set it on the ground by the back door, and walked through the grass around the house by the little barn to the back of Zeus. The whole area was almost pitch black, but my eyes and muscle memory knew each step. I had done this too many times at this hour or late at night.

I raised the camper shell window, and the tailgate lowered slowly. Then I went back to the house. It took seven trips from the bedroom closet out the back door and to the back corner of the house, where I stacked the twenty-five bags—three hundred pounds. I leaned the surfboard against the side of the truck so that if my neighbors down the driveway heard me, they would see the surfboard against the truck and the back camper window open and assume I was heading out for a dawn swell, which was a reasonably common activity for that hour in this community—and my alibi.

Up went the tailgate, slowly, slowly holding the latch open. Then I let it close with a soft click. I slid the surfboard in, the fins catching the tailgate and left to protrude a couple of feet. Then in went a tote and the wetsuits, plus accessories, right into the bed of the truck. I grabbed one wetsuit and a pair of booties to throw on the passenger seat.

I left my little lunch pail on the floor but visible. Slowly bringing the back window down, I used one lightly colored bungee cord attached to the bumper to hold the window down. A moment later, I returned from the barn with the bottle to spray fuel into the bed of the truck and onto the back bumper.

I briskly walked back into the house, checked the fireplace, poured another cup of coffee, glanced around the dark house, and tapped the sign above the front door that read *You are beautiful.* Then I locked the deadbolt, slipped my boots back on, and went back out into the dark morning air. As I approached the truck, I tapped the back windshield, telling Zeus, "Saddle up; we're going surfing."

Looking back, I can only remember a couple of drives after the second year of "the cause." It got to the point where I was driving large amounts of weed somewhere for a good nine months out of the year, a couple of times a week minimum. I merged onto the dark and empty highway. It was a long straight shot to the Trinidad exit, lined with tall redwoods from the Westhaven on-ramp.

There was a logging truck racing north as I merged on, a couple of other big rigs heading south, and me and my large pickup truck Zeus. That was all. It was a quick and relaxing couple of miles listening to Garth Brooks as I had done many times.

When I exited into Trinidad at 6:18 a.m., the sky was just starting to shift from black to gray. From the off-ramp, I turned into the little town of Trinidad toward the four-way stop that acts as the little coastal town's gateway. On the left was the little one-room bait and surf shop, which had its lights on but didn't seem to be open yet. The grocery store wasn't open, and the other little shops were also dark. Their prime hours were during the afternoon.

On the right was the Chevron station, which was open twenty-four hours. The town was free of vehicle traffic. As I approached the four-way stop, I noticed three black SUVs parked in the side parking lot of the gas station. Their orange running lights created enough glow to read the word on the door panels—*Sheriff*. It was a Monday at 6:21 a.m.

Huh, I thought as I came to a full halt at the intersection. I pulled forward. Three on one. I felt like a salmon about to swim upriver past a line of bears and a massive hook. From my experience in the rodeo or just my crazy nature and out-of-the-box thinking, I put my right blinker on to pull into the gas station. I drove through the intersection, passing them on my left, pulled under the well-lit cover of the pumps, and rolled to a stop at the green diesel nozzle. The truck was placed perfectly so they could see the surfboard. The back window was unlocked, and there was apparently nothing I was hiding in my grow-dozer of a truck on this early cold morning.

"Morning, hon!" the clerk yelled from behind the big stove in the kitchen behind the counter. "Out at it early again this morning?"

"Happy Monday, Darci!" I had to yell over the old country music and sizzling grill. "Them breakfast burritos smelling great this morning. I'll take a bacon, crispy with potatoes, light cheese."

"OK, sweetie, coming right up. The breakfast blend over there is fresh. The rest is from some hours ago. Just made it for the boys out there."

I was beyond good on coffee and still riding high on adrenaline and possibly some snowball residue from the night before, but she had created a conversation starter that was perfect for me—or maybe she knew that.

"Yeah, saw them out there," I said, referring to our appreciated men in uniform, still sitting patiently outside in their vehicles. I knew they were right outside the window, but I didn't check. I knew they would be watching our interaction, and I liked that it would take some time for the burrito to be finished. Pouring the coffee gave me some structured distraction from the uneasy feeling hanging over the moment.

Darci yelled again from over the stovetop. "About an hour ago, there was a couple strung-out derelicts across the way at da bus stop. They were yelling and throwing up and all the classic Humboldt, late-night, spun-out antics these characters we deal with nowadays do."

"What, really? Damn." I looked up at the clock above the register. I had six minutes to be at the house with the load, or they would start to worry.

"Yeah. Well, I locked the door for the twenty or so minutes it took for those boys to get here. You're in the clear this morning. They just waiting around to go watch the sunrise at the lighthouse in a few minutes," she said with a wink as she walked the foil-wrapped burrito to the front counter.

"Thanks, Darci. You packing back there? You start early."

"I probably am," she said with a smile. "See you later. Enjoy the surfing."

She turned around and walked back to the grill, laughing. I left a twenty in the tip jar. I got in the truck, took a slight deep breath in through my nose, adjusted the radio, drove past the three deputies, and nodded.

The house was about a mile and a half up the coast. It sat on about an acre with a nice privacy hedge and gate around the front. I was about five minutes late—reasonable but not approved. The gate began opening the moment Zeus's lights shone on the wood carving nailed to its center.

I pulled through and parked around the side of the house by the RV garage. The place was immaculate with its landscaping. It was still cold, dark, and misty. Dew hung from the Japanese maples and rhododendrons lining the softly lit gravel driveway. I could hear the faint sound of the waves crashing against the rocks behind the house. No exterior lights were on; they never were.

I knew the drill. Back the truck up to the gate beside the garage. The gate would be open. Let my eyes adjust to the darkness. Then quietly empty the bed of the truck with the twenty-five cubes. Stage the cubes next to the French doors that led to the master bedroom. Then into the dark bedroom they would go.

Sometimes, I marveled at the creativity of this green vein of business. The covert, just-veiled-enough methods we all simultaneously knew and didn't know. To us in the weed industry, secrets were business as usual. The ability to keep those secrets was vital. The need to deliver on your word was as firm as a statute. The constant anxiety of not slipping up was exhausting. The reward—well, the reward was very satisfying in the short term. It felt like a long rodeo season. Just trying to deliver product to what felt like a never-ending demand over and over again. Holding tight to the reins eight seconds at a time.

CHAPTER 32

The Rush Gets Darker in Winter

ONE YEAR PRIOR—WINTER 2013

THAT WINTER, I was working on the house I had bought, and I remodeled a section to start my plants. I finally had a place to do it. We made a nice secure room. I was secluding myself from all my local friends and anybody but those who worked with me. During the first four or so years, growing was the only major part of my life that I needed to hide and suppress. My whole life seemed broken into two parts—my life behind the gate and most of my life in front of it. I was depressed. I accepted that it was what I was doing; I was just a weed grower.

Every day was becoming filled with drama and riddled with risks. The stories and gossip during elbow talks were turning darker in subject matter. Houses were being shot up, and home and ranch invasions seemed to occur weekly. The downward spiral of the green rush seemed to have started. The itch had become a rash, and now it was an open and infected wound. It was festering in our environment and our community—both for those involved and those not.

The community bulletin board in the grocery store was filled with three types of posts: firewood for sale, missing dogs, and missing persons. The last made up the majority. I had lost a few more friends that year to overdoses.

I lost a close childhood friend who crashed her four-wheeler going to shut her gate, broke her neck, and died along our ranch roads. Noah's son tragically chose to hang himself on the property one afternoon. One of the guys who had ridden his dirt bike and inadvertently diverted the attention of the helicopter pilot all those years before did the same. An Iraq War veteran hired to help with the harvest played Russian roulette with himself around the campfire, as did a close friend and mentor of mine; both lost. Two neighbors shot each other while high on meth, thinking someone was breaking in; it was just the two of them. Another childhood friend died in a DUI on his way back from gambling; his two passengers were hurt badly. One of those passengers, a local grower, later OD'd from an addiction that gave temporary comfort during his own battles. Other friends I grew up with who got into the weed game were getting crops cut, being handcuffed, and having cases thrown at them. "The Hollywoods," as some people had nicknamed the fast-living area around the growing weed industry in Humboldt, was fueling the explosion of self-created celebrity status, living the life of a "pot star."

That was the dark side of the massive, lucrative, and secretive weed game in the rural hills of Humboldt. A war with each other, ourselves, and society was in full bloom. In 2013, many of my local industry friends were quickly getting into harder drugs. Even I started saying, "Sure, I'll have some," more often than not. The cash, the insane entrepreneurial work ethic, the "work hard, play hard" mentality, and the lack of structure were too powerful, providing easy reasons, opportunities, and excuses to unravel at the seams.

It was no problem finding people wanting to buy the product. People came from all over the country saying, "Gimme, gimme."

The county was experiencing an explosion in its economy. Members of "the industry" (as our generation of growers was called) were revered by the public and in a local theatrical play depicting the history and culture of weed in Humboldt. It was true, and it was obvious that members of "the industry" were getting way more confident. Pot stars were becoming easy to spot and stereotype. Girlfriends were wearing $1,000 designer heels and driving Porsches and new, dusty luxury SUVs to dinner, ordering the pricier bottles of champagne and wine. I, too, was becoming guilty on all counts.

You could see it in the sagging eyes of all of us in the industry—the lack of sleep and the aching necks from constantly looking over our shoulders. The trucks were getting bigger; the risks were getting bigger; the losses were getting bigger; the piles of cash and the mounds of drugs were all getting bigger, getting faster, the environmental destruction exponentially expanding across the hills. Wads of cash were thrown around; the bets at the casinos were larger, the losses more compounding on fiscal and mental health. The harvest parties were massive, hosting top DJs from around the country.

The industry had gone from quiet, secretive, and dangerous to loud, blatant, and obnoxious. In a matter of twenty-four months, the golden train had left the tracks, and the golden goose was ready to fly south with her eggs. It was noticeable. The basket was full, and it was dirty. The industry couldn't be tamed, and those involved at the top were beginning to lose hold. Outsiders had flocked in and began eating the golden local eggs.

I was the last neighbor on the mountain out of the original four. Death and destruction, suicide, overdoses, and busts had netted the other three.

Things were getting so "Hollywood." I finally thought, *I need seclusion and calmness.*

And even though I could obtain seclusion and calmness, it worked against me. I created seclusion and calmness on both sides of my life—the Hollywood weed side and the personal life side—where I shouldn't have. I pushed away the woman I was dating by being a man unworthy of dating such a wonderful lady. I even drove away friends who were positive influences. I drove everyone away. And when I did, it just gave me more time and space for bad behavior. Soon, my depression really started kicking in.

Even though I did drugs once a week and drank excessively a few nights a week, I was the healthiest I had been in a while. I found myself in a pattern of trying to overcompensate when I needed to find balance rather than elimination. I was running on the beach, going on hikes by myself, and working out. But I wasn't talking really to anybody.

I realized I couldn't keep a solid relationship. Even the girlfriend I had been dating on and off would come and check on me in off times.

"How are you doing? You don't want to go out?"

"No, I don't want to go to that party. I'm good."

I was beginning to choose to party alone more often than not. Alone with my thoughts, I had tried to take one step toward betterment. Despite my efforts, I was still under the negative influences of drugs and alcohol. Instead of cutting out substances, I had cut myself off from those around me.

The darkness felt like a repeat of what happened right before I got into the industry. I didn't want to be around anybody local—anyone I'd been affiliated with when I started this.

CHAPTER 33

It's Gone

SPRING 2014

IN 2014, a few growers approached me and asked me to help them get into the light-deprivation game. I agreed to help them, although my conscience was screaming at me. *Haven't you learned? You idiot.*

But the thought of more greenbacks and having others grow and take care of it was just too attractive. We were going to be harvesting a full term for them in October. It was planted out in the sun on a spot we leased, neighboring my aunt's land. They were 100 percent in control of it; I just checked on it every couple of weeks.

Simultaneously, our whole operation was going normally. We harvested everything early, and they still had two months to go. Part of our deal was that they could trim and dry in my barn. They trimmed it all and put it in the correct, secure place. I felt it was safest up there.

In December, my now-on girlfriend and I were going to spend Christmas at my river house. We had met right before I went on a four-month trip around the globe, visiting eight countries. We continued to talk as I traveled, and I flew her out to see me in Rio, where we decided to start officially dating. She probably thought I would get out of the growing business for her. The trimming and having tons of women living on your property for a few months a year was not conducive to any long-term relationship.

I should go up there before Christmas and grab the weed, I thought, looking forward to staying at the river house. The few weeks before that, I was thinking I needed to get the product moved—I knew I could get rid of it all right after the New Year. So the day after Christmas, my girlfriend and I drove up.

My girlfriend was a local who had grown up with fear around the industry. She had a job where she needed to keep it very secret even though the people she worked with had partners and spouses who grew. It was tough hiding the secret we all knew.

That was only her second time at one of the properties in two and a half years. She never wanted to see it or anything. It was very hard to manage that dichotomy. I couldn't and didn't blame her for the feelings she had. They were reasonable. They were valid. The industry and local economy were progressing and expanding faster than fear and feelings of disapproval and disgust she and many other locals had felt for years.

We had a tough relationship, but she was supportive as disaster struck.

As I neared my property, I noticed a quad trailer hidden in the trees near the gate, a half mile from where I'd last left it. That was odd—a bad sign. When I got closer—another mile onto the property—I saw that the container was wide open and that the padlock was missing, as was the product. I glanced in for a split second. It was gone.

I walked down to my house, sat on the deck, and almost threw up. I was distraught. I wanted to kill someone, but I didn't know who, although it was most definitely someone local or an insider of our operations. Someone had used my quad trailer to load up the product, wheel it down to the gate, where another vehicle must have been waiting, and steal all the weed—or made it seem like that's how it was done.

"We are going to go back to the river house to stay the night," I said. Shock and anger at myself numbed my boiling blood. After just glancing at the mountains in the distance and feeling the ground beneath my boots, I knew it was hopeless to try to find clues. The scene was cold, and misty clouds hung in the air of that December day. Any evidence would be long gone, and clues weren't going to magically make the product reappear out of the frozen atmosphere. I was too bitter with myself to be mad yet at the thieves.

We picked up a nice dinner and two small bottles of Jameson. Then we sat down along the river shore and drank it all. She went back to the coast, and I stayed at the river for a week and just went to a local full-on backwoods honky-tonk bar and got drunk every day. One of the nights, I closed down the bar, and the bartender I knew came on to me, and I kept that a secret. It happened with another woman a few days later. Up to that point, I partied and drank, but it was always when going to a concert, a college party, or New Year's Eve in Thailand. After the robbery, I started drinking as a way of medicating, suppressing my surroundings and numbing myself to the crazy grind of being an outlaw grower. I drank to help accept that no matter what I did I could never really turn "the business" into an actual business. That was infuriating to my soul. Drinking no longer was a social thing. It was a medication that led to the need for more medication.

I didn't know what was developing at the time, but I started realizing that I drank more when I took myself out to eat. I would have a fine cocktail with dinner and a glass of champagne. Then I would have three or four more cocktails. There were more substances coming into my life. There was more debauchery. There was death occurring all around me. Loss of property and arrests all around me. Loss of product, loss of money, loss, loss, loss.

After a weird ten-day period of drunken poor decisions, a friend of mine had his birthday in Vail, Colorado.

"Dude, I can't spend any money right now," I told him. "I just got robbed."

He insisted. "I'm going to fly you out to Vail. I want you to celebrate my birthday with me. You've been there for me so much."

Years before, I got him and his wife a hotel room one time when they were stranded. He was doing great now.

I went into a fancy weed store in downtown Vail—the line was out the door. They had to buy the building next door for a waiting room. I looked at the line and saw every walk of life. There was an executive from Duke Energy there. There were women in their fifties. It wasn't the stoners I had imagined. My friend was talking to the lady in the lobby, who was giving us our stickers.

When we entered the store, the person in front of us was a sixty-year-old guy from Texas with two FedEx envelopes and a long list. The store had six cash registers going—it was wild. Each cash register had an ATM next to it. I looked at the whole thing in complete awe as I stood in line. It felt like I was at a ski shop or a nice jewelry store, not an efficient, high-end weed store. As I looked over the product, I noticed that the customers were relaxed and laid back.

We finally got to the counter.

"What do you want?"

I had no idea, so I spent $300 on random stuff I wasn't even going to use. As I was walking out, the cashier noticed that my sweatshirt read *Trinidad CA*.

"Oh, the owner is from near there. Northern coast of Cali, right? Let me go get him!"

He came out.

"Hey, you are from Trinidad?"

"No, I'm from near there."

"Oh, nice, you a grower?"

"Yep."

We exchanged small talk.

"Oh yeah, I grew up in Mendocino but never was in it, went to school in Boulder, and then was in real estate finance lending in Denver, and then I got into this," he said.

"Man, it looks like it is super successful."

"Yeah, we've already done close to eighty thousand dollars in sales this afternoon."

"What?"

My mind was blown.

"Yeah. It's a holiday weekend in Vail. We'll probably do about sixty million dollars in retail stores across the state this year."

"What?!" That was my "boom" moment. *OK, I'm doing this wrong. I'm doing this in the wrong place. There is an opportunity to do it right. This is happening. Legalization is happening in California. My Humboldt hamlet of weed is already being left behind in the game it created.*

I knew I needed to change. I needed to make moves. California voted down adult legalization the first time in 2010, but Colorado is a red-and-blue state. A conservative governor supported it, and legalization had passed there in 2012. California would undoubtedly put it on the ballot again—and next time, it would pass. Once the country saw Colorado and Washington go legal without the sky falling, others would follow.

I was living in a place profiting immensely off this that didn't want it to go legal because the sheriffs were making money, the growers were making money, the retail stores were making money, the restaurants were making money, the charities were making money, and the Targets were making money because all the back-to-school clothes were being purchased in cash because the growers were hiring local moms to trim. The whole economic side of it hit me while I was in that beautiful store in Vail.

My whole community survives off this.

We had a university and a hospital, and from what the county staff told us, 78 percent of the economy was run by weed at the time. We had lost logging and fishing, at least compared to their heydays. I could see that we were going to lose weed in the future too.

"This is why I wanted you to see this," my buddy said as we got back in the car.

"Hey, should I put this in the wheel well?" I was concerned that I needed to hide the weed. I couldn't quite grasp that it was legal and we didn't have to hide it.

"What? Why?"

"'Cause it's weed."

"You have the receipt, right?"

"Yeah."

"The state knows. It's all licensed product."

As I tried to wrap my head around the experience, I realized it was a turning point. "I've got to make a change," I said.

I felt clarity in my mind and slowed down to listen to my subconscious—to trust it. I always have the most clarity on airplanes, maybe because I'm stuck somewhere with my ADHD. On the flight home, I realized I'd been doing mass production with B-grade material, winning on quantity rather than quality. In the moments I spent in the store, I realized the emerging legal industry would be won by quality and presentation of products rather than quantity.

A week after I got back from Colorado, I started doing my research. But I still hadn't gotten over the rock-hard ball of anger and need for revenge that was taking anchor in my soul after the theft; every moment required constant effort to suppress it.

I never gave up on figuring out who did it, and I planned to retaliate when they had more to lose. Eventually, I learned the identity of the thieves. But by then I had decided I wouldn't turn to violence but instead learn to live with knowing who did it. It was better than them losing their lives and me getting double robbed by going to jail. I would not let it happen again, and I would thrive beyond my wildest dreams for the life I wanted. I had served the opportunity for theft to them on a silver platter, but they would have to live with the karma of their choices.

CHAPTER 34

Outlaw Outlier

SPRING 2015

AFTER I AWOKE from my month-long bender of booze, pow-ders, and women, and after returning from Colorado, I had to ac-cept who I was. I needed to let go of the alibis and the facades. They had become symbols of the fear that was controlling my life. Safety was important and still valid in certain scenarios, but as a whole, the control had begun to have a negative effect on me.

I turned off my phone for some days, as my relationship was once again shot.

I spent a few days at a lady friend's vacation home near Shasta Lake. During a forty-eight-hour molly binge, I finally accepted who I was: a grower, a weed businessman, a pot farmer, a weed man, whatever you want to call it. Almost eight years into my venture, I was finally able to allow myself to recognize my life for what it was. It was an incredibly powerful feeling.

Two days later, on a cold, crisp February morning, I walked down to the river. When I arrived at the shore, I stripped down completely naked. My head was pounding from the lack of vitamins, excessive drinking, and rare late-night cigarettes. As goosebumps covered my body, I waded out into the slow-running, clear, and frigid waters of the Trinity River.

"Oh, Holy Trinity," I breathed into fog that left my lips. I stood in the water up to my chest until I was numb, then dove completely under.

Moments later, I lay naked in the morning sun on the sand, steam rising from my body. As I dried off, "the itch" returned to my mind. My thoughts were clearer than they had been in weeks—maybe years.

"I'm a grower, I'm a grower," I told myself seven times in a row, a memory tactic I had implemented as a child.

"This is a business, this is a business," I said—again seven times.

"This is a lesson, and this is an opportunity," I said seven times. The damp towel I had wrapped myself in held in the last of my body's heat.

The moments of acceptance immediately followed the frigid baptism. I, the me, the myself, the who I am, was back. So was something else. The authentic itch of my early days, but this time on a leash of experience, wearing a collar of failures. I turned and looked up at the steep switchback trail that rose out of the river canyon. I thought of that famous saying about falling down. "Kid, it's how many times you get back up," I said out loud.

I reached down, picked up my hiking boots, and began walking up the trail barefoot.

"You need to feel every step on the way back up."

It was cliché but fact. The weeks that followed were full of planning, full of financial organization, full of learning, full of hustling. Over the next three months, I would move and broker 1,600 to 2,000 pounds of product. I was locked in and focused on squaring up with what I owed my hired help, my landlord, and my contractors.

I'd always been a super saver, which helped me drastically. So I had savings to pay mortgages and do business again. My business background had taught me to always expect exorbitant earnings to be temporary. I never thought I would make that kind of money again. I just needed a nice nest egg to make the transition. I could only trust myself to make that happen. *Back to working alone again.*

. . .

After getting robbed, I had to do a full grow on my own to pay off a couple of debts and consider the possibility of exiting the industry. I had a lot of savings but didn't want to touch it. I spent the entire spring building a grow alone, wearing my tool bags again, and began yelling "Lunch!" again to Rue and some friends' dogs I watched now and then.

The grow was in the meadow over at my Uncle Bob's cabin, where Rachel and I had lived eight years before. It was difficult living there alone doing all that. I still found her things in the back of junk drawers, in the bookshelves, or hanging in the shed—unwanted reminders reflecting like diamonds in the rough. The excessive solitude and overload of physical labor flowed easily. I started to compare myself to her and what seemed like her better choices. She chose to leave me, leave the industry, and continue on the path that we had originally decided on together as the reason for getting into the industry in the first place: a stepping stone, a leg up on our schooling and career trajectories.

I was back to doing it all alone on a large scale. I had employees running the mountain, but I was working full-time again on my own grow. It was seven greenhouses, 20 by 110 feet long, to be handled by only one person.

. . .

Efficiencies in engineering were the key. I had three alarm clocks. One sat on the little table on the right side of the couch. Another was on the kitchen counter. The third was my phone, placed on the bedside table. The first sang loud into the silent night at 3:58 a.m. The second was at 4:04, and my phone chimed at 4:10. The goal was to always be able to turn off the phone alarm before it sounded.

After turning off the kitchen alarm, I reached for the box of matches, turned the knob on the old RV stove, and lit the burner under the tea kettle. I walked over to the old La-Z-Boy chair with a cheap rug in front of it, grabbed my Carhartt pants, balanced my sleepy body on one leg, and put on the first half of my work jersey. Then I'd throw on the ratty long-sleeve shirt and sit in the chair to lace my Kmart steel-toe boots.

Right at that moment, the kettle whistled. Walking back across the room and past the woodstove, I reached up with my right arm and turned on the camping lantern hanging from the rafter joists over the kitchen area. The yellow glow filled the room as I turned off the gas to the stove.

As the tea steeped, I grabbed the big headlamp hanging on the front doorknob, turned on the green light, and wrapped my head with the elastic strap. Then I grabbed the 500k-candle spotlight and shined it through the window of the front door. It was imperative to check the porch, outdoor kitchen area, and yard for any unwelcome large furry overnight visitors before opening the front door. Once it was verified clear out front, I stepped out into the dark early morning air of the mountain. Taking the spotlight, I scanned the tree line, the driveway up to the cabin, and down past the little shed toward the six greenhouses below, then flashed it once more to ensure no eyes were peering back, no shadows moving between the thickets.

"Clear."

Next, I stood on the porch, the front door open, and filled my custom belt with my framing hammer and tactical knife. Then I tossed the strap of the spotlight over my head and shoulder, letting it hang on my right side. My breaths were slow and full over the next three or so minutes in the dark silence of the woods, standing there on the porch, living my isolationism, smelling my steeping tea, double-checking my safety. Even walking sounds can make one's heart stop when alone in the woods in the dark at 4:00 a.m. This morning was all good, though. All clear and ready for the next hour of work in the blackness of the night.

The tea went down smoothly, and the cold water from the sink on my face added to my pre-tarp ritual. Last, I grabbed my gloves off the little red table next to an old wooden folding chair on the porch and started my march to the tarps.

It was the fifty-third morning in a row. Twenty-one more to go. I was in the home stretch to that other green—green paper. I had become seasoned in my routine. The neighborhood deer, bears, and foxes had all become annoyed and uninterested in my obnoxious tasks at such an early hour.

One morning after pulling the six large tarps over the green-houses, I was scrambling my eggs on the outdoor stove and watching the last stars. The planet Mercury was flickering on the horizon. I remembered the question I had asked Trey in the garden shop in those early days: "Do you know anyone who has ever retired from this industry?" I realized growing wasn't worth it. The goals I had in life didn't seem obtainable by growing, no matter the fiscal reward. The negative reputation, banking problems, and lack of a sched-ule—I no longer had a regulator on myself. I had taught myself how to regulate the itch of the industry, but I was over it.

. . .

One evening that October, after the incredible success and bounty of my solo grow, a family friend of mine, a successful businessman, had flown in some other businessmen for an annual trip where, each year, they played poker and fished at an ocean house. He invited me to join them for an evening.

"Come have some beers in the evening. I want you to meet some of these people. I think it would be cool for you—healthy for your age and situation."

They were real estate investors and imported goods wholesalers. One was a big shipping logistics guy from Seattle who shipped computer products from Asia to the US. Apparently, he was part of the shift from making a lot of computer chips in Palo Alto and Seattle to moving the manufacturing to Asia and then importing the chips.

I was telling the logistics guy my story, and I said, "I got into this. I don't know why, and I don't know if it's who I am or if it can be scaled successfully. I'm starting to question all my ideas because it's a bad time."

I asked them as many questions as I could about their businesses, how they got started, what were their biggest mistakes, if they liked what they did, how they exited or whether or not they should exit at all.

In the middle of telling me a story about his business, a man named Bill asked, "What are your cost percentages? How much is your overhead, I mean."

After I went over the previous year's financials and the current year's costs, they seemed more impressed and eager to help with some guidance.

"The future of this industry here seems so uncertain," I said. "An inevitable extinction."

"Shoot, kid, all business is uncertain, but that weed can grow a lot easier and probably better elsewhere. One can be hill rich but will never be wealthy; there's a difference, you know."

"These numbers look outstanding but not lasting. I'm out. Like *Shark Tank*, get it?"

"Ha. Yeah, I get it. I hope these problems aren't lasting either, 'cause I think I'm out too." I laughed.

"You have issues now, not problems. You need to prepare your mind to deal with a new set of problems. The problems of doing business correctly. Come back and tell me your problems when you've got a hundred and fifty mouths to feed every two weeks and countless orders and vendors you're tracking daily."

"You're being modest with those numbers, Bill," another man said to him.

"Get out now or jump fully in. Either way, get out of here, then come back annually and play poker with us. Be relentless."

"I'm not sure it's for me anymore," I said.

They all paused for a few minutes as we watched a couple of seagulls circle the shoreline below the deck and settle on a rock for a late-afternoon hunt.

"You've got to read this book *Outliers*," one of the men said.

"What?"

"Go camping with your dog or something. Go on a little road trip and take your fishing pole. Take things you had before you got into this weed and just go back to being a chill guy, like a carpenter or whatever, and just go camping and take this book. Tell your girl-friend, 'I can't talk to you for a couple of days. I'm going to go read.' Then make your decision after you read this book."

I thought about my fishing pole and tent collecting dust in the barn—the thoughts I had of those nights in the barn while looking at them. His suggestion seemed like a sign.

Not long after that evening, I drove up to the Oregon coast and had a great time. I sat down and read the book *Outliers* by Malcolm Gladwell. His thesis was that your age, geography, where you are born, the year you are born, and things like that play into different successes and "divine opportunities" in different things.

For example, something like 80 percent of NHL all-stars were born in January because of the way the cutoff worked. Until they were ten years old, they played with older people. And then all of a sudden, there was a switch and they became the oldest. Steve Jobs was born in Palo Alto, right next to where the original computer companies were contracting with the military, and had access to their defunct computer parts for super cheap. The book was about having the right experience, being in the right place at the right time, and knowing that having the right access can lead to an odd business destiny.

I thought about my life, my childhood, my love for the woods, my skill sets, the current status of the laws in the industry, the timing, and how it all related to my life. I was truly an outlier in the weed industry. Maybe I wasn't an "outlaw," like the old farmer had told me at the gas station before that lightning storm drive. But I was an "outlier." My life, place, experiences, and timing all fit the thesis of the equation. Sum = I am an outlier in this cannabis industry.

"I'm going as legal as possible," I said as I finished the last page and closed the book. "This is my career."

$$\cdot\ \cdot\ \cdot$$

After reading *Outliers*, I took stock of my situation over the past years. I sold to some dispensaries in my second year but got ripped off every time. I left four pounds at one dispensary and they closed a few days later. Another time, I drove down to Southern California and got half the price I would have gotten had I stayed in Humboldt.

After a couple of years, we started overnighting the product to San Diego via an in-state courier service. I flew down in the morning, got to the house before the package arrived for the imaginary gal, then took it to the owner of a dispensary in the Gas Lamp district of San Diego, grabbed the donations, and flew home that night. I did that on the Alaska Airlines flight every other Tuesday for almost nine months. The product was sold at that dispensary in San Diego and the Disabled Veterans of America clinic in Oceanside near Camp Pendleton.

In the first and second years, I tried to do things by the book-ish but soon realized that just sitting and waiting for buyers to come to Humboldt and shop was the easiest and safest approach, just not the closest to a legal framework. But now, something had to change. That change was me.

I hired a local attorney who had been the sitting DA during my early growing years. I was determined to do it legally and start looking at stores openly operating under Proposition 215 because of what I had seen in Colorado, where it seemed so accepted without the stigma.

Since cannabis was already a billion-dollar industry in California at that point, there was no stopping it without getting the National Guard or something. I made a few quality business plans, got a few high-net real estate developers to consult with me, and started pitching. Everywhere I went to pitch that plan, meaning every municipality, they said, "Absolutely not. Nope, we don't need that."

I pitched everyone I could—members of the commercial real estate community, people with access to the county supervisors, successful and prominent architects and engineers with connections to the local building department. I showed them downtown Aspen, Colorado. I showed them videos and the approval process in Aspen, Boulder, Seattle, and Denver. They kept saying no. I got the most nos in the Emerald Triangle. It was constantly no, no, no.

Once I accepted that "no" was going to happen, things got a lot easier. I just kept going to places and conferences where yeses were happening. I went to a massive event at the Universal Orlando resort, where investors from all over the country and Europe gathered. *This is nuts. I'm in Orlando, Florida, where weed is incredibly illegal, and everybody is here openly meeting and talking about investing.*

During one of my trips to Colorado, one of my guys called from the grow. "Hey, they are evacuating all of our houses. A fire has started."

"You know what?" I said. "If it burns, it burns. There is nothing I can do. I got to have this time."

The ability to look within and admit you have done all you can is empowering, and so is the ability to accept it.

CHAPTER 35
The Call of the Owl
MAY 2015

I ATTENDED A CONFERENCE in Sacramento about legalization hosted by 420 College. I started studying. It was time to get in on the ground floor and make a change. The conference focused on the legal formation of a corporation and California's Proposition 215, the gray area. It was what you needed if you were going to build an as-legal-as-possible, not-for-profit cannabis business in California. It was my out. While, well, staying in.

I was feeling the itch of excitement, of developing something that might bring our hiding to an end. But I also feared the potential loss of the industry. Was the county finally admitting to the reality that weed was the tree of the county—not the redwood? As I spoke to engineers and local planning personnel to dig deeper into the amount of excavation work, permitting, and the like, my construction past and experience started to take hold.

After the conference, my mind processed new possibilities as I typed the report and one-sheets I was working on for the county and the newly formed Cannabis Alliance. I glanced out the same cabin window Rachel and I had used as a vent when we dried our first couple of crops.

She had called a few days earlier at six in the morning. It was evening her time. I had been loading up the truck at the cabin to head to the mountain.

"You've been spotted in my dreams lately," she said. It was the first time we'd spoken since our airport goodbye five years earlier.

My emotions fluttered.

"It didn't look good," she said. "You didn't look good."

Over the staticky line, I tried to tell her the new direction I was trying to go.

"You still growing on those mountains?"

"Yeah."

The topic changed as my answer affirmed her dreams and why she had called. Her voice played again in my head as it had constantly in the days since that call. *Get out of those hills. The Universe has a different plan for you now.*

I was bitter at the truth. I looked down into the meadow at the wheelbarrow, drying in the midafternoon sun, and the concrete pads I had poured that morning. I hadn't etched any names, dates, or sentimental statements like I had with her and other coworkers in the past. I was back to being alone in that cabin again for five months, eight years later.

Even though I was on a new path to going legal, my literal trajectory had stalled. Despite everything, I was in the same mountains where I had started. No longer was I damned if I did or if I didn't do what I had been doing the way I'd been doing it. Recreational use of cannabis by adults was legal in two states. The industry was shifting, even if only by subtle little shakes on the Richter scale.

You were in my dream. Her voice tornadoed through my mind again.

"You need to get out of those hills," she had said. "I used to tease you and try to guilt trip it out of you, help you hear your own consciousness, help you finally resolve that constant itch, as you call it. Now I'm telling you, get out of those hills. You've done all you can. You've conquered that goal, proved yourself a mountain man, and proved your self-sufficiency, but it's going to prove greater than you in a short time. I can feel it."

I also realized during that call that no part of me missed her or us. My detachment from those feelings gave an even stronger unbiased, acceptable, and partially unwanted truth to her dream. I trusted her fully for the first time in years.

The sun was a couple hours from setting. The direct orange glow began piercing through the windows, warming the space. Rue and three other dogs from the neighborhood were sleeping on the warm back deck. The shed hairs from their backs danced slightly from the afternoon breeze and floated into the surrounding trees. The constant pounding from a neighboring well that was being drilled all afternoon had disappeared, finally. It was quiet and calm in the valley and in my head.

"Come on, Rue."

She jumped to her feet and shook her body. I did the same. Some years before, each time the dogs stretched or shook, I'd started doing it as well. It was surprisingly helpful for the body and mind.

"Load up."

She ran through the house, her paws losing traction from the overexcitement. She was through the front door, off the porch, and into the front seats of the side-by-side souped-up golf cart in one bound. I tossed a faded beach chair, a cushion covered in dog hair, and a shotgun for protection into the small utility bed. In the center console, I placed two bottles of expensive wine and my canteen of iced lemon water. I gave Rue a knuckle handshake, and we drove up to The Rock.

After the chair and the Rue cushion were set up, I stripped completely naked, uncorked the first bottle of wine, and sat facing west—facing the future. "Face toward the Lewis and Clark unknown," as we used to say.

Being naked in nature when making my most important decisions or preparing for a life season change had become a thing of clarity and comfort. My mind was free to analyze and contemplate, allowing the rest of my body to be completely vulnerable, taking away the shackles and falsehoods of luxuries and the constraints of clothes down to the bare self so I could make the right choice. I wrapped my hand tightly around the neck of the bottle.

I repeatedly lifted my arm to guzzle delicious fermented grape juice and listened to the automatic firearms sing throughout the valley below. I chose to think quickly through each year from that morning, the most recent summer before, and back to the first drive up with Uncle Bob. I visualized each whole season and offseason. I remembered rest and exhaustion, confidence and fear, royalty and hunger, joy and sadness. I thought of all the different people I had worked with, people who had worked for me, people I sold to, people I bought from.

I made sure Uncle Bob received his 40 percent for the first three years. We could have bought a property for cheaper at that point, but we never planned on continuing. Failure and circumstance made that happen.

Jarod gave me the original plants because he believed in passing it on, giving another person a shot at it. I always kept that giving spirit with me and never forgot that if it weren't for those first free and incredibly healthy plants and an opportunity, I would never have taken the fork in the road into the weed industry or succeeded.

I thought of rushing water, and I thought of dried plants, heavy buds, and heavy molds. I thought of beautiful meteor showers in August and of hallucinating at angry skulls scolding me in the dark night skies of October. I was reminded of all the failures and the loss of plants due to hailstorms, windstorms, bears, bugs, mold, laser-cut gates, and upset stomachs. I thought of being robbed, losing product in transition, and crashed and dented vehicles.

Forest fires.

Rattlesnakes.

Hunters.

Helicopters and airplanes.

Travels.

Death.

I thought of Trey's list of things to watch out for and avoid. I thought of how most of them had been checked off with experience. I thought of the overwhelming burden of secrets my cranium had to hold in and carry through my daily grind. I thought of the days Rue almost died. I thought of the days I should have died. I contemplated my arrogance, how I wouldn't look back or focus on the past. I had learned the only way to break a cycle and not create a new version of your own past is to reflect on it and learn from it.

I hadn't taken a moment like this in ages. I thought back to the times I had taken a moment. They had all been right before a major life paradigm shift. I visualized all the years like a whole amusement park ride. It was some chaotic, colorful, and exciting game board. I kicked a couple of large timber ants off the tops of my toes.

"Flashback," I joked to myself.

As I came back to recounting my journey on the green brick road over the years, where I was, where one would have thought I should have been, and the vicious back-and-forth of self-sabotaging thoughts, a couple of things were clear. I loved the ride—all of it. Even the parts I hated, I loved. I loved how hard it had been physically and how destructive it had been emotionally—my graying hair and drooping eyelids. I marveled with excitement over how dangerous, sexy, stupid, and brilliant it was, and I was, all at the same time. I thought of all the breakups, the dates, and the pure human wildness unfit to write about.

Then I paused my thoughts and brought myself back to the most important thing: the plants. I smiled at just how much I loved the plants. From their strong seeds to how they first cracked their little seed shells and out popped a start, the two small green leaves that stretched to a height where they couldn't hold themselves up, the exploding foliage like the true weeds they were, the shift toward flowering and the color changes in the final weeks before harvest.

I smirked at the testosterone boost I always got from the business process, the transport logistics, and the commerce of it all. I was proud of the colossal magnitude of the industry. I loved the perfect little safe balance in a gray area of geographic and judicial safety where it lived. I thought of the legal advancements the industry had experienced since I started my livelihood that only consisted of offerings from a plant. At that thought, goosebumps covered my naked body. I rose out of the chair to let more rays from the evening sun reach me. The wine immediately warmed my stomach and lifted my bloated cheeks in a smile.

I reflected on, compared, and processed the data, read the past, and admitted to the inevitable writing on the wall. Subconsciously, as I stood gazing out over that valley at a couple hundred large rural parcels containing various greenhouses and flats for the season planting ahead, I accepted the data. I accepted what it was telling me.

"I can't do this anymore. At least not out here, nor do I want to. Listen to your own screaming subconscious before it loses its voice."

Seconds after saying that out loud, Rue looked up and behind us from her cushion, then up and over me. I turned to find what her eyes had been tracing. A large owl flew no more than ten feet from us, slowly passing. Any slower and it would have fallen out of the sky. It hovered just on the edge of The Rock, twenty feet in front of us, searching for possible dinner options, perhaps. The sun's rays highlighted such detail in the feathers of its skull and perfect symmetry of its wing tips. A long moment later, it turned back and glanced at Rue and me.

I naturally held the bottle of wine up in a toast and salute. The owl's head turned forward, then it dove down across the hillside like a rocket through the wooded watershed. I watched until it disappeared into the glare of the sun.

"Wisdom flying westward, Rue. Damn, if that ain't a sign of conviction in a decision, I don't know what is."

Rue lowered her head, snuggled her snout further into the cushion, and shut her eyes. But it was the message I needed. When the first transcontinental railroad across the United States was finished in 1869, the owner drove a golden spike into the ground to join the Central Pacific Railroad and the Union Pacific Railroad. This was my perilous golden spike in life's path of fate. It was the confirmation of a change. In Greek mythology, the goddess Athena was thought to symbolize wisdom and was often depicted with an owl nearby. That was probably inspired by the owl's big eyes and solemn appearance. The Greeks also thought owls had an inner light that let them see at night.

"I'm really done this time," I said. With a "cheers" for the sun, I poured a sip out to the owl.

Rue's ears perked up, and her nose and eyes stayed down. I heard a quad engine coming up the ravine. Moments later, I caught a glimpse of it as it approached on the switchbacks below our wine lookout. It was anti-Babylon Noah and his dog. I put on my clothes, surprised to see another person but excited about who it was. *Right on time, Universe.*

After a few moments of catching up, I told him my decision.

"I'm done out here. The industry ain't crushing it no more; it's only crushing me."

"I've been watching it crush you for years, brother," he said.

"I know."

"How can you be done when you've got five thousand two-foot-tall plants under those greenhouses ready to be planted in three weeks?"

"It will have to be after this season sometime," I thought out loud, realizing my preset internal goals. "Maybe after two seasons."

"Shoot, you ain't done, kid. You're the king of the rodeo out here," he replied, opening his arms and hugging the sun's warming rays and the sight of the Pacific on the horizon. "You're just in a bunch and tipsy with your thoughts 'cause she called a couple days ago. From that empty bottle I see under your sweatshirt and the half you got left in your hand, you seem to be overtaking me lately on the throne of the devil's juice."

"It ain't the devil's juice," I said. "It's only if we allow the devil to ride the raft on in as we pour it down our throats. Follow?"

"Good luck holding him back on that liquid current," he mocked me. We both chuckled, knowing all too well the juice owned us. We didn't own the juice.

"You have said you're done before every round-the-world trip you've gone on these last few years, and at the start of every year, you say, 'I think this is the last for x, y, z reasons.' Just never seem to make it that far down the alphabet of affirmation in your false statements."

He was right; I had said all those things. We stood motionless as a spotter plane traveled overhead from an early spring surveillance and reconnaissance mission.

"An owl came and said hello to Rue and me here ten minutes ago. I came up here to make the decision."

"Oh," he said and paused. "Brother, well then, the decision has been made. Make the date."

"Date?" I asked, still visualizing the weightless strength of the owl, defying gravity with the silent wisdom it ushered into our surroundings as it hung in the updraft in front of me.

"The last day you will be a grower in these hills. What day will it be, brother?"

I thought for a moment as the screech of a red-tailed hawk echoed against the rock face.

"October sixteenth, 2016, brother."

"Don't tell me. Tell these mountains. Tell this rock. Tell the rain in the clouds above. Tell that setting sun out there. Tell Jesus. Tell Buddha. And most importantly, tell yourself. Tell yourself with such strong permanence and perpetuity that you wouldn't ever be able to backtrack on the oath you are telling yourself."

We stood silently for another twenty minutes, a common occurrence in our friendship, watching the views of nature broadcast.

"October sixteenth, 2016," I said stern and low six times. Then I took a deep breath and glanced a couple of miles into the distance as the lights came on in one of the greenhouses tucked into the hillside. I said it a seventh time at the top of my lungs.

"October sixteenth, 2016! Amen."

I went to the cart and grabbed the shotgun, walked back up onto The Rock, and unloaded three rounds into a rotted snag.

Noah gave me a hug. "Good pray, brother, good pray."

The sun disappeared into the swells on the horizon.

The decision had been made, and a deadline had been set. Noah left The Rock while Rue and I packed up our belongings, empty bottles, and used shotgun shells. As I was about to start the side-by-side, I looked east at the purple, darkening sky. Stars began to appear alongside bright reflections from the setting sun.

"Stars, stars, stars," I said softly, and Rue howled.

There are moments in all our lives when a fork in the road becomes a life-altering shift.

It was time. It can be a hard battle with your ego, with your self-honored accomplishments. It can feel like you're quitting—like you're throwing in the towel.

But it's not quitting, and you're not throwing in the towel. You are reassigning and rebalancing the table of life, as Bob liked to say. If you know there is something greater out there for yourself, then go forth toward that.

Sometimes you have to disassemble to rebuild.

CHAPTER 36

Orange Glow

FALL 2016

BY FALL 2016, I was building a life in Sacramento. I'd found a business partner, William, and we were working to build our business. However, I still needed funds to build the Sacramento operation, so I had the three operations built, planted, harvested, and finished up on the mountain. The new venture would cost way more to build than anything I had ever done in Humboldt. It was so chaotic trying to do everything all at once. But it would be legal—finally.

I told everyone I was getting out and starting over in Sacramento. I had lost so much weight that summer that close friends told me, "Hey, you have got a new opportunity, but you are going downhill, and you can't keep up with everything."

I realized they were right. I didn't want to half-ass either location. So in September of that year, I decided to honor my vow to the mountain in the owl's presence. It was time to make good on my words.

I rented a place and told my uncle and aunt to sell the property. The logging company would soon sell parcels around them, causing the price of theirs to drop. Saying goodbye to the land was very hard, but it was the solidification I needed. I spent a day up there with Bob to clean up and say my final goodbyes.

Legal weed was a completely different business. Everything in Sacramento was done inside big warehouses, so I didn't bring a single piece of equipment down from the mountain. I sold all kinds of stuff and gave away a lot to my friends who were still growing. All my friends thought I had gotten busted. Everyone said things like "Do you have a pending case? Why are you giving me these tens of thousands of dollars' worth of equipment?"

"Because I'm done. I'm actually done."

"Yeah, but why?" they asked.

It was the opportunity I was looking for. I had to go so I could adhere to the deadline of October 16, 2016, I had given myself. I knew God and the Universe weren't going to throw me another bone like that.

. . .

I had lived in cities before, but it was difficult living in a big city after years of small-town and rural-property living. I lived right in Midtown. It was hip and artsy, with lots of music and bars. The light pollution from the orange glow of the streetlamps shone in my windows as I tried to fall asleep each night and blocked my ability to watch the stars overhead on the back balcony. I was completely alone and running through my savings. In Humboldt, I had built my whole life according to plan. I had my own home, my vacation house where I went to relax, and my friends, my relationships, and my very comfortable financial circumstances. I left everything behind. It was a different type of itch, less about damned if I do or damned if I don't—less about survival than my start had been. I had assets and financial security and was willing to risk all of it again for a more stable daily routine, for happiness and scalability.

I wouldn't take a paycheck for almost the first year and a half after I moved to Sacramento as I was building the new business with William. Construction was in full swing by May of 2016, plants were planted in August, and our first harvest would be on the first of December. Even though we were quickly working toward our first harvest, it seemed like I was questioning my decision daily. I continually reminded myself that I had made a choice on the mountain to change my life on October 16, 2016.

The goal was to harvest more often with three large rooms and sell wholesale to dispensaries. I continued to attend conferences and High Times events, learning the California culture as best I could.

So I was living very cheap. I had furnished my apartment with used Ikea furniture, a folding table, and a nice air mattress. Drinking was easily the most expensive part of my life. I was drinking four or five nights a week just to have bar talk. There were a lot of times when I thought, *What have I done?*

I thought back to when I first asked Trey at the garden shop, "Do you know anyone who has ever retired from doing this, anyone who has had a career, per se?" He knew one or two people who had retired with a pile of cash. One moved to Baja, Mexico, and the other one moved to wine country. I was still hustling, investing, and risking, trying to make it a career—unwilling to settle for the status quo I had been living.

I was also still incredibly angry about being robbed. I had a huge chip on my shoulder, and I was trying to drown it with alcohol. I was starting to become an angry and snarky drunk.

Eight months into my new life, it was difficult not having friends or a consistent romantic partner, but I wasn't ready to let many people in on what I was doing—until fate stepped in.

During a company meeting with my business partner, our architect, and a few others, I was seated next to a plumber named Mitch whom I'd met a few months earlier. I'd hired his company to do some work at the new business.

We were going over blueprints for the three grow rooms, about 2,500 square feet each. And right in the middle of the meeting, he turned to me and said, "I want you to meet somebody."

"OK. What do you mean?"

"This gal, Jessica. I want you to maybe go on a date with her and meet her."

"Mitch, I told you I am not dating anybody. This is Ty time. I'm eight months into this. I'm loving some parts of it."

"No, no. You've got to meet her."

"No, it's not happening," I said. I thought that was the end of it.

A few hours later, I was driving north after picking up my dad at the Sacramento airport. Half an hour into the drive, Mitch called me, and I clicked the Bluetooth setting so he was on speaker.

"So I set it up," he said. "She's coming to my house on Halloween, and you guys are going to meet. She's great."

"Mitch, I told you!"

He cut me off. "Nope. I already talked to her."

Apparently, he'd done the same thing to her. She wasn't interested in meeting anyone, but Mitch told her I'd already said yes—peer pressure at its finest.

We were still a few days from Halloween, so I said, "I'd like to talk to her before."

I called her and talked to her on the phone, and we really hit it off. She knew somebody I knew, and we were able to lurk on each other's profiles on Facebook.

By the time Halloween came, I was digging the conversation and was really looking forward to meeting her. An hour before the costume party, I decided to buy her flowers. Then, soon after, with bouquet in hand, I walked down the street in my pirate costume toward my friend's house. The streets were full of people in costumes and those scurrying home from work to prep for the big night.

I spotted her instantly. She was dressed as a classic witch.

I walked up to her on the street, bowed in my best Johnny Depp pirate impersonation, and said, "It's nice to meet you, m'lady."

She replied with a curtsy so graceful that Her Majesty, the queen herself, would have been proud. So there we were—the witch and the pirate—walking hand in hand, laughing, talking, and falling fast despite our efforts to avoid meeting one another. It was the Universe working its magic.

A month later, as we walked hand in hand under the orange glow of the streetlamps along the tree-lined roads of Old Sacramento, I asked her, "Would you like to take a road trip five hours north?"

My Promise to the Land

2018

FOR THE FIRST YEAR AND A HALF in Sacramento—half of 2016 and all of 2017—we were still operating under the gray medical market, which was very gray, even in California. In that period, I was open and honest with the local municipalities, police departments, and fire departments. I really wanted to be known. We knew legalization was coming because Proposition 64 passed. We were doing everything we could to operate legally before licenses were given out and applied for. But to bring in income during that time, we still had to sell under a gray area of legality. That was the only way we could afford to pay for the license and everything once it came.

The overtness of some of my counterparts in Sacramento took some time to get used to; they were way more willing to discuss and flaunt their "weed incomes," whether true or not. I would just stand quietly and listen. I was surprised at their lack of fear of having their homes invaded and robbed or having the IRS on their backs. They loved to flaunt shiny things. I guess it was just a different culture. But I honestly didn't feel like I fit in. Nor did it feel safe to.

At the time, I'd vowed not to sell our product to any of my old Humboldt connections. That was part of my complete disconnection from my past, and it meant that I had to eliminate any possibility of returning to those old connections as a plan B. I knew I could sell all the weed instantly if I reached out to old contacts. But I really wanted to create a wall between that life and this new one. In fact, I hid my past so well that my employees thought I had just gotten into the weed industry.

It took some time to grow the new business. The company was back to doing lots and lots of small weekly transactions instead of working with large bulk buyers. A year before, in Humboldt, I would have moved a hundred pounds to one person. In Sacramento in those early years, we had to conduct transactions of three pounds to thirty shops to make the same amount. But our persistence paid off. When it was fully legalized, we were ready with product to ship and sell.

• • •

These days, I start every week with a walk-through of our SEVEN LEAVES facility, which Jessica helped name. I talk to the plants and say "thank you" to each room and thousands upon thousands of ladies.

As of the publication of this book in 2024, we have more than fourteen rooms, and our total production is around fifty-four thousand square feet. We have thirty to forty-five active barcodes at any given time and are in nearly four hundred stores statewide. Our products are all over the country and Europe because people are buying our products in bulk at legal stores and shipping it to wherever they are from.

We harvest forty-nine times a year now, and it takes seventy-five to eighty full-time personnel to make the operation run smoothly.

We have a contract with an HR firm, a contract with a payroll firm, a contract with our bookkeeping company and our accountants, and too many attorneys to mention.

Sometimes, I can't believe I'm actually the head of this company and that it is doing all right. I'm a firm believer that once you can afford it, even if you can't pay yourself for a while, hire great people with skill sets and experience that you do not have. Your job is to give them the arena, vision, guidelines, and tools they need to succeed and allow the company to stay in business.

· · ·

As for the Humboldt property, my aunt and uncle finally had a buyer at the start of 2017, and I needed to start doing several final sweeps to make sure it was clean. I was also going to clean up my house to rent it out. Jessica and I were serious, and she agreed to come with me to the property. It was the first time her eyes were fully opened to what I'd been doing out on those mountains all those years.

She harbored no judgment—only honesty and encouragement. Our relationship continued to deepen. There was no drama, not even during hard conversations and difficult periods. No fighting. No infidelity. Just genuine connection, respect, and fun.

Ten months after I met Jessica, I was clear-minded. I knew what I did and didn't want. I didn't need any more time to make the decision. People used to say, "When you know, you know," and I was starting to feel that. I wanted to marry Jessica. My friends had seen our relationship grow and the positive changes I'd made, and they were on board too.

I needed to check on my house up in Humboldt to get it ready for the next set of renters. I wasn't willing yet to fully detach from that part of the land. On my drive back down to Sacramento, I decided to take the old route down through Santa Rosa—the same drive I had made repeatedly when I drove five hours north. I wanted time to think.

Out there in the not-too-distant future was another itch. *Marriage*. And in 2018, that itch was scratched.

. . .

As well as everything was going on so many fronts at the beginning of 2019, I knew I needed help with my alcohol use. I tried going to AA but didn't resonate with the program. The way my relationship with alcohol manifested was different from that of many of the people in my group. I heard stories about robbing family members and selling precious belongings to maintain addictions. I couldn't relate, but I still needed support. So instead, I found a therapist and started going to counseling for drinking and the damage done from living such a secretive double life. Nobody knew the extent of my past. That was a rough road. But it was incredibly helpful to talk through everything in a place where I wouldn't be judged and where I felt safe to decompress.

"Dr. Helpful" was very encouraging, and I had sessions with him for fifteen months. I stopped seeing him in March 2020 for two reasons. One, the pandemic happened. And two, our daughter was born in April 2020.

I did get drunk a few times in 2020, but it was different. I was a father to a baby girl who needed me to always be present. My wife deserved the same. At some point, I had a realization. "OK, I'm good. I'm not doing it anymore."

The same year, the buyers for my aunt and uncle's property defaulted on their payments, and they got the land back. The mountain had spoken—the new owners couldn't get the land to work with them. Uncle Bob called to sell it to me. He had only a few months left to live. They wanted me to have it at an incredibly low price. My aunt felt like I had already been paying for the property. It was true—I had been visiting the area and keeping the land in good shape for all the years it was in my care. Her one request was that

I wouldn't cut any of the trees and would turn it into a nature conservancy before I die. Uncle Bob just wanted to know that the funds would be added to his wife's account so he wouldn't have to stress about her financial future while he was quickly declining.

I knew I needed to return to the land and clean it up again. I'd heard rumors that the people who'd purchased it had littered everywhere, and I couldn't bear the thought of them demeaning the land that way, especially not after my experience tripping on acid where I'd connected so strongly to the land and its history.

I made a plan to go up there for a couple of weeks with contractors and really clean the property up. I asked Jessica if she wanted to come with me. In true Jessica fashion, she agreed without hesitation to go and help me clean up the mountain.

• • •

At the start of the story of this book, cannabis was illegal in every state of the United States. By the time this book is published, twenty-four states and the District of Columbia have legalized recreational cannabis for use by adults. Approximately eight other states have possible plans to vote on or legalize within the next eighteen months. Countries like Thailand, Germany, Czech Republic, Spain, Israel, South Africa, Uruguay, Columbia, Canada, and the United Kingdom all have forms of medicinal or recreational industries in place or fast emerging. The industry is maturing and expanding, with billions in investment dollars and billions in sales.

I have shared my story to give a better inside understanding of the historical period and place of the Humboldt County green rush. To educate, entertain, and deliver to the reader real and relatable emotions, risks, struggles, hilarity, successes, and pains about what it was like to be operating as a large-scale grower and mover in those early days. Within the secret life behind the locked gates of the Emerald Triangle weed world, brotherhoods and sisterhoods were formed as we navigated our rebellious farm life and logistics for an ever-hungry national demand for our regional product.

There are numerous told and untold stories from "behind the gates" of the Emerald Triangle cannabis industry. I urge other living and surviving members of this industry to document those histories. Since this story is just one of the many accounts of that lifestyle, I could only share a portion of my personal stories, and there were so many more chapters that didn't make the final cut. I hope more books, short stories, films, spoken words, and even paintings from other pioneers, both legacy operators and modern ones, will be created and shared. It is important that the risks, the sacrifices, and the ultimate revolution find a path toward tomorrow's customers and the marketplace.

Although this has been my livelihood for the last seventeen years, it is still a hustle. But so is almost every other business, job, position, rank, duty, or command. It has truly become my career. I can now check that box off Trey's original list as well. Will I get to ride off into some fantasy sunset like they do at the end of movies or careers? Who knows and who cares? I am blessed with the sunrises and sunsets I get to catch today.

I'm no longer the young man, wild in his itch and ready to jump on whichever angry bull is eager to kick me off this weed rodeo. I'm more middle-weeded in my age, less focused on trying to always grow more, sell more, and build more. Now I focus on ensuring the well-being of the company's financial securities and supporting the team.

Still, this industry is like a river that is ever-changing, ever evolving. But like the consistency of the Sun in the sky, so is the consistency of the cannabis plant in my adult life. She means the world to me; she is the "other lady" in my life. She has shown me the world's cultures and wonders. She has tested and blessed me to the edges of both extremes. She has introduced me to incredible people, including my wife. She has brought me closer to the elements—earth, water, fire, and air. She has guided my journey along the ladder, cliffs, curves, and climbs of capitalism. She has seen me at my worst. She has seen me at my best. She is one of my closest friends. She is family.

Monthly, I'm reminded of when Uncle Bob turned up the neighbors' driveway that May afternoon and Jarod gave me those first forty plants. The destiny and gesture are never forgotten and have spawned a new level of philanthropy in my life. I'm so blessed to be able to provide and pay it forward.

· · ·

I still go up to the mountain for a few nights each year, five hours north of where I live now. As my truck makes the last few turns and climbs to the first Forest Service gate, the inevitable nervousness covers my body and mind as I approach my annual pilgrimage and handshake with the mountain. I look forward to bringing our children—my daughter and my son, who was born in December 2022—to the land when they are a little older.

I still notice the indented tree to the left that I slammed into that first day by the gate. Legend has it that I can still be found a few days out of the year walking around those mountains naked in tattered construction boots with a hand-carved walking stick decorated with a single feather and leather lacing around the top.

There are moments when I am still surprised that I did not write this book from a jail cell. I lived on the edge of a life behind bars, literally and figuratively, for years, and I got lucky. I also played the game as smartly as I could since possible felony convictions haunted my every move. So many others were not so fortunate, and that is not lost on me. Perhaps being the one who got away is anticlimactic, but I like to think of it as an opportunity.

. . .

Under the stars, I remember Rue running and barking with excitement, chasing after creatures. Rue was mine for ten years until she passed away, and she looked like a German shepherd puppy her whole life.

I hear Uncle Bob's voice telling cheesy bits of old-man wisdom and reminding me to turn off the water main and pick up any piece of man-made trash. On my fortieth birthday, I visited the mountain alone to spread Rue's ashes and the ashes of a private thank-you letter to Uncle Bob in a place they both dearly loved, the same place that made me who I am.

Above all, I've listened to the land behind those locked gates and honored it. And it has blessed me beyond my wildest dreams.

About the Author

Ty Kearns was born in Humboldt County, California, during the summer months of 1983, the same months CAMP (the Campaign Against Marijuana Planting) was created in the state of California. He grew up in a community where much of the economy was supported by marijuana cultivation and transactions.

From 2004 to 2007, he worked in the construction trades swinging a hammer and building spec-home neighborhoods. In 2006, he won an award for a business plan he wrote for building low-income single-family homes with used rice straw from the Central Valley rice farmers. After presenting this idea at the Collegiate Entrepreneurs' Organization conference in Chicago that year, he got a loan to build a spec home and start his development company. That home was sold in June of 2007 right before the housing crash. Then in 2008, facing financial difficulties from the great recession, he made marijuana his livelihood.

Kearns started from humble beginnings, planting his first crop in the mountains of Humboldt County. With hard work and perseverance, he founded and owned the Humboldt Cannabis Center, which was Proposition 215 compliant, while simultaneously attending college, graduating with a degree in energy management and design.

Anticipating the inevitable changes in the industry, Kearns made the bold decision to shut down his operations in Humboldt and move to Sacramento in 2016, where he cofounded SEVEN LEAVES. Since its inception, Kearns has been involved in every aspect of the company, from gathering funding and painting walls to completing licensing applications and financial reports.

Today, with seventeen years in the cannabis industry under his belt, Kearns is the CEO of SEVEN LEAVES and president of MTG Investments. The success of SEVEN LEAVES has allowed Kearns to work *on* the company instead of in it day to day. His passion for the industry and his drive to succeed in the face of change continue to propel SEVEN LEAVES forward.

As a board member of the Sacramento Asian Pacific Chamber of Commerce, Kearns has been instrumental in sponsoring the "Cannabis Talks" series and policy and industry study missions to Colorado and Canada. He has also taught classes for the Cannabis Opportunity Reinvestment and Equity (CORE) program in Sacramento, helping social equity cannabis entrepreneurs and employees better understand and prepare for the industry. And he has presented at various conferences on the electrical energy impacts of the cannabis industry on the power grid.

Beyond the cannabis industry, Kearns enjoys real estate and is still passionate about construction and building with recycled materials and innovative solutions. He reads books and makes art to calm his mind. He strongly believes in supporting charitable organizations close to his heart. Curious about the peoples, cultures, and wonders of world, he has traveled to over thirty countries. He is an avid outdoorsman, enjoying mountain biking, river and stream fishing, and meditating in the wilderness. His other passions are picnicking and going on dates with his wife.

Kearns is driven and passionate about succeeding in the fast-changing cannabis industry, and proud of his place in it. He believes it takes a union of the Boots and the Suits, legacy experience and dynasty building, for longevity in this ever-changing and emerging industry. With the news of rescheduling, the number of states now legalizing marijuana, an election year, and other nations fast approaching legalization, he felt it was a perfect time to release *Five Hours North*. It is time to celebrate history and some of the pioneers of the modern industry.

Kearns currently lives in Placer County, California, with his wife and two children.

Acknowledgments

I would like to thank: the Plants, the "Ladies;" the champions of Prop 215, YR. 1996; the "itch;" people who enjoy weed; the Mama Bear; public radio, NPR, KMUD, KHSU, and Giants Baseball Radio Broadcasting; Ace Hardware; the natural wonders and beauty of Humboldt and Trinity Counties; Buddy's Towing; the Rock Slide Bar and Grill; Frank; Tractor T; everyone who worked with us over the years; Darci at the Chevron; Trey; Trinity River Garden Center; Mad River Gardens; Farmer Browns; Farm Tek; "Toby," our resident squirrel; Cal Fire; logging company next-door; USFS, for protecting our nation's forests; Lil Sweetie Stove by Vogelzang; the Mountain Springs; Kmart and WinCo Foods; Mr. Washington; books; Ma and Pa; James; Coleman Camping Products; Black Contractor Bags; Alice; the folks at the Fancy Restaurant; the state of California; the Rain and Snow; the Stars; the Sun; Security Company Eureka; Fortuna Welders; the Dirt; all the surrounding animals, even the rattlesnakes; the Dogs: Diesel, Distance, Kona, Bear, Sandy, Paco, Luna; Giuntoli and Sunny Brae veterinarian hospitals; the Poseidon Twins; our pumps; newspaper and matches; the Arcata Recycling and Reuse Center; those who stole from me, the damn thieves; Humboldt Waste Management; the Department of Fish and Wildlife; the Mexican restaurant in Willow Creek, CA; Barn Builders; the Millyard and J.; Frank, the Old Mechanic in Willow Creek, CA; U-Haul rentals; Don's Rent-All; Honda Power Equipment; Carhartt;

warm, dry socks; tarps; Rachel; Noah; Jesse; Smiles; my business partners; the Dodge Ram, Zeus; the Ford Ranger, Rick; my back and hands; Oregon Gene; the Green Key; the natural springs; my aunt; the Mountain; the saying, "You're damned if you do. You're damned if you don't." Thank you all and apologies to those I didn't list!

To the industry of today—I'm proud of us. I am also proud of the voting citizens of this country for continuing to legalize cannabis and expunging the records of those with nonviolent crimes of possession and small amounts of peddling. It surprises me and motivates my soul daily, witnessing the spread of legalization and a broader acceptance of the cannabis plant across the United States and the rest of the globe.

To the anchoring and sailing vessel that is the cannabis culture—I love you. Because my current role in the space and life has placed different daily priorities in my lap (running a large cannabis company and keeping everyone employed while staying true to my roots and navigating the emerging marketplace, as well as staying relevant, hip, and profitable), I am now a hybrid of Boots and Suits.

To the cultures of cannabis—from the aficionados to the smoker's clubs, movers and shakers, influencers, and pop-ups, to the folks reviewing their favorite flowers, terpenes, hash, rosin and carts—thank you. Onward with these trends, innovations, discussions, and camaraderie around all that this plant gives and creates for us. Thank you for mapping the future of this industry. What the culture is doing can't be knocked off by the big, heavily funded behemoths of this space. Authenticity is just that—authentic. And you can't fake or make synthetic authenticity.

The pioneers of cannabis growing before me couldn't believe I was willing to build massive greenhouses full of weed out in the open. I still pinch myself, knowing the industry and consumers have brought the space to where it is now, with massive brands and Pot Stars known worldwide, creating a multitude of careers. Folks are openly advertising cannabis jobs in every sector of the cannabis industry. This would have been unimaginable that day when I first drove up the mountain with Uncle Bob. I look forward to watching the worldwide sprawl of cannabis continue to press forward.

I want to say thank you to the Humboldt County community of schools, folks, festivals, coaches, family, family friends, coworkers, landlords, realtors, bosses, shop keepers, bus drivers, park rangers, tribal members, professors, past girlfriends, fire fighters, attorneys, college students, my aunt and uncle, my brother, and my parents. Thank you for raising me as a young boy.

To the Sun, the Sky, the Mountains, the Rains, the Snow, the Watersheds, the rugged, unforgiving terrain, and cannabis plants of Humboldt County—thank you for cultivating me into a man.

And to my wife and my children—thank you for being the light that is my life. I love you, I love you, I love you.